D0427434

BREAKING GROUND

Adventurous New Plays from
Adventurous Theaters

BREAKING GROUND

Adventurous New Plays from Adventurous Theaters

Edited and with an Introduction by

Kent Nicholson

Plays by

Glen Berger

Adam Bock

Gordon Dahlquist

Dan Dietz

Naomi Iizuka

Julie Marie Myatt

Stage & Screen
New York

Great Men of Science, Nos. 21 & 22
Copyright © 1997 by Glen Berger

Five Flights
Copyright © 2001 by Adam Bock

Delirium Palace
Copyright © 2001 by Gordon Dahlquist

Tilt Angel
Copyright © 2000 by Dan Dietz

17 reasons (why)
Copyright © 2002 by Naomi Iizuka

Cowbird
Copyright © 1999 by Julie Marie Myatt

CAUTION: Professionals and amateurs are hereby warned that the plays represented in this book are subject to a royalty. They are fully protected under the copyright laws of the United States of America and of all countries covered by the International Copyright Union (including the Dominion of Canada and the rest of the British Commonwealth), the Berne Convention, as well as all countries with which the United States has reciprocal copyright relations. All rights, including professional, amateur stage rights, motion picture, recitation, lecturing, public reading, radio reproduction, such as CD-ROM, CD-1, information storage and retrieval systems and photocopying, and the rights of translation into foreign languages, are strictly reserved. Particular emphasis is laid upon the matter of readings, permission for which must be secured from the Author's agent in writing. See individual plays for contact information.

ISBN: 1-58288-049-2

Printed in the United States of America

⇛ ACKNOWLEDGMENTS ⇚

This anthology would not have been possible without the assistance and encouragement of the following individuals: Liz Duffy Adams, Cassie Beck, Elizabeth Bennett, Glen Berger, Adam Bock, Kirsten Bowen, Gordon Dahlquist, Bart DeLorenzo, Dan Dietz, Naomi Iizuka, Morgan Jenness, Joyce Ketay, Todd London, Julie Marie Myatt, Jason Neulander, Sean San Jose, Casy Stangl, Lisa Steindler, Kelly Stuart.

⇒ CONTENTS ⇐

⇒ INTRODUCTION ⇐

Breaking Ground
Theater Is Everywhere

There is theater happening all over this country. We are often led to believe that theater is in dire straits, an irrelevant art form with a dying audience base that simply can't speak to the numbers or contain the intensity of its high impact media cousins, film and television. But there is theater happening all over this country. In my own community of San Francisco, our local theater service organization, Theater Bay Area, reports a company membership of over three hundred. Yet I can count the number of large theaters in the Bay Area on one hand. These larger theaters, mostly members of The League of Resident Theaters (LORT), receive the lion's share of attention and produce high quality, high budget productions that speak to the largest audiences.

But what about the rest of these theaters? Who are they? Where do their audiences come from? Who are the artists working in them? The answer to that question is as multifaceted as the theaters themselves. There are, however, a large number of these companies who exist because they are tired of the conservative tendencies of these LORT theaters. They believe that theater works best when it exists on a community level. They believe that it works best when it takes risks and tells it like it is (or at least like they see it). They believe that theater needs to speak a different language if it is to speak to a younger audience. And they believe that they can best do this by producing new plays by writers who share this vision and will help them achieve it.

In recent years, we've seen a disturbing trend in many of the LORT companies. I like to call it the McFranchising of American Theater, which occurs when major LORT houses around the country start producing the same two or three new plays in their seasons. At the point at which HBO produced a movie version of *Dinner with Friends* did we really need to see more than ten productions of that play? (No disrespect to Donald Marguiles or his play; they're both wonderful.) These small theaters, which create and produce risky theater, are the antidote to this McFranchising.

They take the chance on unknown writers. They introduce theater to a different demographic, often for the price of a movie ticket. They don't do it for money, nor do they do it for the attention. They do it because they believe in the innate power of theater to transform a society and a culture. They do it because they need to speak to their community and are trying to find alternative means by which to do that. They do it because they believe in what the theater has to offer.

As one might expect, younger, idealistic artists are often the founders of these theaters. In some cases they are recent college graduates; in other cases they are established, working artists whose desire for challenge has led them to find a new outlet for their work. Many simply desire an artistic home, having felt disenfranchised by the mainstream. Most small companies begin with similar roots.

The theaters represented in this anthology are among an elite group. They represent a small portion of the theaters that have heard the siren call, taken up the challenge, and begun the process of implementing a new vision of what theater can be. They have done this by identifying voices in their community and bringing those voices to light. The playwrights represented in this anthology are among the brightest talents in this country, and, fortunately, the theaters represented in this anthology understand that this is the case. Without the vision of these companies, these writers might go unknown and unproduced.

What's most remarkable about the work here is the success that all of these plays have achieved in their own communities. Without exception, the work of these artists has won critical and audience acclaim. And almost without exception, the artists represented in this volume have been completely ignored by the mainstream theaters in these very same communities. This book is an attempt to amend that error: to tell the nation that there is theater happening all over this country.

In San Francisco, Encore Theatre and Campo Santo regularly produce original works that speak with vibrancy and immediacy. It was Campo Santo who introduced the dynamic work of Naomi Iizuka to the Bay Area. Naomi's work has been produced all over the country at some of the greatest theaters, yet she had been ignored in San Francisco. Campo Santo took the chance and now has a relationship that includes plays written exclusively for their company. Naomi's play *17 reasons (why)* was created by interviewing residents and exploring the community of the Mission District (where Campo Santo performs). Upon leaving the theater, patrons were confronted with the very locales they had just seen recreated onstage. In fact Campo Santo only produces plays in world premieres that have been written for them. (And they only produce world premieres.) They have introduced writers to the community and the art form. Novelists such as Denis Johnson and Dave Eggers have created work for this vibrant company. As a result, they speak directly to their community in a way that transcends activism and proves the potential for immediacy that theater, more than any other art form, possesses.

Encore has produced regional and world premieres of contemporary dramatists. They have been immensely successful in bringing attention to the work of young local artists with distinct visions. Adam Bock's runaway hit *Five Flights* ran for five months and was named one of the top ten cultural events of the year in the *San Francisco Chronicle*, right up there with the San Francisco Giants World Series run and the Gerhard Richter retrospective at the Museum of Modern Art. Pretty remarkable for a theater company that has a limited budget and works out of a theater that seats only seventy-five people. Adam's lovely work teaches us that theater can be emotional without relying on sentimentality. Like many theaters, Encore was created by a group of actors, and still maintains their roots in this regard. They prove, again and again, the power of live performance. There is nothing quite like seeing truly great performances in an intimate setting.

There is a common belief that there is no theater in Los Angeles. Circle X and Evidence Room prove that this is, in fact, a tremendous lie. L.A. has one of the most vibrant theater scenes I've ever encountered. Bolstered by the immense amount of talent that exists in the acting community, these two theaters have managed to carve out a niche for their own brand of experimental and avant-garde work. In a town as media savvy as L.A., it can be quite a relief to see the straightforward productions of Circle X. Founded, like many L.A. theaters, as an acting ensemble, Circle X isn't content to simply produce work that showcases their individual abilities. They believe strongly in the power of community and of the art of theater. They have consistently presented some of the best world premiere work in the country and have an eye for talent that is unparalleled. Helping bring the work of Glen Berger to the attention of Angelinos (and to the rest of the country), they helped discover one of the most unique voices creating work today. Berger's attention to historical detail and his innate sense of the absurd make for a wickedly unique theatrical experience. *Great Men of Science, Nos. 21 & 22* is a perfect example of this experience. By focusing on the true story of two minor but unwittingly important figures in scientific history, Berger brings into question whether science is in fact methodical or entirely accidental.

Evidence Room quite simply produces some of the most dynamic work in this country. Consisting of artists whose love is the theater, the attention to detail in their productions demonstrates that love with alarming clarity. The work they do is among the most challenging being written. Gordon Dahlquist's play *Delirium Palace* is a sampling of the kind of work they present. Dahlquist's vision of delirium, his constantly shifting landscape, and his constant questioning of identity in this noirish vision of society is intoxicating, delirious, and visionary in production. Evidence Room challenges their audiences with these dystopian visions on a regular basis. Having produced the work of Edward Bond, Charles Mee, and Gordon Dahlquist, they never let their audiences rest. Except for when they produce their living *Comic Strip*, a weekly serial performed late-night that lets the steam out of their intense productions. Immensely popular, it is a testament to their quality that Evidence Room can maneuver through this multiplicity of styles and genres. They are stalwarts of the community providing needed performance space, coproductions, and vitality to the L.A. theater scene.

Minneapolis has one of the most vital small theater scenes in the country. They also have one of the most vital midsize and large theater scenes in the country. Similarly to New York and Seattle, it can truly be called a theater town. So how does a company stand out in this environment? They produce high quality work. Eye of the Storm has been attracting attention to itself for some time. They produce the work of some great contemporary artists, such as Edward Albee and Paula Vogel, presenting the much sought-after regional premieres of these artists' work. They have also made commissioning of local artists a cornerstone of their development, and plays they have commissioned have gone on to major productions. It cannot be denied that this company has enriched the local and national landscape in ways we may not even be aware of. Julie Marie Myatt's *Cowbird* stands as a perfect example of the power of this small company. Myatt's work is extraordinarily delicate. In reading it, we can hear the voice of a generation of urban dwellers, lonely, disenfranchised, and searching for the things that will make them feel whole. While living and working in Minneapolis, Myatt created a body of work that speaks from the heart, lovingly and achingly, through the medium of theater. Truly beautiful works, they carry their theatricality through the performers' bodies and an expression of visual discourse with the text through images and slides. It takes a tremendous company to convey the intricacy of Myatt's work. That's how Eye of the Storm stands out in a theater town like Minneapolis.

When one speaks of Texas, one doesn't usually conjure images of great theater. But nothing proves more that theater is happening all over the country than the dynamic environment being created in Austin by the presence of Salvage Vanguard Theater. Introducing artists such as Dan Dietz, Karen Hartman, and Ruth Margraff, not just to Austin audiences but to the theater world at large, Salvage Vanguard has become a place where one can look to see who the next dynamic theater writers are going to be. An imperative, the name Salvage Vanguard Theater better describes their aesthetic than anything I can think of saying does. They are salvaging the vanguard of American Theater. If one needs to understand more about the plays in this anthology or the philosophies that drive many of the artists represented here, I encourage you to look to Salvage Vanguard's website, www.salvagevanguard.org, and read the manifesto "Why We Hate Theater." Dan Dietz's work *Tilt Angel* expresses the dynamism that is this company. A resident playwright there, Dietz's experiments in lyricism, language, and musicality bring a freshness and exuberance to the medium that is rare.

There is theater happening all over this country. It's also happening in Portland (Theater Schmeater), Atlanta (Dad's Garage), New York (where do I begin?), Chicago (Famous Door), and basically anywhere you find a community of artists who have a vision large enough to bring something new into their community. These six plays represent the slimmest minority of the truly great work that happens in these communities on a regular basis, often overlooked by the mainstream. I encourage everyone to dig a little deeper, look a little harder, and discover the unexpected that is most likely happening right down the street from where you live.

—Kent Nicholson
San Francisco
2003

For everyone who
has ever taken a risk
on something new.

Great Men of Science, Nos. 21 & 22

by Glen Berger

All rights reserved. Except for brief passages quoted in newspaper, magazine, radio, or television reviews, no part of this book may be reproduced in any form or by any means, electronic or mechanical, including photocopying or recording, or by an information storage and retrieval system, without permission in writing from the publisher.

Professionals and amateurs are hereby warned that this material, being fully protected under the Copyright Laws of the United States of America and all other countries of the Berne and Universal Copyright Conventions, is subject to a royalty. All rights including, but not limited to, professional, amateur, recording, motion picture, recitation, lecturing, public reading, radio and television broadcasting, and the rights of translation into foreign languages are expressly reserved. Particular emphasis is placed on readings and all uses of this book by educational institutions, permission for which must be secured from the author's representative, Joyce Ketay, The Joyce Ketay Agency, 1501 Broadway, Suite 1908, New York, NY 10036, (212) 354-6825

≫ BIOGRAPHY ≪

Glen Berger was head writer for the Mask and Wig Comedy Troupe at the University of Pennsylvania before relocating to Seattle where he was a member of Annex Theatre and saw produced *This End Up* and *The Kaywoodie Briar*, among others. *The Birdwatcher* took first place in the 1990 New City Playwrights Festival. In 1993, he received an Emerging Artist Grant for *Bessemer's Spectacles*, and he was the 1994 playwright-in-residence at New York Stage and Film. His *Great Men of Science, Nos. 21 & 22* won both the 1998 *L.A. Weekly* Award and the 1998 Ovation Award for Best Play. He was a Sloan Foundation Science and Technology Fellow at the Manhattan Theatre Club, where he is currently writing a musical, *On Words and Onwards*, about the evolution of language. His play *The Wooden Breeks* was nominated for Best Play by the *L.A. Weekly*, and has also seen productions in Juneau and Atlanta, with a U.K. production scheduled for the summer of 2003. His one-person show *Underneath The Lintel* was first seen in Los Angeles in June 2001, where it won the Ovation Award for Best Play. It ran Off-Broadway from October 2001 to January 2003, and has several other productions scheduled, including Seattle, Sydney, Paris, Athens, Tel Aviv, and Washington, D.C. Glen also writes for the children's PBS animated series, *Arthur*. He has been a member of New Dramatists since 2001.

≫ PRODUCTION HISTORY ≪

Great Men of Science, Nos. 21 & 22 by Glen Berger
Produced by Circle X
at The Lost Studio
March 20-April 26, 1998
Directed by Jillian Armenante

Cast

Alice Dodd ....Chatelet
Matthew Allen Bretz..Vaucanson
Jim Anzide..Spallanzani
David Wichert..Condorcet
Paul Morgan Stetler ....Lecat
Melanie van Betten ....Housekeeper
Bob Clendenin ....Abbe

Designers & Technical Staff

Ann Mulhall ....Stage Manager
Gary Smoot..Set Designer
Dan Weingarten..Lighting Designer
M. E. Dunn ....Costume Designer
David Hakim & Mikael Sandgren............Sound Designers
Jillian Armenante ....Music Selection

Circle X Theatre Company

Circle X is a not-for-profit, ensemble theater company dedicated to highly provocative and boldly theatrical productions of new and rarely seen plays. We believe in imagination over budget, adrenaline over inertia, and excellence over all. Through our art and action, we help cultivate a better community.

Circle X Theatre Co. was founded in early 1996 by seven artists drawn together by a common dream of creating an artistic home. By the fall of 2000, the company has grown to approximately fifty members and established itself as one of the most artistically substantive theatre companies in Los Angeles. Circle X maintains an open-company policy, and never charges dues. Admission to the company is gained through participation (artistic, technical, or both) in the production process.

Since its inception, Circle X has been home to eleven full-scale productions, eight of them world premieres. We have received three Ovation Awards and thirteen nominations, two *L.A. Weekly* Awards and five nominations, and five Garland Awards. The Ovation Award for Best Play and the *L.A. Weekly* Award for Best Production both went to *Great Men of Science, Nos. 21 & 22* in 1998. Last season, our world premiere of Paul Mullin's *Louis Slotin Sonata* received the *L.A. Weekly Award* for Best New Play, two Garland Awards and, most recently, an Ovation Award nomination for Best Writing-New Play. Also from last season, Circle X's production of *Fathers and Sons*, written by company member, Brian Senter, has been nominated for the Ovation Award for Best New Adaptation. Circle X mounts four or five full productions each season.

While we are honored by the accolades we have received and appreciate the recognition of our work, it is not for awards that we set out to produce live theater. Our artistic process is the challenge and the bond that drives our company. Ensemble feedback during our reading series, as well as encouragement of director-driven projects from within the company, make for a highly collaborative atmosphere in which company involvement is passionate and dynamic. Our emphasis on innovation goes beyond our selection of thought-provoking, highly theatrical plays, it extends into everything from design, performance and direction to administration and marketing, creating the aesthetic for which Circle X is known. In the years to come Circle X looks forward to refining its high theatrical and community ideals as well as continuing its evolution as an organization that challenges and champions the community it serves.

—Circle X Theater Ensemble
2003

— ACT I —

Life, the Canard

The Story of Jacques de Vaucanson's Great Labour

SETTING AND CHARACTERS

Characters

Jacques de Vaucanson
Gabrielle du Chatelet
Abbe
Le Cat
Lazarro Spallanzani
Citizens #1-#4, Member of Academy, etc.

Note for Act I Set

Slide projection suggested. Consider as well utilizing projection screen as a screen for eighteenth-century-style silhouette/tableaus.

Note for Act I Music

Music is strongly recommended for the production. Modern, yet evoking the eighteenth century, intricate, repetitive, and stirring.

Time

1738

(Lights up slowly to reveal GABRIELLE DU CHATELET, dressed as the Goddess of Reason. She sings—)

CHATELET: *(Singing.)*
>Awake my Paris . . .
>Stir from thy slumberings!
>The worlds you now strive in
>Shall be snuffed and forgotten,
>come the Dawn . . .
>Bid farewell and return to
>This one Dream we share . . .
>Paris . . . Awake . . .
>Embrace the streets
>Embrace the anvils
>And sewers
>And markets
>And furnaces

(Dim light up slow on tableau of VAUCANSON asleep in thinking pose.)

>And you . . . Jacques de Vaucanson . . .
>Great hope of our time . . .
>Whose mind burns with the
>Incandescency
>Of Genius . . .
>Now Dispel the mists from your eyes
>So you may dispel the great mist from ours
>So we may be brought
>Ever nearer . . . ever nearer . . .
>To the Age of Light . . .
>Leave your dreams behind . . .
>Behold! . . . the world . . . is thine . . .

(We see drawings of Moon and Sun. A ticking watch increases anticipation.)

VAUCANSON: With its face always facing us, The Moon in this Minuet, moving counterclockwise, six tenths of a mile with every tick of the clock, bids Paris adieu for the day, and now we bow to the Sun, and Morning comes as Morning must! *(The city awakes with cock crow and stirring music.) (Thinking to self in studio.)* A hammer, in a 34 degree arc, strikes a nail, one two three four times and Pause . . . *(We see a man hammering a notice of heavy paper, one two three four times, pause. Then utter silence while—)* And in the pause, in a puddle . . . the birth of a gnat. For now, at least, it lives. A fifth time hammer to nail and one more for good measure—

(The hammerer hammers once and one more for good measure.)

HAMMERER: The Annual Contest, sponsored by the Royal Academy of Sciences, has today been made public! Devised for the year of our Lord Seventeen Hundred Thirty Eight!

CITIZEN #1: *(Reading notice.)* "With the highest Degree of Persuasiveness, Prove or Refute the following statement, uttered by the eminent mathematician Abraham de Moivre—"

(Projected on a screen, or on a large banner unfurled, de Moivre's statement is written, and visible throughout the play. We hear the voice of de Moivre, and, perhaps, see a rendering of de Moivre, with moving mouth.)

VOICE OF DE MOIVRE: "The Apparent *Randomness* of Events in Nature—

CITIZENS: The Apparent Randomness—

VOICE OF DE MOIVRE: Will, if subjected to Calculation, Reveal an *underlying Order* Expressing Exquisite Wisdom and Design."

CITIZEN #1: *(Reading.)* "Prove or Refute."

(For the following section, Citizens #1-#5 move with precision in a sort of minuet in the "street." ABBE is to the side, unseen by citizens. VAUCANSON remains in studio.)

CITIZEN #2: What minds have turned to this question!

CITIZEN #3: To prove or refute is to prove or refute the existence of God—

VAUCANSON: Dear Lord grant me the courage and wherewithal to unveil Your secrets . . . Surely You do not mean them to be secrets forever . . . And surely now our gnat touches down on a hat. The right elbow bends, the hand is carried upward, and by pressure of thumb, the hat, with the gnat . . . is lifted.

(The right elbow of ABBE bends, he takes off hat and bows.)

CITIZEN #4: *(To CITIZEN #2.)* Have you heard from D'Alembert?

CITIZEN #2: *(Excitedly.)* Oh yes—in affirmation of de Moivre, he will show that Newton's Third Law of Motion applies to both freely-moving *and* stationary bodies.

CITIZEN #1: And what, pray tell, of Fontanelle—

CITIZEN #3: —the secretary of the Royal Academy is refuting the possibility that random events are anything but random. He said, and I quote, "It is beyond the reach—"

VAUCANSON: A gnat in the nose.

CITIZEN #3: —of scientific investigation . . . !"

VAUCANSON: A sneeze.

(ABBE sneezes.)

CITIZEN #1: And what of Jacques de Vaucanson?

VAUCANSON: A sneeze.

(ABBE sneezes.)

CITIZEN #1: And what of Jacques de Vaucanson?

(Long pause.)

VAUCANSON: A sneeze.

(And an enormous sneeze from ABBE.)

CITIZEN #4: Jacques de Vaucanson!

CITIZEN #2: A most promising young scientist—

CITIZEN #4: Startling—

CITIZEN #3: Insolent—

CITIZEN #1: Jacques de Vaucanson!

CITIZEN #2: Yet I have heard he has overreached himself this time—

CITIZEN #3: It is a mathematical problem, and he is known for mechanical things—

CITIZEN #1: His rooms have been given over to every manner of machinery—

CITIZEN #3: He returns his meals uneaten—

CITIZEN #1: Only the Jesuit, the Abbe de Fontaine, knows just what he labours on—

CITIZEN #4: Yes, the Abbe, whose fondness for Vaucanson is rivaled only by his fondness for a drink—

(The ABBE, a dissipated older Jesuit, enters, carrying a parcel under his arm and putting a flask surreptitiously to his lips.)

CITIZEN #2: And I say! Isn't that the Abbe now—

VAUCANSON: A gnat near the mouth now flies to the eye—

ABBE: I have been—

(ABBE swats gnat by eye with hand.)

VAUCANSON: A miss.

ABBE: —requested by Monsieur Vaucanson not to reveal the nature of his work. You will see soon enough.

CITIZEN #3: And that parcel you conceal from us—is it not for your young upstart?

ABBE: You will see soon enough.

CITIZEN #1: But you must give us something!

ABBE: I gave him my word—

CITIZEN #2: But he's the only one missing from our list—

(CITIZEN #4 reads from his checklist, and checks "refute" or "affirm" in turn.)

CITIZEN #4: Clairaut will examine the variables in magnesia and quicklime.

ALL: Refute!

CITIZEN #4: Maupertuis will address the case of the polygon curve.

ALL: Refute!

CITIZEN #4: Couboursier will account for the irregularities in the observed motion of the planets.

ALL: Affirm!

CITIZEN #4: Burke will forecast the month in 1751 when Halley's Comet shall return—

ALL: Affirm!

CITIZEN #4: Lavoisier will show that Halley's Comet shall *never* return—

ALL: A refutation!

VAUCANSON: If I can but do it . . .

CITIZEN #3: So you won't let on?

CITIZEN #2: Come come, what is Jacques concocting?

VAUCANSON: If I can but do it—

CITIZEN #4: All of Paris wants to know—

VAUCANSON: Eyes will weep in gratitude—

CITIZEN #1: Divulge this at least: Will Vaucanson affirm or refute de Moivre's statement?

CITIZEN #2: Will he affirm or refute de Moivre's statement?

(The music builds. We hear the rumble of carts on cobbles, the tension builds, and as church bells ring out across the city—)

ABBE: Affirm! He will affirm! And with a ringing declaration that will bring tears to the faithful and turn all the treatises of the Fontanelles and Buffons into so much bumf!

VAUCANSON: From the noblest man to the humblest gnat. Life!

CITIZEN #3: *(To ABBE.)* Your neck, Monsieur.

(ABBE swats neck, smashing gnat.)

VAUCANSON: And Death—
ABBE: *(Exiting.)* Good day!

(Music intensifies, isolated light on VAUCANSON.)

VAUCANSON: *(Passionate to tears and heroism.)* —Nothing is random . . . Nothing is random, and I will prove it . . . Employing
Newton's laws of attraction by which the tides behave and the
planets are known to rotate; Using calculations plotting the
movement of the stars themselves across the heavens; utilizing
a system of springs and weights, gearwheels, cogs and escapements of my own construction fashioned in ratios of proven
mathematical laws and proportion . . . I will create . . . a Duck
. . . that flaps its wings, eats, and excretes . . . just like a duck!

*(The music ends, the stage clears. We then hear a number of insis-
tent knocks on the door of the garret of VAUCANSON. We
become aware of the quack of ducks. VAUCANSON is deeply
engrossed in hard thought and pained study and intense labor.)*

ABBE: *(Through door.)* Monsieur Vaucanson, it is I—
VAUCANSON: *(Quite in the middle of work.)* It's open.
ABBE: It's not open.

(Pause. Then knock knock knock.)

VAUCANSON: It is open.
ABBE: Jacques it's locked.
VAUCANSON: It isn't. You have to push.
ABBE: I am. I am pushing.
VAUCANSON: No, push . . . push.
ABBE: I'm pushing.
VAUCANSON: Hold the handle and push.
ABBE: For God's sake, it is locked.
VAUCANSON: It is not locked. I was occasioned to unlock it an hour
ago.

(Pause. More knocking. Pause.)

ABBE: Jacques. The door is locked.

VAUCANSON: I'm telling you it's open, stop knocking and push.

ABBE: Jacques, we do not have much time—

VAUCANSON: *(Half to self.)* I know . . . I know . . . in less than nine months I'm to present to the Academy a deterministic, dynamic model that yet will elucidate irregular, unpredictable behavior . . . how . . . how to accomplish all that needs doing when I haven't a sou to my name and I've lost my peruke . . .

(Pause.)

ABBE: What? Your what? Jacques, I can't hear you . . . Look, I have something here to show you if you would only— *(Tries door again.)* . . . I think it will be a great aid in the solicitation of funds . . . Please, I beg of you open the—

(VAUCANSON pulls on door, unfastens bolt, opens door.)

VAUCANSON: It was locked after all. My apologies. Everywhere I turn, unexpected Impediments.

ABBE: You look terrible.

VAUCANSON: The work . . . The work involved . . .

ABBE: There's food outside the door—

VAUCANSON: Leave it outside.

ABBE: *(Retrieving it.)* You must try to eat a little.

VAUCANSON: I cannot.

ABBE: When was the last time you ate?

VAUCANSON: I don't remember. I can't even look at it.

ABBE: It is nourishment.

VAUCANSON: Put it out of sight.

ABBE: If you want it, it's over here.

VAUCANSON: Fine.

ABBE: Do you see? Over here.

VAUCANSON: Fine!

ABBE: Jacques, how are you proceeding . . .

VAUCANSON: *(Erupts.)* What contrivance can I use to make this artificial duck take up the corn and suck it up quite to its stomach I don't know! I don't know! I don't know! *(Calming.)* ... the obstacles seem ... insurmountable ...

ABBE: But can you do it?

VAUCANSON: There is this. If I do not manage it, another will, in time. For all knowledge will be Man's, in time. I know I am at least fifty years ahead of my time. Perhaps sixty. But perhaps this idea of mine is eighty years ahead of its time.

ABBE: And what then?

VAUCANSON: I'll have no choice but endeavor to stride yet another twenty years in nine months and only hope it wasn't thirty years I needed to traverse.

ABBE: What? Look, Jacques, sleep, there's such a thing as that ...

VAUCANSON: I know, but when I finish. If I finish.

ABBE: And then it will be the sleep of the just.

VAUCANSON: Oh more than that my friend, more than that. With such exuberance will the angels dance in Heaven that the crowns will fall off of their heads!

ABBE: And yet you do not believe in heaven.

VAUCANSON: Not as such. Sit and I will explain to you the whole of my beliefs.

ABBE: Jacques de Vaucanson doubles over, clutches his abdomen, profanes the Lord and takes off his trousers.

(VAUCANSON doubles over in great pain.)

VAUCANSON: Jesus ... God ... !

(VAUCANSON hastens to unbutton trousers, and hops about from foot to foot to stifle the intense pain and refrain from urinating.)

ABBE: What is it? Do you need the chamber pot?

VAUCANSON: Where's the chamber pot ...

ABBE: Is it your bladder again?

VAUCANSON: The stones, oh the stones ...

(VAUCANSON finds chamber pot and runs behind the silhouette screen.)

ABBE: I thought you were improving . . .

VAUCANSON: No, if anything the spasms are more frequent.

ABBE: Haven't you seen a doctor?

VAUCANSON: No time. Or money . . .

ABBE: The suffering you endure . . . and yet still you continue . . .

VAUCANSON: *(With trousers at ankles, appearing from behind screen.)* We must . . . We must persevere . . . it is all we can do . . .

(He runs back behind screen. In silhouette, we see and hear VAUCANSON urinating.)

VAUCANSON: *(Whilst urinating.)* But what is this you were saying at the door—something about something to help us solicit funds?

ABBE: Oh yes, I was thinking we needed some sort of device to—

VAUCANSON: *(Due to volume of urinating.)* What? I can't hear you—

ABBE: *(Raising voice to compete with urinating.)* I was saying how I thought it would be—

VAUCANSON: I'm telling you, I can't hear you—

ABBE: *(Raising voice still louder.)* Well just that it occurred to me—

VAUCANSON: Damn it, can't you see I'm occupied!? A moment is all I ask!

(VAUCANSON yelps in pain, finishes urinating, and emerges trouserless.)

ABBE: How are you?

VAUCANSON: Miserable.

ABBE: But are you taking anything for it?

VAUCANSON: *(Pulling out a small flask.)* Just this.

ABBE: What is it?

VAUCANSON: Turpentine.

ABBE: Does it work?

VAUCANSON: In theory, it should break down the stones, the stones being either calcium oxide or calcium phosphate or magnesium ammonium phosphate but I don't know. From time to time, I pass gravel. Perhaps that is a good sign.

ABBE: Perhaps.

VAUCANSON: Well there's nothing to be done.

ABBE: Surgery?

VAUCANSON: Never again. But friend, what is this about a device for raising money?

ABBE: I'm concerned about your gravel.

VAUCANSON: Never mind my gravel, if we can raise enough money to enable the realization of this duck I will be happy to pass the Alps in my urine. The Alps.

ABBE: Well. I thought to myself, how can we make our plea for funds more compelling, and this old Jesuit looked no further than another old Jesuit who invented . . . this.

(He opens the box he was carrying to reveal a Magic Lantern.)

VAUCANSON: A Magic Lantern?

ABBE: What do you think?

(ABBE has set up Magic Lantern and random slides are "projected.")

VAUCANSON: I think in elucidating some of the finer points in our fundraising presentations, yes the device of Jesuit mathematician, biologist, and physicist Athanasius Kircher, who died in 1680, will be quite effective.

ABBE: *(Showing random slides.)* And if not, the images can still be most pleasing to look upon. "If what we say is confusing to you, at least take solace in viewing this picture of . . . *(He changes the slide.)* a trout."

VAUCANSON: No! They must they must understand that we are furthering the case that God's world is not a whimsical and capricious one.

ABBE: And that of course is why, in the end, I am assisting you—

VAUCANSON: I do not deserve it. You have found suppliers and have been my invaluable liaison, you have raised much-needed funds, you have gone above and beyond—

ABBE: No, I'll hear no more of it. I once did you a terrible wrong.

(A historical presentation utilizing magic lantern. We hear a hymn sung by a choir, and see slides depicting gears, orreries, angels, etc.)

Jacques de Vaucanson, you once had designs of being a Jesuit. You were twelve years old, a novice, and you constructed a mechanical angel. It opened its mouth in song and flapped its wings. "Just like an angel," you said. "Just like an angel indeed," said I. "How should you know how an angel flaps its wings? How naive, how presumptuous, nay blasphemous, to reduce a heavenly creature to cogs! cogs and gearwork!" "Look here you bitter ruinous old man," said you, "I wanted to see an angel come to life. You are beholding a year's labour." "And now," said I, "you will behold a moment's effort." And I smashed the angel to pieces in front of you. And you, twelve years old, replied, "Father . . . Man and Woman once lived in a Paradise. But this first paradise was *dependent* on their ignorance. With the first taste of knowledge, they were cast out. But it is you who are naive and presumptuous, nay blasphemous, if you believe God constructed this miracle of a world so that we may appreciate it as a blind man appreciates a painting. Just as Newton has revealed the laws governing the planets, that the planets move with a clockwork precision, those same laws must by necessity govern the natural world, and when we at last fully understand these laws, we will understand what God wants of us, what his intentions are and what our purpose is, and when we under-stand that, we will no longer be His helpless bawling child groping in the darkness, but His *helpmate* and His true friend and that will be the Second Paradise, the Lasting Paradise, the paradise dependent not on ignorance, not on ignorance, but on understanding, and we cannot turn back, no, not out of fear, not now." And with that you threw down your cassock, slammed the door, and left the Jesuits, striding through the city streets to your destiny.

VAUCANSON: Naked, for I wore nothing underneath my cassock.

ABBE: Yes.

VAUCANSON: Impassioned.

ABBE: Yes.

VAUCANSON: And I have carried that vision to this day, and now this!—something much better, something real and observable . . . something true . . . for yes like an angel, a duck too is God's creation, yes?

(Silence.)

VAUCANSON: Why are you silent?

ABBE: I have just hit my funny bone. I am in great pain.

VAUCANSON: *(Out of patience with his friend.)* Have you arranged a presentation.

ABBE: For next Tuesday, but I'll need a list from you tomorrow of the images we'll want to project, as well as a list of more necessary materials you require for your construction as another shipment goes out Friday.

VAUCANSON: Yes.

ABBE: And perhaps knowing there will be some money for your cogs and springs will permit you to sleep a bit easier?

VAUCANSON: Yes but . . . No . . .

ABBE: No?

VAUCANSON: No, for there is a further difficulty that threatens to undo all our good intentions . . .

ABBE: A further difficulty . . .

(Pause.)

VAUCANSON: My ratios . . . I have lost all of my ratios.

ABBE: Your ratios?

VAUCANSON: Yes . . .

ABBE: Are they important?

VAUCANSON: The duck cannot be made without them.

ABBE: And you cannot reconstitute the ratios?

VAUCANSON: Perhaps, but it would take me weeks of lost time, for they are built on discoveries that have taken me years to uncover through sweat and toil and miserable nights.

ABBE: And you don't know where you have misplaced them.

VAUCANSON: No . . . no, I know . . .

ABBE: You do know?

VAUCANSON: Yes.

ABBE: Then the difficulty—

VAUCANSON: The difficulty . . . the difficulty . . . oh god, the difficulty . . . is that . . . I am in love with Gabrielle-Emilie, the Marquise du Chatelet.

(Lights up on tableau of CHATELET.)

VAUCANSON: She has green eyes and had Euclid and Virgil memorized before she was twelve. Handsome, headstrong, passionate, and the first to translate Isaac Newton's Principia Mathematica into French . . . Who is like her? I . . . I never want to leave you.

(VAUCANSON is now lying in bed. It is evening. Distant strains from a ball are heard. Perhaps a slide with title "Three Weeks Previous.")

CHATELET: But Jacques, your work—that must come first.

VAUCANSON: My work, yes. This contest of which you've just informed me intrigues. But how can I prove that events in nature are not random?

CHATELET: Not with pen and paper—

VAUCANSON: No, you're right, not a treatise. I need to create . . . a living testament!

CHATELET: Your submission to the Annual Contest will be nothing short of genius . . .

VAUCANSON: If I can but manage it.

CHATELET: You will.

VAUCANSON: I don't know . . . Or no, yes, yes I will. I am with you and somehow nothing seems out of reach . . . Must we still keep the two of us a secret?

CHATELET: We must.

VAUCANSON: Your husband the Marquis.

CHATELET: My husband.

VAUCANSON: Come back to bed.

CHATELET: I am expected downstairs.

VAUCANSON: From here you can hear the ball—

CHATELET: But I'm the one who threw it—

VAUCANSON: You have set the dance in motion—now, as God does, let it run, in perfect harmony, without you.

CHATELET: *(Kissing him.)* No . . . no . . . I really must return, and you must go . . .

VAUCANSON: I can't bear it!

CHATELET: Go forth and astonish the world.

VAUCANSON: I'll do my astonishing from this bed.

CHATELET: That's not what the Academy has in mind.

VAUCANSON: Who would even think to disprove de Moivre?

CHATELET: Well, Fontanelle for one.

VAUCANSON: Let him try.

CHATELET: François Arouet for another . . .

VAUCANSON: Ah. François Arouet.

CHATELET: Yes. François Arouet.

VAUCANSON: François Arouet?

CHATELET: Yes, François Arouet.

(Pause.)

VAUCANSON: By François Arouet you of course mean Voltaire.

CHATELET: Yes.

VAUCANSON: *(Feigning nonchalance.)* So you have heard from him? Voltaire?

CHATELET: Yes.

VAUCANSON: So he is back from Prussia?

CHATELET: Yes.

VAUCANSON: And you have spoken with him.

CHATELET: I have spoken with him.

VAUCANSON: But did you not say yourself . . . *(Now erupting.)* that you were through with him?!

CHATELET: Only I can keep his imagination in check. The mischievous man must be kept out of mischief, his wings clipped. Whereas you . . . your wings require nothing less than the sky's infinite expanse.

VAUCANSON: But all the same, do you not find his company anything but trying?

CHATELET: No . . . no . . . There were poetry readings, and picnics . . . laboratory experiments . . . Our coach last year overturned on a freezing winter's night and help had to be sent for . . . When the servants returned, how amazed they were, for they found us curled up together in a pile of cushions and Russian rugs, deep in a snow drift, identifying the outlines of the lesser constellations . . . *(We see slides depicting constellations of Delphinus, Cepheus, etc.)* That for one was a beautiful night . . .

VAUCANSON: It sounds indeed beautiful. *(Brooding—)* Even if you took me as a lover only to spite him . . .

CHATELET: No Jacques, don't believe it—

VAUCANSON: Even if I am merely a pawn in a lover's quarrel, it has backfired, for I am smitten, utterly, and there isn't a set of calipers in the universe that could measure the length and breadth of it, and I will devote myself to convincing you—

CHATELET: Make this contest then the definitive argument—work and prove Voltaire and his skepticism are misguided . . .

VAUCANSON: I will Gabrielle, I will, yes, let me show you . . .

CHATELET: Done then.

VAUCANSON: And perhaps, in the meantime, you should not see the man.

CHATELET: Voltaire? No, I will still see him.

VAUCANSON: So you will still see him?

CHATELET: Yes.

VAUCANSON: I see. So you will still see him then.

CHATELET: Yes.

VAUCANSON: As a friend.

CHATELET: Yes, as a friend.

VAUCANSON: Good. For he is an old friend.

CHATELET: Yes.

VAUCANSON: So as a friend. *(Pause.)* And as a lover?

CHATELET: You mustn't fret over such things.

VAUCANSON: I mustn't fret because of course you will not see him as a lover, or I mustn't fret because it will just upset me tremendously?

CHATELET: The latter.

VAUCANSON: The latter.

CHATELET: I have seen him. I am still seeing him, and in fact, he is on his way here as we speak.

VAUCANSON: As we speak?

CHATELET: Yes.

VAUCANSON: Where are my trousers. Where are my trousers! He is approaching as we speak?! How could you invite him here?! Mon Dieu! What do you see in that man!

CHATELET: You have a rare and noble spirit Jacques de Vaucanson . . . But he is wittier.

VAUCANSON: For holding nothing sacred he is to be admired?

CHATELET: Perhaps you are right.

VAUCANSON: Perhaps not.

CHATELET: He declared de Moivre's statement the desperate hope of a febrile old man.

VAUCANSON: He said this? When all of nature argues against it?

CHATELET: He often speaks of you.

VAUCANSON: Does he.

CHATELET: He has great admiration for you.

VAUCANSON: Does he.

(A servant enters.)

SERVANT: Monsieur Voltaire has arrived.

VAUCANSON: God my god . . .

CHATELET: You will return to the dancing?

VAUCANSON: No.

CHATELET: Where will you go?

VAUCANSON: I need some air.

CHATELET: He would like to meet you.

VAUCANSON: Yes, and you and all your guests can have fun at my expense. Gabrielle . . . Gabrielle . . . I can prove him wrong, and if I do succeed, I must know, I must know . . . will I have your favour? Will you pledge yourself to me alone?

(Pause.)

CHATELET: It's likely.
VAUCANSON: That is enough.
CHATELET: *(Handing him peruke.)* Take this.
VAUCANSON: I am missing a shoe.
CHATELET: By the window, and please do not be upset.
VAUCANSON: I'm fine I'm fine. But I have to go. Fine then . . . I'll be off.
CHATELET: Your peruke is crooked.
VAUCANSON: My peruke?
CHATELET: Jacques de Vaucanson, scientist, lover, erupts with an expletive—
VAUCANSON: Fuck my peruke!
CHATELET: Right hand clutches, throws down peruke, and off he storms, slamming door, leaving peruke.

(VAUCANSON throws down peruke, turns, storms out of room, slams door. Lights up again on ABBE.)

ABBE: So you threw down your peruke . . .
VAUCANSON: Yes, and I felt great about it. At the time.
ABBE: But what does all that have to do with your ratios?
VAUCANSON: The ratios are in my peruke.
ABBE: Ah, I see. You keep your ratios in your peruke.
VAUCANSON: Yes.
ABBE: And when was this?
VAUCANSON: I don't know . . . three weeks ago.
ABBE: Well good god man, get them back!
VAUCANSON: *(Tortured.)* I can't . . . I can't . . . because . . . no doubt . . . Voltaire is there as we speak . . . they are in each other's arms as we speak . . . *(Pause. VAUCANSON broods.)* But friend, perhaps you could retrieve my peruke.
ABBE: *(Matter-of-factly, in one sentence—)* I would do anything for

you, but you know in this instance that I cannot. I am that man's sworn enemy after I criticized his work on Newton and he denounced me in his pamphlet Le Preservatif, and I responded with the stinging condemnation La Voltairomanie; and we who once were friends! But of course, he still thinks I should be indebted to him but it is because he is under the mistaken assumption that it was he alone who sprung me from prison after the spurious charge that I corrupted young boys.

VAUCANSON: Damn damn this peruke. As if I hadn't other things to think about . . .

ABBE: Do you think it's still in the bedroom?

VAUCANSON: *(Resigned.)* Perhaps a servant has carried it away . . . or thrown it away . . .

ABBE: *(Alarmed.)* Yes, oh Christ, or thrown it away. Look, We must take a coach there together immediately—

VAUCANSON: *(Spurred to action.)* You'll make inquiries with the servants, and perhaps I can enter the bedroom, if it is unoccupied, via the window . . . and seek out the curséd hairpiece!

ABBE: We'll find the fastest coach.

VAUCANSON: Until then, every moment is a moment lost.

(The ABBE and VAUCANSON exit. Lights up on Minuet Interlude. Stirring violin, harpsichord. CHATELET, dancers. VAUCANSON and other characters take their places in minuet.)

CHATELET: Before we can consider the Minuet, we must consider the complexity and harmony inherent in a single step! We must go Neither fast nor slow—The former is Folly, the latter is Indolence. And Above all, no affectation; the steps must progress naturally, and yet in each step, there is effort, there is premeditation. The knees boldly stretched—The legs slightly turned outward—Head upright, waist steady—With the left arm forward, we advance the right foot . . . We have begun . . .

(A knock on VAUCANSON's door. Door opened tentatively. LE CAT enters. Finds no one. Makes himself comfortable. Peruses papers scattered about. LE CAT glances at his pocket watch. As

diagrams of setting sun, and of rising moon, are projected, LE CAT muses—)

LE CAT: Though standing still, and still as still as it has always stood, the Sun, notwithstanding, steals from view as we pirouette west to east never ceasing never ceasing, and Evening descends as Evening will . . .

(VAUCANSON enters worse for wear.)

VAUCANSON: My pardons, I attempted travel this morning only to reach midway and watch the wheel of our carriage fall off and roll away and now the wheel and day are lost . . . irretrievably . . .

LE CAT: Monsieur Vaucanson.

VAUCANSON: Do I know you?

LE CAT: You do not. But it is an honor to meet you, I have heard much of your abilities.

VAUCANSON: How did you get in?

LE CAT: The door was open.

VAUCANSON: No, no I locked it.

LE CAT: It was unlocked.

VAUCANSON: It must have been locked.

LE CAT: But it was not.

VAUCANSON: It was locked, surely.

LE CAT: No.

VAUCANSON: But I take pains to secure the door whene'er I leave.

LE CAT: It was not secured.

VAUCANSON: Are you sure?

LE CAT: I am quite sure.

VAUCANSON: The window perhaps?

LE CAT: I did not come in through the window. And no, I did not spontaneously generate from that plate of meat.

VAUCANSON: I did not wish to suggest that you had. My pardons if you thought I thought you had generated spontaneously from that plate of meat. I suppose the secrecy I cloaked my project in was a privilege I'd have to relinquish sooner or later. You've been here long?

LE CAT: Long enough to examine your sketches. An artificial duck that stretches its neck to take corn from your hand!

VAUCANSON: *(Growing excited again.)* Yes, from the hand! then swallows it greedily, and doubles the swiftness in the motion of its neck and gullet to drive the food into its stomach where it will be digested by dissolution, not trituration as some would have it. The matter digested is conducted by pipes quite to the Anus, where there is a Sphincter that lets it out.

LE CAT: So you have set out to refute de Moivre's statement.

VAUCANSON: No, I have set out to prove de Moivre's statement.

LE CAT: But you are constructing an artificial duck.

VAUCANSON: Yes sir, were you not listening?

LE CAT: If you don't mind my saying so, you will never accomplish it.

VAUCANSON: So far, Courage and Patience have overcome everything. And now if you'll excuse me, I have much work to do, Monsieur . . . I'm sorry, what was your name?

LE CAT: Le Cat.

VAUCANSON: Le Cat? If you are Le Cat then you are the most celebrated surgeon in Paris.

LE CAT: I am Le Cat, and if you please, undress, and I shall look at your penis.

VAUCANSON: My penis? Ah, you have heard of my adversity.

LE CAT: I have.

VAUCANSON: Madame du Chatelet recommends you highly, but I cannot afford a doctor.

LE CAT: Do not worry about the cost, for it was Madame who sent me here. I was with her this morning.

VAUCANSON: This morning?

LE CAT: Please, your trousers.

VAUCANSON: You were with the Madame this morning?

LE CAT: Yes, Monsieur Arouet was distressed at her condition and had me summoned.

VAUCANSON: Monsieur Arouet?

LE CAT: Yes.

VAUCANSON: François Arouet?

LE CAT: Yes.

VAUCANSON: By François Arouet you mean of course Voltaire?
LE CAT: Yes.
VAUCANSON: He was there was he . . . Voltaire . . .

(VAUCANSON, trouserless, picks up a very large book and reads a page to hide his thoughts while LE CAT speaks.)

LE CAT: Oh yes, they are much in love, I don't usually believe in such tripe but you can feel it in the air, their love . . .
VAUCANSON: Fine.
LE CAT: —and early this morning he was alarmed to find Madame suffering from great swoons and any amount of vomit.
VAUCANSON: My God is she all right?
LE CAT: In a manner of speaking. She is pregnant.
VAUCANSON: *(To self, with delight.)* Great swoons . . . and any amount of vomit . . . are two reactions contemplated then suppressed by this scientist upon hearing the news of a pump beating in tiny 2/4 counterpoint to the greater pump above it and all this occurred in the time it took for a large book to slip from the hands and fall at a velocity proportional not to its weight but to the time elapsed in its falling.
LE CAT: *(Rewinding to previous line.)* In a manner of speaking. She is pregnant.

(The book falls from the hands of VAUCANSON with a thud.)

VAUCANSON: I see.
LE CAT: Yes, and true to her nature, she said never mind her, she would foot the bill if I went straight away to the studios of the suffering Jacques de Vaucanson.
VAUCANSON: *(Failing to disguise excitement.)* But this is . . . this is staggering . . .
LE CAT: Is it.
VAUCANSON: . . . How truly . . . miraculous . . . for her . . .
LE CAT: Yes, well Shall we get on? If you may, please bend from the waist to 85 degrees.
VAUCANSON: *(Bending.)* A child . . . Well! . . . And how pregnant is she?

LE CAT: There is another eight months before the infant receives the first of many rude shocks . . .

VAUCANSON: Eight months . . . yes, that would do it . . . amazing . . . amazing . . . a tiny life . . .

LE CAT: Well you seem certainly more moved by the event than Voltaire . . .

VAUCANSON: *(Sobered.)* Oh yes, Voltaire. How did he take the news?

LE CAT: I can't say favorably. After all, in less than a month, Madame's husband is expected home from the military campaigns in Corsica—

VAUCANSON: *(Still more sobered.)* Oh yes, her husband . . .

LE CAT: *(Examining rectal area.)* There's quite a scar I see . . . You've had surgery before?

VAUCANSON: Three years ago.

LE CAT: It's a perilous operation. One's chances of survival are quite small.

VAUCANSON: That fact was made known to me only afterward. How close . . . how close I came to obliteration . . . And all for a stone.

LE CAT: A trivial death is the most appropriate sort of death for it does not obscure, nay in fact it underscores, the irrefutable insignificance of individual life. Don't you agree?

VAUCANSON: No I do not, and the stone they removed was the size of a tennis ball.

LE CAT: I don't doubt it.

VAUCANSON: And I still pass gravel in my urine. No, never the knife again.

LE CAT: Well, if you change your mind, I have developed techniques that avoid many of the complications caused by this sort of surgery in the past.

VAUCANSON: What sort of complications?

LE CAT: Well, sterility for one.

(Pause.)

VAUCANSON: Sterility?

LE CAT: You were made aware that a procedure like the one you endured almost always results in sterility.

VAUCANSON: *(Devastated.)* Sterility. No. No I was not made aware.

LE CAT: Do you have children?

VAUCANSON: Do I have children?

(A slide is projected—a lateral view of the male reproductive system with penis.)

LE CAT: It's a lateral cut of the perineum to reach the urethra, where the stone is impacted, and the slightest slip of the knife will sever the vas deferens which connects to it.

VAUCANSON: *(Profound dejection.)* And the vas deferens carries the juice of the testicles.

LE CAT: Yes. I'm sorry to have to tell you but it's a near certainty. I thought you knew . . .

VAUCANSON: *(Half to self.)* . . . and we can be reasonably assured then that Voltaire has not the same curse upon him . . .

LE CAT: I should say he has amply proved otherwise . . .

VAUCANSON: . . . no little chicks . . . and my life will end with me . . . and all that will live on . . . is my work . . .

LE CAT: And all because from the same tube men emit both waste and life . . . which perhaps is why waste and life are so difficult to distinguish from one another . . .

VAUCANSON: You say so, but I do not think so . . .

LE CAT: You do not think so, but think of Needham, who through the tube of his microscope witnessed in a teardrop the swarming of little eels so small that a cluster of a million could not be discerned by the human eye. A cluster of a million! And no doubt this universe is but another teardrop, containing all of mankind and all his great grand history besides. Blot it up with a handkerchief and who, pray tell, will take notice?

VAUCANSON: You may well ask!

LE CAT: I needn't ask, for I know the answer. No one. And no thing.

VAUCANSON: No sir, no sir, no event goes unfelt, and even the flap of wings on a fly may no doubt be amplified through space and time into a thunderclap, for all things are ineluctably connected—

LE CAT: I assure you sir, the stars stand aloof, and so do I.

VAUCANSON: You can try, but I tell you not a particle in the universe can make such a claim, much less a surgeon—

LE CAT: —One who sees all this soup of living and dying for what it is—a dish of laughable insignificance.

VAUCANSON: There is nothing laughable and nothing insignificant. Do you not see that in the infinite chain of beings, our earth, our body, are among the necessary links? In every droplet of sea water you'll find Needham's little eels. Look and you'll see the movement of one little eel affecting and affected by other little eels, and other little eels still other little eels, until the entire droplet is affected, and each droplet affecting other countless droplets until it is the very sea that is affected, yes the sea, that engenders clouds, and the clouds that furnish the rain that nourishes the earth that binds the moon that makes the tides that affects the ships, and sailors on ships, and the wives of those sailors on ships and the handkerchiefs of those wives waved at departing sailors on ships, and the teardrops in those handkerchiefs and the eels in those tear drops, the eels sir, the eels sir . . . To say nothing of the sailors' wives' grandfathers.

LE CAT: To say nothing is right. You have said nothing as to the purpose of it all. To what end?

VAUCANSON: That we will discover in time, and in the meantime we have this . . . this dance . . . And there is no begging out of it—you say you stand aloof, but a man who says he has left a ballroom has done nothing of the sort. He has merely stepped outside and under the stars and into an even greater, all-encompassing, incomparable Minuet.

LE CAT: A Minuet. If this Universe is a dance, sir, it is nothing more than the spasmodic dance of a boy who has just burned his tongue.

VAUCANSON: *(The gracious host.)* Yes, well, thank you doctor. Now if you don't mind, I have much work—

LE CAT: I have some suggested courses of treatment—

VAUCANSON: Thank you all the same, but I'm not interested, you can tell Madame Chatelet I said as much—

LE CAT: Madame Chatelet, yes, I nearly forgot—she sent this on to give to you.

(LE CAT hands VAUCANSON his peruke.)

VAUCANSON: My peruke! Say what you will Le Cat, but I will prove all your doubts wrong with this!

LE CAT: With your peruke?

(But VAUCANSON realizes the ratios are not to be found.)

VAUCANSON: Le Cat, did you not perhaps from this wig see slip a slip of paper as you traveled from Chatelet's?

LE CAT: No.

(Pause.)

VAUCANSON: No matter . . . No matter. But if you would be so good as to survey your carriage.

LE CAT: Of course. May I ask what the slip contained?

VAUCANSON: Merely . . . effort.

LE CAT: It occurs to me that as I was riding here I espied a spider within your peruke and I shook the peruke violently outside the window, dislodging the spider—

VAUCANSON: —and perhaps the paper—

LE CAT: It is possible.

VAUCANSON: Where was this?

LE CAT: Some miles between Paris and Cirey on the King's Highway.

VAUCANSON: Can you be more specific?

LE CAT: No.

VAUCANSON: Right, fine, thank you. I will show you now the door—

LE CAT: Thank you all the same but I can find it myself. I wouldn't recommend across this floor any unclad feet . . . *(Notices toes of VAUCANSON poking through large holes in his stockings.)* My dear sir, your feet—

VAUCANSON: Yes.

LE CAT: They're webbed.

VAUCANSON: An incomplete separation of the digits. My father's feet were the same.

LE CAT: Were they . . . And his father's before him?

VAUCANSON: I don't know.

LE CAT: Because it is a trait known to pass from one generation to the next.

VAUCANSON: Is it?

LE CAT: But of course, Sterile Sam, the trait will end with you . . .

VAUCANSON: *(Through gritted teeth.)* Yes. It will end with me. And now the door—

LE CAT: Webbed feet. So that is why you've set out to construct of all things, a clockwork duck.

VAUCANSON: No, actually . . . that hadn't occurred to me . . .

LE CAT: Come sir, surely—

VAUCANSON: No, it is coincidence.

LE CAT: Pure accident! And here you are constructing a duck to prove there is no such thing! How then did you fix upon the idea specifically of a duck?

VAUCANSON: Do you really want to know?

LE CAT: I do.

(We hear crickets, frogs, distant ducks.)

VAUCANSON: *(Carrying shoes.)* How the sky was awash with stars that night of the ball at du Chatelet's chateau . . . It was about three weeks ago, I was in a disagreeable mood, I needed air, but just as I was taking my leave for the evening I was foolishly convinced in participating in that vexatious game wherein all the shoes of all the guests are piled in one enormous pile, and when all was said and done, I wound up with shoes that resembled mine in every respect except they were too small by half. As I roamed the grounds wet with dew— *(We hear the sound of a man vomiting into a body of water.)* I heard coming from the banks of the pond—

(More vomiting, and revealed, in silhouette, LAZARRO SPALLANZANI. Pitiful groans heard from the man as well. Italian accent, clearly exhausting for him to communicate with

*VAUCANSON, and a struggle for VAUCANSON as well. By end of
scene however, they are finishing each other's sentences.)*

VAUCANSON: The punch at Madame Chatelet's gatherings tends to
be quite strong.

SPALLANZANI: I cannot-a-speak-a French.

VAUCANSON: You are Italian.

SPALLANZANI: Yes, so . . . how you say . . . shove off.

VAUCANSON: My pardons. Never mind.

SPALLANZANI: But what is it that you said. I must try. I must try.

VAUCANSON: Merely that you've had too much to drink . . .

SPALLANZANI: No, no, I never drink! It is . . . the after-effects . . .

VAUCANSON: Yes?

SPALLANZANI: of . . . what is the word . . . oh to hell with it.

VAUCANSON: No, no, what? You must try. The after-effects of what.

SPALLANZANI: The after-effects of . . . experiments I performed on-
a myself.

VAUCANSON: Experiments? For the contest sponsored by the Royal
Academy?

SPALLANZANI: No. I did not know the contest it had-a been made
public yet.

VAUCANSON: It hasn't, but perhaps you had gotten wind—

SPALLANZANI: No, I do not have wind! But you found out this contest? From whom?

VAUCANSON: I have only just now been informed by Madame du
Chatelet.

SPALLANZANI: Ah, they say-a she is a most-a remarkable woman.

VAUCANSON: She is . . . most remarkable . . . *(Aside.)* And what with
Voltaire having just returned, I for now must extinguish all
thought of her, or I will surely torment myself to oblivion . . .

SPALLANZANI: *(Half to self.)* I do not know why I am here. Perhaps
I should leave.

VAUCANSON: Were you not invited?

SPALLANZANI: No. Yes. I mean France. This . . . Earth.

VAUCANSON: Well take your leave then, although I hear there will
be fireworks later.

SPALLANZANI: The fireworks will never come . . . How do you say in French . . . How-a vain-a is all-a human thought!

VAUCANSON: Your French is sound, but not your conclusion.

SPALLANZANI: How-a petty is all our ideas!

VAUCANSON: You are overwrought.

SPALLANZANI: Petty! And how-a poor our glories and-a all our labors!

VAUCANSON: No. Shush!

(Pause.)

SPALLANZANI: How-a wretched we are!

VAUCANSON: Quiet.

(Pause.)

SPALLANZANI: Wretched.

VAUCANSON: No. Cease and I will tell you the topic of this year's contest.

SPALLANZANI: I am very sick.

(While SPALLANZANI retches with volume and violence, VAUCANSON recites.)

VAUCANSON: The contest is thus.
     Prove or refute the following statement:
     The Apparent Randomness of Events in Nature
     Will, if subjected to Calculation,
     Reveal an underlying Order. . . .
     Expressing Exquisite Wisdom and Design

SPALLANZANI: I did not get any of that. Once more please.

VAUCANSON: The Apparent . . . Oh what's the point . . .

SPALLANZANI: No no, you must tell me . . . you must try . . .

VAUCANSON: *(Miming/gesturing as best he can, but ridiculously.)*
     The Apparent Randomness of Events in Nature—

SPALLANZANI: The apparent randomness . . .

VAUCANSON: *(Miming.)* Yes—Will, If Subjected to Calculation,

SPALLANZANI: yes . . .

VAUCANSON: *(Miming.)* Reveal an Underlying Order

SPALLANZANI: An Underlying Order—

VAUCANSON: *(Miming.)* Expressing Exquisite Wisdom and Design. Prove or refute.

SPALLANZANI: Ah yes, and tell me, will you prove or refute?

VAUCANSON: Prove.

SPALLANZANI: How.

VAUCANSON: *(Clutching SPALLANZANI.)* I don't know, but I must . . . *must* think of something, Everything depends on it!

SPALLANZANI: Tonight my mood is black, yes, but I don't see how it can be done without much deceit.

VAUCANSON: No, I cannot believe that.

SPALLANZANI: It is all foul and pointless endeavorings. Instead of vomiting into this duck pond, I should drown myself in it. But the problem . . . is that I can swim, and I would swim through the muck and the lily pads back-a to the edge despite myself, yes? It makes-a no sense, why I should cling to this . . . dunghill.

VAUCANSON: You are feeling low after a failed experiment, that is all. I have often felt the same way.

SPALLANZANI: Perhaps.

VAUCANSON: What experiment were you working on before being forced to abandon it?

SPALLANZANI: *(Becoming animated.)* It concerned-a . . . Life!

VAUCANSON: Excellent!

SPALLANZANI: How inert matter somehow becomes flesh . . .

VAUCANSON: For instance?

SPALLANZANI: Seména.

VAUCANSON: What?

SPALLANZANI: *(With heavy accent.)* Seména.

VAUCANSON: *(Not getting it.)* One more time.

SPALLANZANI: Seména!

VAUCANSON: One more time.

SPALLANZANI: Seména!

(Pause.)

VAUCANSON: *(Straining.)* One more time.

SPALLANZANI: Oh to hell with it.

VAUCANSON: *(Timidly trying again.)* Semena?

SPALLANZANI: I said forget it!

VAUCANSON: Fine.

SPALLANZANI: *(Under breath.)* To hell with everyone.

VAUCANSON: I'm sorry?

SPALLANZANI: I said to hell with you!

VAUCANSON: Well to hell with you!

SPALLANZANI: Just-a leave me alone, eh? I want to be just-a with the pond and the frogs ...

VAUCANSON: Fine. You have your liberty. The croaking's too loud for me anyway.

SPALLANZANI: They are seeking mates.

VAUCANSON: *(Walking away, to self.)* And they'll find nothing but heartache and despair—

SPALLANZANI: The female frog, she lays her 20,000 eggs, and the male sprays his semen-a on top of them, and in one week, tadpoles.

VAUCANSON: *(Stops, now realizing.)* ... semen ... Semen!

SPALLANZANI: Yes! Yes! Semena! Inert matter! And in one week, tadpoles! How? How is this possible?

VAUCANSON: Yes—How indeed. What is it in the semen that creates life?

SPALLANZANI: No one knows, but I can tell you that it is the same for both man and frog.

VAUCANSON: Ah but look here, man is not a frog.

SPALLANZANI: Is man not a frog?

VAUCANSON: I say to you Man is not a Frog.

SPALLANZANI: The difference, it is trivial.

(Duck quack and frog croak at minimum volume.)

VAUCANSON: I don't know his name, but Impulses from the gastrointestinal tract of my fellow scientist have been sent to his brain. The brain then sends back impulses that precipitate spasmodic muscular contractions. The pressure generated forces up the contents of his stomach, namely: bile, three prunes, and a dollop of porridge.

SPALLANZANI: I do not-a know his name, but in the pelvis of this fellow, the muscular sac, holding a half a pint of urine, is irritated by a calcium concretion floating in the urine, and suddenly begins persistent-a rigid contractions.

(Beat. Then VAUCANSON is attacked by an intense bladder spasm, and almost simultaneously, SPALLANZANI begins retching with violence and misery. Quite prolonged. VAUCANSON attempts to stifle pain and prevent from urinating, while desperately attempting to undo his trousers but a button becomes stuck. He rolls on ground, he stands up again, fighting with button. Frog croak and duck quack quite voluble.)

VAUCANSON: *(With violence.)* I can't undo the button! Come button! Cursed button!

(SPALLANZANI, retching now waning, has collapsed on ground, and crawls toward VAUCANSON. VAUCANSON has sudden realization that his bladder is emptying into his trousers.)

VAUCANSON: Oh God . . .

(VAUCANSON sinks to ground.)

SPALLANZANI: Your pants, they are damp.
VAUCANSON: You see a man in trousers humiliated.
SPALLANZANI: Do not be embarrassed.
VAUCANSON: This wretched wretched bladder . . . I'd sooner not eat or drink anything again—
SPALLANZANI: No, no . . . We eat and we grow into men.
VAUCANSON: Ah, again—inert matter into living matter . . .
SPALLANZANI: Yes, food! That is it. In our stomach . . . a . . . a . . .
VAUCANSON: Yes, yes . . . a . . . a . . .
SPALLANZANI: A . . . how you say—
VAUCANSON: a . . . a . . . Transubstantiation!
SPALLANZANI: A what?
VAUCANSON: Food into flesh—

SPALLANZANI: Yes! Yes! That is it!

VAUCANSON: These were the experiments you conducted?

SPALLANZANI: My rival Reaumur, damn him, he persuaded a duck to swallow a sponge that the duck then regurgitated.

VAUCANSON: Go on.

SPALLANZANI: But are the juices in the human-a stomach like those in other beasts? That is the question. So I myself swallowed not just a sponge, but many-a bags of chemicals.

VAUCANSON: You shewed admirable conviction—

SPALLANZANI: But I could not vomit them up again! Reaumur's duck, he could, the duck could and I could not. And now I think the packets have broken open for I vomit all the time, and with blood.

VAUCANSON: I have seen a human carnival performer who swallowed stones for a living and then regurgitates them at will. You might have hired someone like him to swallow your packets.

(Pause.)

SPALLANZANI: I did not think of that.

VAUCANSON: Nevertheless, yours was a worthy experiment.

SPALLANZANI: And yet I am sure I would find the gastric juices similar between man and duck.

VAUCANSON: But look here, man is not a duck.

SPALLANZANI: Is man not a duck?

VAUCANSON: I say to you Man is not a Duck.

SPALLANZANI: The difference, it is trivial.

VAUCANSON: No. Our nobility, our reason, puts us in a different class altogether from the duck . . .

SPALLANZANI: And yet . . . look . . . look at one of those creatures . . .

(SPALLANZANI points at duck by pond, we hear gentle quacking.)

SPALLANZANI: See! It walks, it flutters its wings, it feels irritations—

VAUCANSON: Yes, you're right, it runs away, it comes back again—

SPALLANZANI: —it-a makes a complaining sound, yes? It feels pain—
VAUCANSON: —it shows affection—
SPALLANZANI: —it has desires, it gets-a pleasure from this or that . . .

(Music more stirring, up on frogs and ducks.)

VAUCANSON: Yes you're right, it certainly shows all the emotions that you show! . . .

(Music more stirring still.)

SPALLANZANI: —and it eats and eliminates just as you do.
VAUCANSON: Better than I do!
SPALLANZANI: And here they say that it has-a no soul—that it's just a machine—
VAUCANSON: A machine? Oh no my friend, it is—
SPALLANZANI: No, that spark of life, it will never be explained.
VAUCANSON: We do not know it yet, but do not call that unknowable. Good god sir, are we not scientists? There were mysteries all around us that we . . . *we* have exploded! The formulas for that duck may be more complex than those of a clock—
SPALLANZANI: Hah! A hundred million times more complex—
VAUCANSON: —fine! yes! but a hundred million is still a *finite* number, of course it is! And therefore, with time, *attainable.* I assure you sir, we are living equations—
SPALLANZANI: —machines then—
VAUCANSON: —but how exquisite the Design . . .

(Music now shimmering, inspiring—)

SPALLANZANI: *(Clutching VAUCANSON's shoulders, with tears.)* My god . . . it is true . . . it is true! . . . Signore, we are living in a utopia . . .
VAUCANSON: *(Clutching SPALLANZANI, with tears.)* I know . . . I know, my friend . . .
SPALLANZANI: —under this canopy of stars . . .

VAUCANSON: —aneath the music and whirrings of the spheres, it is truly—

SPALLANZANI: —the best of all—

VAUCANSON: —possible worlds—

SPALLANZANI: —where even those ducks—

VAUCANSON: —yes, those flapping excreting ducks by a stagnant pond are—

SPALLANZANI: —a glorious necessity—

VAUCANSON: —and contain within their atoms—

SPALLANZANI: —the blueprint—

VAUCANSON: —of the universe! . . . *(Growing excited at a thought forming in head—)* . . . indeed . . . indeed—

SPALLANZANI: *(Pointing to the ground, ecstatic.)* —Holy God, Signore—You have-a my shoes!

(Music still more stirring, and fireworks begin to be set off. A great booming, and slides of flares.)

VAUCANSON: *(Ecstatic, clutching SPALLANZANI even tighter, and completing thought—)* Nothing is random! . . . Nothing is random, and I will prove it! . . . Employing Newton's laws of attraction by which the tides behave and the planets are known to rotate; Using calculations plotting the movement of the stars themselves across the heavens; Utilizing a system of springs and weights, gearwheels, cogs and escapements of my own construction fashioned in ratios of proven mathematical laws and proportion . . . I will create . . . a Duck . . . that flaps its wings, eats, and excretes . . . just like a duck!

(Musical coda. The slides change to another picture. SPALLAZANI has exited.)

VAUCANSON: Any questions?

(It becomes clear that VAUCANSON is now in the midst of a fundraising presentation. The ABBE is assisting with the Magic Lantern slides.)

CITIZEN #1: Why a duck?

VAUCANSON: I believe I have just explained to you why a duck.

CITIZEN #2: It is a clockwork.

VAUCANSON: Yes.

CITIZEN #2: Will it tell the time?

VAUCANSON: Of course not! But! Study the movement of the humerus in the wing and you will observe the same mathematical ratios that send Mars around the Sun, watch the duck stretch out its neck and you are witnessing the formulae that predict the curl of smoke from a pipe, steam from a kettle, the shape of a cumulus cloud or a plume of dust from a cart, in short, you will observe chaos itself made sensical by mathematical principles!

CITIZEN #3: Good God, you are creating the universe—

CITIZEN #2: What you propose sir is impossible!

VAUCANSON: Impossible?

CITIZEN #2: Of course you do not want to hear such an opinion.

VAUCANSON: No, no . . . tell me the things that are not possible, for those are the things that I will do . . . I require a minimum of funding and your names shall be attached to an undertaking that will be spoken of centuries hence!

(Montage, with much music. We see VAUCANSON hard at work, e.g., filing gears, tearing down designs from the wall, crippled by bladder spasms. We then see projected a landscape, with a road stretching on. We hear birds whistle, and the lowing of cows.)

ABBE: How large is this strip of paper?

VAUCANSON: Yea long.

(Pause.)

ABBE: And you propose we should walk yet a mile further on this road in search of it?

VAUCANSON: Have we a choice? I can little believe that such ratios, so vital to this work, nay, essential to the completion of it, will not return to my possession.

(Long pause.)

ABBE: But Jacques, the odds . . .

VAUCANSON: Blast the odds! Odds are irrelevant! This duck was meant to be made!

ABBE: I say . . . *(Spying scrap of paper on ground.)* Jacques! Jacques!

(They dive for the scrap. VAUCANSON reads scrap.)

VAUCANSON: *(Disappointed.)* No, it is not the ratios. It appears to be a strip torn from a love letter.

ABBE: Here on the King's Highway?

VAUCANSON: It was a blustery day on November 12th. Perhaps in a man's hand is pressed a letter from his Love just as he is taking his leave. In his carriage he reads with great anticipation, but finds that instead of cooing phrases, she is calling it off. "Enough," she writes. "I wish it done." The man shreds the letter and scatters it to the wind, and here a scrap descended, to lie befouled . . . in a ditch . . .

ABBE: Well that's certainly one possibility. *(Concerned by VAUCANSON's narrative.)* Jacques . . . How fares Madame Chatelet?

VAUCANSON: I wouldn't know.

ABBE: You have not heard from her?

VAUCANSON: I have not. Nor have I thought of her. *(Pause.)* I never think of her.

(Thunder rumbles. A storm begins.)

ABBE: *(Hopeful that they can now go home.)* Shall we give up?

(Pause. The rain falls hard.)

VAUCANSON: No!

(Thunder claps. Montage continues. Much music. We see VAUCANSON building the framework, studying the movements

of makeshift wings, drinking turpentine, running over list of more materials needed.)

VAUCANSON: Read it back to me.

ABBE: *(Reading.)* "One worm gear with 112-toothed wheel and threaded cylinder, 2.8 inch diameter, 20 feet of copper wire 11 pound torque, and additional amounts for the cubitus of the right wing. Also feathers. Mallard."

VAUCANSON: Good.

ABBE: But you have not found the ratios?

VAUCANSON: I will have to reconstruct them.

ABBE: Do you have time?

VAUCANSON: Plenty. If I do not sleep.

(Montage continues, with VAUCANSON tearing down designs from the wall, crippled by bladder spasms, fighting sleep, finally falling asleep. Darkness. We then hear, softly, CHATELET singing the opening song. Lights up. JACQUES, at table, head resting on palm, slowly awakes, and singing softly next to him, an eight-months pregnant CHATELET.)

VAUCANSON: You?

CHATELET: You.

VAUCANSON: Am I awake?

CHATELET: I promise.

VAUCANSON: . . . I dreamt . . . I don't even remember, except I stood naked with months of work for naught and a deadline in less than a day . . .

CHATELET: No, you have still nearly a month . . . And you will shape infinity into the dimensions of a duck . . .

VAUCANSON: But my dream, so vivid . . . all that work . . . and no indication that they were all calculations in futility . . .

CHATELET: Dreams are for the dead . . . You can dream . . . but you can do more than dream . . .

VAUCANSON: Yes, I can make the duck drink, play in the water with his bill, and unleash a gurgling noise like a real living duck, but

with no assurance that I will not awake and find it was all yet
again for naught . . .

CHATELET: Then awake and begin again, so long as you find yourself awake—strive! What more can you do?

VAUCANSON: With every atom of my being, I love you . . . I love
you, and I know *how* all things move, yes, but *what* is it that
moves them? What? And suddenly I am convinced that it is this
love for you. For without you, all the world would seem lifeless
and inanimate, I know it. And if I know now the how and what,
I still will never know why . . . why do all things move and why
do I persist in loving you when you are clearly in love with
someone else and carrying his child?

CHATELET: Jacques de Vaucanson . . . Why do you think I've come
to you? Because I have decided at long last to choose the man
whose vision offers mankind a glimpse of things to come . . .

VAUCANSON: *(Looks around the room, then realizes—)* Me?

CHATELET: There are many who say what you are attempting cannot be done—

VAUCANSON: So many raspberries have been blown at me, the air
is fragrant with fruit . . .

CHATELET: And yet you have faith . . . and I don't want to live with
someone without it . . . the faith that all humanity tries as hard
as it can, that we all mean well . . . that History may prove us
wrong, but we did what we thought best, with what we had—

VAUCANSON: Yes . . . Faith. It is slow but I know progress comes
daily even though I cannot see it . . . But how maddening in its
pace . . .

CHATELET: Everything, from the wing of a dragonfly to the invention of the harpsichord, everything, everything, everything was
built on trial and error.

VAUCANSON: Yes, yes it's true . . .

CHATELET: From the powder in your peruke to Newton's First Law
of Motion . . .

VAUCANSON: Yes.

CHATELET: The door hinge, and the pendulum clock.

VAUCANSON: And domestic livestock breeding.

CHATELET: And soap-manufacturing—

VAUCANSON: —and knowledge of the lymphatic system—

(By now a bit of intellectual/romantic play between them, which brings them closer.)

CHATELET: —and stained glass—

VAUCANSON: —double-entry bookkeeping—

CHATELET: —and the Gregorian calendar

VAUCANSON: The cultivation of the cabernet grape—

CHATELET: —intercolumniation

VAUCANSON: —and the moldboard plough

CHATELET: —and the bagpipes.

VAUCANSON: And dephlogisticated air

CHATELET: Plus the banquet couch—

VAUCANSON: —and belaying pins on ships.

CHATELET: And the parasol—

VAUCANSON: The flintlock—

CHATELET: —bobbin lace

VAUCANSON: —the crosstitch

CHATELET: —the mapping of Africa

VAUCANSON: —and the shoemaker's awl for pegging shoes!

CHATELET: Yes.

VAUCANSON: They all came about through struggle—

CHATELET: *(By now in embrace—)* —so Patience. Mankind is still in its infancy.

VAUCANSON: Yes—

CHATELET: I have faith in you . . . have patience with me and we will construct a life together—

VAUCANSON: *(Beginning to feel giddy.)* Upon trial and error—

CHATELET: Yes.

VAUCANSON: And you truly mean it.

CHATELET: Not only do I mean it, I'm quite o'erwhelmed about it—

VAUCANSON: *(Beaming for first time in play.)* You're quite o'erwhelmed? How . . . most . . . excellent good.

CHATELET: And Jacques perhaps, perhaps the child is yours . . .

VAUCANSON: No no no, it's not, it's not . . . but no matter . . . I don't mind . . .

(Pause.)

CHATELET: Well . . . I should go . . .
VAUCANSON: I want to be with you.
CHATELET: No, I mustn't stand in your way . . . but such days ahead . . . I can taste them on my lips . . .
VAUCANSON: *(Tears of happiness.)* Yes . . . yes . . .
CHATELET: *(Nearly exiting, then turning around and saying matter-of-factly.)* Oh, I nearly forgot. I found this scrap of paper in my bedroom. I don't know if its important. It appears to contain a number of different ratios . . . and it's in your handwriting . . . Have you been looking for it?

(JACQUES seizes scrap of paper. Montage with still grander music. JACQUES in untucked shirt, wrench clenched in teeth, tearing down designs from the wall, bending duck prototype with pliers, etc. Musical coda, then a number of insistent knocks on the door. VAUCANSON is deeply engrossed in hard thought and pained study and intense labor.)

ABBE: *(Through door.)* Jacques . . . Jacques, it is I—
VAUCANSON: It's open.
ABBE: It's not open.

(Pause. Then knock knock knock.)

VAUCANSON: It's open.
ABBE: Jacques it's locked.
VAUCANSON: It isn't. You have to push.
ABBE: I am. I am pushing.
VAUCANSON: No, push . . . push.
ABBE: I'm pushing.
VAUCANSON: Hold the handle and push.
ABBE: For God's sake, it is locked.

VAUCANSON: It is not locked. I was occasioned to unlock it an hour ago.

(Pause. More knocking. Pause.)

ABBE: Jacques. The door is locked.
VAUCANSON: I'm telling you it's open, stop knocking and push.
ABBE: Jacques, we don't have much time—
VAUCANSON: *(Half to self.)* I know . . . I know . . . in less than ninety-six hours I'm to present to the Academy a deterministic, dynamic model that yet will elucidate irregular, unpredictable behavior . . .

(Pause.)

ABBE: What? Jacques, I can't hear you . . . Look, I have news of grave import that perhaps you have not heard, I beg of you, open the—

(VAUCANSON pulls on door, unfastens bolt, opens door.)

VAUCANSON: Who continues to lock my door against my wishes?! Everywhere I turn, unexpected impediments!

(The ABBE looks distraught, despite efforts to hide it. Though also clear that he is no longer the sot he was at beginning of play.)

ABBE: You look terrible.
VAUCANSON: The work . . . The work involved!
ABBE: There's food outside the door—
VAUCANSON: Leave it outside.
ABBE: *(Retrieving it.)* You must try to eat a little.
VAUCANSON: I cannot.
ABBE: When was the last time you ate?
VAUCANSON: I don't remember. I can't even look at it.
ABBE: It is nourishment.
VAUCANSON: Put it out of sight.

ABBE: *(Putting it behind screen.)* If you want it, it's over here.

VAUCANSON: Fine.

ABBE: Do you see? Over here.

VAUCANSON: Fine! Now what is this about news of grave import . . .

ABBE: Yes . . . I will come to that. Jacques, how are you proceeding . . .

VAUCANSON: I don't know if it's progress, or if I'm just going in circles. I have not left my rooms for weeks. So many different moving parts in such a small automaton . . .

ABBE: I'm worried about you, Jacques, sleep—there's such a thing as that . . .

VAUCANSON: Do you know where mankind would be if he always got a proper night's sleep? Still in the mud! We are the only creature who has said, "I am tired, but until I am finished, I will not sleep"—I will not sleep—

(A knock on the door. The ABBE opens it to reveal LE CAT.)

LE CAT: Abbe, you are here? So you have told him?

ABBE: No . . . I have not told him.

VAUCANSON: Told me what?

(Silence. A pause long enough for VAUCANSON, and perhaps audience too, to understand fully that CHATELET has died in childbirth.)

VAUCANSON: Oh god . . .

LE CAT: You could feed all the pigs in all the farms in France for a month I'd wager from the trough containing nothing but our hard-won knowledge . . . And I think the pigs wouldn't notice a whit of difference between it and their usual fodder . . .

VAUCANSON: I disagree.

LE CAT: The ultimate cause of things has no more regard to good above ill than to heat above cold . . .

VAUCANSON: No, I disagree. But tell me Abbe, why was I not informed . . .

ABBE: I was summoned by Madame du Chatelet to be present, for she was enduring a labor long and difficult but your work she did not want to disturb.

VAUCANSON: How did Voltaire receive the news?

ABBE: He is in bed, having fallen down the stairs. His servant attests that he saw his master throw himself down on purpose . . .

VAUCANSON: The child?

ABBE: . . . A girl . . . It struggled 'til morning, then it too . . .

LE CAT: And so we see our man's seed, hell-bent on producing life, has instead produced nothing but death . . . I once asserted that a trivial death had the most befitting irony . . . but a death in childbirth quite eclipses it.

VAUCANSON: You say these things out of fear Le Cat.

LE CAT: Cynicism. I have seen too much of the world to feel otherwise.

VAUCANSON: And that assertion is uttered out of naiveté . . . for contrary to your belief you have not seen enough to know . . . to know truly the way of things . . .

LE CAT: I have seen enough to know that life is little more than the momentary difficulty when swallowing your slaver.

VAUCANSON: No.

LE CAT: It gives one nothing but nausea to see you stand here and say that our lady's death was all part of god's shimmering plan—

VAUCANSON: *(Obviously struggling heroically with grief.)* Her death . . . Madame du Chatelet's . . . death . . . so as her life . . . has and will continue to have generated incalculable consequences, and the world is altered irrevocably for her having lived in it, and died in it, just as the world had been influenced and adjusted step by step again and again before our time until it produced, as one of its near-innumerable effects, a child who would become Gabrielle-Emilie, patroness of the Sciences, and she might have perished when she was three, before anyone knew her or loved her, she might have succumbed to smallpox or consumption, or been run down by a carriage, or had her brains dashed out by a Hessian soldier when but a girl but it was not till now and it was this and so—

LE CAT: And so we will not find you throwing yourself down stairs?

VAUCANSON: No. Now if you will excuse me doctor, I have much work—

LE CAT: I should say you do.

(LE CAT turns round just as he is about to exit.)

LE CAT: Tell me . . . What did you mean . . . that I said what I said out of fear?

VAUCANSON: What is your fear, Le Cat? The fear of striving for not a scrap of recompense . . . The fear that all the faithless share— that you will never find meaning in your loves and labours, so why even attempt . . .

LE CAT: *(Profoundly sobered.)* Yes . . . perhaps you are right . . . I am . . . moved by your vision, Jacques de Vaucanson, the magnitude of your undertaking . . . your fortitude . . . You are a bulwark . . . a bulwark . . . and I thank you for it . . . I thank you for it . . .

(LE CAT exits.)

VAUCANSON: Abbe . . . Was there much suffering?

ABBE: *(Lying.)* No. All in all she succumbed most peaceably . . . but Le Cat does not know what I know . . . that the construction of your duck was motivated in no little part by your feelings for Madame Chatelet.

VAUCANSON: Yes . . .

ABBE: Where then do you stand with the project . . . Will you wash your hands of it?

VAUCANSON: Abandon the work?

ABBE: Perhaps you should give up.

VAUCANSON: No, no surely you understand the sincere necessity of completing it.

ABBE: I am relieved. Is there anything you need?

VAUCANSON: This is a list. The last.

ABBE: I'll go then. And Jacques . . . thank you . . .

VAUCANSON: Thank you?

ABBE: You, and who would have thought it, but you have replenished my faith in God. May your endeavor be blessed my son.

VAUCANSON: Abbe . . . Were there any last words . . .

ABBE: None to speak of. Madame du Chatelet's last words were regarding her child . . .

VAUCANSON: The daughter.

ABBE: Yes.

VAUCANSON: Abbe . . . was there much suffering?

ABBE: Yes. Much.

VAUCANSON: What were the words?

ABBE: She shook out of her delirium long enough to ask, "*Et comment ça va mon petit canard?*" She expired soon after.

VAUCANSON: Petit Canard . . . why canard? Why a duck?

ABBE: Barely noticeable, but the child's toes were incompletely separated . . . lending an appearance of webbing.

(Stirring music. In silhouette, we see a representation of VAUCANSON's Duck, slowly moving. The duck sits atop a platform, underneath of which is a vast complex network of gears, cylinders, etc.)

We can never fully know and contemplate the obstacles this great man has overcome to construct such a—

CITIZEN #2: It is an object of wonderment—

CITIZEN #3: That he will be made a full member of the Academy, that is certain!

CITIZEN #4: It must tour Europe—

CITIZEN #2: It will be the inspiration and awe of the continent—

CITIZEN #4: And England, birthplace of Isaac Newton—

CITIZEN #3: When once wound up, the machine performs all its different operations without being touched again—

ABBE: I will provide you an in-depth description of the movements of the duck, including the random stammer—

MEMBER OF ACADEMY: It is the Greatest Proof Yet Constructed that there is Wisdom and Design behind all Creation . . .

VAUCANSON: *(To self, still in shock.)* Dreams are for the dead, and while you are awake . . . strive . . .

CITIZEN #4: *(With tears.)* That is not merely a duck up on that pedestal, it is mankind, it is all of us, our lives . . . He has captured the very essence of Human Existence . . .

VAUCANSON: *(To self.)* Mankind is still in its infancy. We try, stumble, fall, fail, and try again, and we come ever closer in our toddling steps toward the open arms of our Maker . . .

MEMBER OF ACADEMY: Congratulations, Jacques de Vaucanson. You have done just as you said you would. Through months of labor, Employing Newton's laws of attraction by which the tides behave and the planets are known to rotate; Using calculations plotting the movement of the stars themselves across the heavens; Utilizing a system of springs and weights, gearwheels, cogs and escapements of your own construction fashioned in ratios of proven mathematical laws and proportion you have created a duck that flaps its wings, eats, and excretes . . . just like a duck.

(Pause. Music builds. VAUCANSON watches duck and then—)

VAUCANSON: Yes.

(Music building to end. VAUCANSON watches the duck flap its wings, stretch its neck, and excrete. And repeat . . . Repeat . . . Repeat . . . Repeat . . . Repeat . . . Slightest change on VAUCANSON's face as he watches the duck. A slightest indication for first time in play . . . of doubt. Stirring Music.)

— ACT II —

A Frog He Would A Wooing Go . . .

The Story of Lazarro Spallanzani's Great Labour

Characters

Housekeeper: Old woman. Italian accent.
Spallanzani: Near death, or so he believes. Italian accent.
Vaucanson: Elderly, near-senile.
Condorcet: Middle-aged. Preferably same actor as Abbe of Act I.

Time

1794

(Darkness. With candlestick and bowl, HOUSEKEEPER. Wind heard outside, whistling and banging the shutters. Distant bark of dog. Room dimly seen. Room clearly cold, dank, and draughty. Much clutter on desk. Preferably a bust of Reaumur, or portrait of Reaumur on wall. HOUSEKEEPER lights a candle with her candle. Sets down bowl of porridge. Faint croak of frogs. In candlelight, we see old man asleep with head on desk table: SPALLANZANI.)

HOUSEKEEPER: Signore . . . ? *(Pause.)* Signore . . . ?

(She has in hand a pail containing a few scraps of coal and a small shovel, having picked up these two articles by the grate, the small stove in the room. With shovel she bangs on pail. Or perhaps she bangs on the chamber pot. Great clatter either way. Lights should remain rather dim for first few pages of play.)

SPALLANZANI: Don't wake me up, let me dream! *(Clatter continues.)* Damn it, let me dream! Let me dream! The answer was there! *(Clatter continues.)* Fine! Fine! All right Housekeeper, all right, enough with the banging.

(Clatter ends.)

HOUSEKEEPER: My pardons Signore. You are up?
SPALLANZANI: Yes.
HOUSEKEEPER: What did you dream? An answer?
SPALLANZANI: To hell with my dreams. Why don't you let in the light?
HOUSEKEEPER: The light?
SPALLANZANI: Yes, by all means, let in the light.

(HOUSEKEEPER opens drapes. No light is let in for it is still dark.)

HOUSEKEEPER: Look at that—completely dark. I don't see why you must awake so early.
SPALLANZANI: Experiments. *(HOUSEKEEPER makes to exit.)* No, don't leave me alone until we are sure we have awoken.

(Pause. SPALLANZANI and HOUSEKEEPER in dim light. Frog croak.)

SPALLANZANI: All right, I'm up. Get out.
HOUSEKEEPER: Eat your breakfast while it is hot.
SPALLANZANI: I am eating it, I have been eating it. Now leave me alone.

(Pause. SPALLANZANI, head propped in hand, closes eyes in thinking pose. Opens eyes.)

SPALLANZANI: You linger?
HOUSEKEEPER: To be sure you do not return to sleep.
SPALLANZANI: How many times do I have to explain to you that I sometimes must think with eyes closed, but I'm not sleeping, now get out, I have much work!

HOUSEKEEPER: Yes, signore.

(She exits. He closes eyes, forehead on palm. She enters.)

HOUSEKEEPER: Signore? *(We hear gentle snoring.)* Signore?

(She again brings shovel to pail in a frightful banging.)

SPALLANZANI: Yes, I'm up, this time I'm up, enough with the banging. Enough with the banging! Do you want a beating?

HOUSEKEEPER: I am sorry Signore, I am only doing as you requested. I do not enjoy it.

(She sets down chamber pot. SPALLANZANI has his morning vomit into the chamber pot.)

SPALLANZANI: Fine.

HOUSEKEEPER: You are very unreasonable in the morning.

SPALLANZANI: Fine.

HOUSEKEEPER: "Do you want a beating" indeed.

SPALLANZANI: When I say I am up I am up.

HOUSEKEEPER: But perhaps you will go back to sleep—

SPALLANZANI: I couldn't sleep now if I slit my wrists, the dreams I dreamed I'll never see again . . .

HOUSEKEEPER: What did you dream?

SPALLANZANI: Let me ask you a question about pants. You've sewn pants before, yes?

HOUSEKEEPER: Of course.

SPALLANZANI: *(Indicating pants he wears.)* Well take these pants for instance. How many different parts do they consist of?

HOUSEKEEPER: What sort of question is this?

SPALLANZANI: Just answer it.

HOUSEKEEPER: It is too early for such questions.

SPALLANZANI: *(Off behind screen to pass water.)* It is never too early to learn. What time is it? Where's my watch?

HOUSEKEEPER: 4:30 o'clock.

SPALLANZANI: 4:30! No! Why did you let me sleep so long, it is nearly dawn!

HOUSEKEEPER: You did not go to bed till nearly two o'clock.

SPALLANZANI: Yes.

HOUSEKEEPER: Sleep is necessary. Look! See! Completely dark.

SPALLANZANI: Dark now, but soon dawn will come, and even before the dawn, the dawn chorus—

HOUSEKEEPER: All the birds and their cheery songs—

SPALLANZANI: *(Derisively.)* Cheery songs . . . all the racket of the birds and who can concentrate with that? And then just when it has subsided, the street cries: the fresh fish and old chairs to mend. And kettles to mend. And sprats alive o! And knives to grind. What is a sprat? A kind of snail?

HOUSEKEEPER: A herring.

SPALLANZANI: *(Derisively.)* Sprats alive. And buy a bird cage, and have your boots cleaned. Buy a door mat. Onions fine onions. Broom, broom. Spring radishes. And just when this settles down—

HOUSEKEEPER: Not spring radishes.

SPALLANZANI: Yes, well they cry spring radishes. I hear it. And just when this settles down—

HOUSEKEEPER: Not spring radishes. Not until spring.

SPALLANZANI: Don't interrupt. It is nearly spring. No doubt there's an early batch to buy.

HOUSEKEEPER: This early, none worth buying.

SPALLANZANI: No of course none worth buying, they are never worth buying—

HOUSEKEEPER: Not to you, they play havoc with your stomach and intestines so I am not to buy them.

SPALLANZANI: Yes.

HOUSEKEEPER: They give you wind.

SPALLANZANI: No, it's not wind, how many times do I have to explain to you that it isn't wind, It's my fragile gizzard from years of scientific experiments. What would I care if radishes gave me a little wind, I live alone.

HOUSEKEEPER: I live with you.

SPALLANZANI: Yes you live with me. Technically. But you . . . what would you mind with a little wind.

HOUSEKEEPER: It is no hardship to avoid purchasing a radish if it means less wind.

SPALLANZANI: *(Erupts.)* It isn't the wind I'm talking about but ulcers and great vomiting upon these floors you have cleaned with such diligence, feed me a radish and I'll vomit my life away. *(Broods.)* Why did you bring up radishes in the first place? It is always radishes. Why yet again are we talking about radishes? Where are you going, stay here. It is nearly five o'clock in the morning, do you understand, I don't want to talk about radishes, to hell with your radishes, soon the dawn chorus will begin, and then the street cries, and when that subsides, the horse-clopping, the carriages on the cobbles to hell with your radishes and the rabble and all the rest of it and it won't be quiet again until it is quite dark!

(Beat.)

HOUSEKEEPER: And even then, the dogs.

SPALLANZANI: Yes, and then the dogs. And crickets.

HOUSEKEEPER: No, there are no crickets in the city.

SPALLANZANI: I hear them.

HOUSEKEEPER: Frogs, there are frogs in the city.

SPALLANZANI: The frogs are different.

HOUSEKEEPER: And frogs.

SPALLANZANI: Never you mind about the frogs.

HOUSEKEEPER: I do not like them.

SPALLANZANI: They are not here for you to like, they are here for an experiment that posterity will thank me for. Or not. To hell with posterity, I know at least its success will stick in the craw of our rival Reaumur.

HOUSEKEEPER: I do not like a hundred frogs in the house.

SPALLANZANI: Go away Housekeeper, you can take the porridge with you.

HOUSEKEEPER: You have not eaten.

SPALLANZANI: I am not hungry.

HOUSEKEEPER: It stinks in here.

SPALLANZANI: Fine.

HOUSEKEEPER: How long have you been wearing those clothes?

SPALLANZANI: These clothes? I just put them on.

HOUSEKEEPER: Oh did you.

SPALLANZANI: Get out.

HOUSEKEEPER: What are you doing with the frogs.

SPALLANZANI: You wouldn't understand.

HOUSEKEEPER: Are you dissecting them?

SPALLANZANI: No.

HOUSEKEEPER: Why not?

SPALLANZANI: Would you like me to needlessly dissect my frogs?

HOUSEKEEPER: They would then be dead.

SPALLANZANI: Then by your leave, I shall first wheel the frogs past you in a cart for you to jeer at? All the innocent little frogs?

HOUSEKEEPER: Some are innocent, but most are surely sympathizers to the crown.

SPALLANZANI: You have officially been in France too long.

HOUSEKEEPER: Yes. Yes I have.

SPALLANZANI: *(Briefly sobered.)* Yes . . . we have. Have you seen the guillotine in action?

HOUSEKEEPER: Yes.

SPALLANZANI: *(Broods.)* Well at least it isn't a lingering death . . . It's over quickly.

HOUSEKEEPER: Not with all the speeches that are made.

SPALLANZANI: Those poor pointless souls . . .

HOUSEKEEPER: They say it is only the elite they do in.

SPALLANZANI: The elite? Oh stay out of it all Housekeeper. The elite! Do you know who they're in for next? Half the members of the Academy! It seems we scientists have been consistently singled out by the royalty for special treatment. Quite right! Anyone can see looking around here that I in particular have had special treatment.

HOUSEKEEPER: You are that piece of farmland that gets the extra dung.

SPALLANZANI: Yes, that must be me. Do you know what they've done with my friend Condorcet?

HOUSEKEEPER: Who?

SPALLANZANI: Condorcet!

HOUSEKEEPER: You have a friend?

SPALLANZANI: Yes! Though not for long. They've run him out. He's been hiding these last two months. And he! The secretary of the Academy no less! *(Broods.)* No, Housekeeper, the frogs in this experiment will not see death or dissection . . .

HOUSEKEEPER: Then what sort of experiment do you have in mind that involves a hundred frogs?

SPALLANZANI: You wouldn't understand.

HOUSEKEEPER: Does it concern semen

SPALLANZANI: Yes, as a matter of fact, it does.

HOUSEKEEPER: All your life it is semen.

SPALLANZANI: All *your* life it is semen, all everyone's lives, it is semen, it is semen.

HOUSEKEEPER: It is no good.

SPALLANZANI: Were it not for semen, Housekeeper, it is well believed you would not exist.

HOUSEKEEPER: Yes, that is what I mean.

SPALLANZANI: Ho ho. Such sentiment. Wasn't it you going on about the birds and their pretty songs?

HOUSEKEEPER: What are you doing with the frogs and their semen?

SPALLANZANI: Nothing. I have spent a miserable week getting nowhere doing nothing on what could have been the most important series of experiments of my life. Perhaps. Perhaps not. But they are surely my last experiments.

HOUSEKEEPER: Why your last? Are you near death?

SPALLANZANI: *(Quite serious.)* Yes. I am near death. *(Beat.)* Oh no. Do you hear that.

HOUSEKEEPER: What.

SPALLANZANI: The peeping. It has begun.

(Dawn chorus increases in intensity.)

HOUSEKEEPER: So it has.

SPALLANZANI: The dawn is nigh and then it will be night and what have I to show for it.

HOUSEKEEPER: You have much to show for it.

SPALLANZANI: I have nothing to show for it. I have evacuated my life away.

HOUSEKEEPER: You are respected and admired in scientific circles.

SPALLANZANI: How should you know that.

HOUSEKEEPER: You told me.

SPALLANZANI: Get out. You have wasted the best part of my day. The part before the beginning.

HOUSEKEEPER: And the stove?

SPALLANZANI: Leave it.

HOUSEKEEPER: No coals?

SPALLANZANI: We are not made of coal.

HOUSEKEEPER: No we are not made of coal. But some of us are made of flint.

SPALLANZANI: What?

HOUSEKEEPER: Of flint.

SPALLANZANI: What is this?

HOUSEKEEPER: Before I take your leave, I will ask you one last time for permission to buy fabric.

SPALLANZANI: Thank God this is the last time.

HOUSEKEEPER: Your answer then still is no?

SPALLANZANI: I am not made of flint, and you are amply provided for.

HOUSEKEEPER: Flint, and I have petitioned humbly three times in as many months for—

(*From outside window: "Fresh fish!" "Old Chairs to mend!" "Sprats alive! Sprats alive o!"*)

SPALLANZANI: Didn't I tell you! Damn it to Hell! Close the window!

HOUSEKEEPER: It is already closed.

SPALLANZANI: Already closed! Well then we must seal the edges with wax—

HOUSEKEEPER: Why?

SPALLANZANI: To shut it out of course!

HOUSEKEEPER: You can't shut it out Signore.

SPALLANZANI: Can't I now.

HOUSEKEEPER: It is impossible. It seeps in.

SPALLANZANI: We'll see about that. A wall of cork perhaps.

HOUSEKEEPER: It is impossible.

(Meanwhile, from outside window, we hear various street cries—)

STREET NOISES:

> Old chairs to mend!
> Kettles to mend!
> Buy a bird cage!
> Knives to grind!
> Have your boots cleaned!
> Dust o! Dust o!
> Buy a door mat!
> Onions fine onions!
> Broom, broom!
> Spring radishes!

(At "spring radishes" SPALLANZANI points to window triumphantly.)

HOUSEKEEPER: Ah. Spring radishes.

SPALLANZANI: You see! You see! And on the First of March.

HOUSEKEEPER: It is not the First of March. It is the Ninth of Wind.

SPALLANZANI: *(Apoplectic.)* Curse you woman, radishes do not give me wind!

HOUSEKEEPER: You are a testy man. I am talking about the new calendar.

SPALLANZANI: What new calendar. What are you saying.

HOUSEKEEPER: It is the ninth of Wind. *(Beat.)* Ventose. *(Beat.)* Wind.

SPALLANZANI: *(Impatient.)* Yes wind. *(Then realizing—)* Oh no . . . have the revolutionaries even done something to the calendar now?

HOUSEKEEPER: They have revolutionized it, why have you not heard about these things.

SPALLANZANI: I have better occupations. And we are not French, we are exiles.

HOUSEKEEPER: Liberty, Equality, Fraternity.

SPALLANZANI: Shut up.

HOUSEKEEPER: Wind is the sixth month. The first month is Vintage Month, the second is Fog, the third Sleet, then Snow, then Rain, now we are in Wind.

SPALLANZANI: And there are still twelve months?

HOUSEKEEPER: Yes. Thirty days a month. But ten days a week. Every tenth day a day of rest.

SPALLANZANI: Idiots. They say they are for the people, then institute less rest.

HOUSEKEEPER: I thought you would be in favor of less rest . . .

SPALLANZANI: What I do I do, but I would not impose a calendar of my habits upon the people.

HOUSEKEEPER: Oh you wouldn't?

SPALLANZANI: What?

HOUSEKEEPER: There happen to be people in this very house.

SPALLANZANI: What are you talking about? What people? When was this calendar decided?

HOUSEKEEPER: In October. I mean, in Fog.

SPALLANZANI: In fog is right. Do they realize that they still cannot convince the earth from revolving around the sun in nothing less than 365 days and thirty days times twelve months is 360. What will they do with five extra days?

HOUSEKEEPER: Those will be feast days. They are named Virtue, Genius—

SPALLANZANI: I don't care about any of this. Get out. The Royal Academy in havoc, my good friend Condorcet in hiding and much abused, a cantaloupe in the street turns out to be a severed head, my stomach's all atwist, leave, please . . .

HOUSEKEEPER: *(Finding fabric.)* What is this?

SPALLANZANI: Please leave.

HOUSEKEEPER: Signore!

SPALLANZANI: What? What does it look like!

HOUSEKEEPER: A bolt of taffeta.

SPALLANZANI: It is exactly a bolt of taffeta.

HOUSEKEEPER: How long have you had this.

SPALLANZANI: A week. A miserable week.

HOUSEKEEPER: And you have not told me?

SPALLANZANI: Told you what?

HOUSEKEEPER: Signore, I don't understand.

SPALLANZANI: What.

HOUSEKEEPER: But thank you, it is very fine.

SPALLANZANI: Thank you? No, no, it is not for you.

HOUSEKEEPER: This is not for me?

SPALLANZANI: No it is not for you.

HOUSEKEEPER: It's not?

SPALLANZANI: No.

HOUSEKEEPER: Who is it for then?

SPALLANZANI: Who do you think it is for?

HOUSEKEEPER: There is a woman in your life?

SPALLANZANI: Unfortunately.

HOUSEKEEPER: *(Clarifying.)* Other than me there is a woman in your life?

SPALLANZANI: Please get out.

HOUSEKEEPER: I will not get out. Who is this taffeta for? Signore, I wish to register a grievance.

SPALLANZANI: Bah.

HOUSEKEEPER: I have petitioned humbly three times in as many months for fabric so that I can replace the timeworn and insupportable articles I now possess and each time you have said no no too expensive, too extravagant, no, no what do you need new dresses for—

SPALLANZANI: *(Overlapping.)* What do you need new dresses for? Who are you trying to impress.

HOUSEKEEPER: There is such a thing as decency.

SPALLANZANI: There is such a thing as economy.

HOUSEKEEPER: You can nearly see through the ones I have.

SPALLANZANI: No one cares, no one cares.

HOUSEKEEPER: They are very old.

SPALLANZANI: This is all very old. Do you know how little money I possess?

HOUSEKEEPER: Yes, and to think now a whole bolt for some

woman I have not even seen, it is not right—

SPALLANZANI: Oh so now you must approve all my women?

HOUSEKEEPER: Yes, all your women.

SPALLANZANI: All the countesses and concubines slinking about here—

HOUSEKEEPER: Tell me who she is.

SPALLANZANI: There is no woman.

HOUSEKEEPER: Then who is the taffeta for?

SPALLANZANI: For me of course.

HOUSEKEEPER: For you?

SPALLANZANI: For me, for me.

HOUSEKEEPER: But look at this sheen! You will look embarrassing. You are too old to parade about in—

SPALLANZANI: *(Interrupting.)* I am not going to parade about—

HOUSEKEEPER: You will be that thing, a fop—

SPALLANZANI: Get out.

HOUSEKEEPER: They will see you and cut off your head. And you knew my situation, and you who profess to eschew all such fine things, and here . . . Do not expect me to make any taffeta pants for you—

SPALLANZANI: I am worn out before dawn.

HOUSEKEEPER: I will not make pants for you to parade about after—

SPALLANZANI: Woman, the taffeta is not for me.

HOUSEKEEPER: Oh now it is not for you.

SPALLANZANI: It is for my experiments.

HOUSEKEEPER: Who is this woman.

SPALLANZANI: I am worn out before dawn!

HOUSEKEEPER: I demand an explanation!

SPALLANZANI: You demand?

HOUSEKEEPER: I don't see how you can use taffeta in an experiment.

SPALLANZANI: Oh so you don't believe me.

HOUSEKEEPER: No.

SPALLANZANI: Well I am.

HOUSEKEEPER: Then explain it then. *(Pause.)* Please. *(Pause.)* I would like to know.

SPALLANZANI: It is very involved. You wouldn't understand. It is scientific.

HOUSEKEEPER: Then I will quit your service.

SPALLANZANI: Quit my service?

HOUSEKEEPER: Yes.

SPALLANZANI: After thirty . . . thirty—

HOUSEKEEPER: Yes, after thirty—

SPALLANZANI: No, forty—

HOUSEKEEPER: After forty-one years of service, yes. With relief.

SPALLANZANI: And where will you go?

HOUSEKEEPER: Back to Pavia.

SPALLANZANI: What, Italy? It is under siege.

HOUSEKEEPER: I will go back to Pavia with pleasure and be done with you.

SPALLANZANI: But I am near death.

HOUSEKEEPER: I am sorry that I will miss the end.

SPALLANZANI: So go. You wouldn't understand, so why bother explaining.

HOUSEKEEPER: I have petitioned humbly three times in as many months for fabric—

SPALLANZANI: I know—

HOUSEKEEPER: —so that I can replace the timeworn and insupportable articles—

SPALLANZANI: I know—

HOUSEKEEPER: —I now possess and each time you have said—

SPALLANZANI: Yes, yes, I know what I have said.

HOUSEKEEPER: So to hell with you, goodbye.

(She is at the door, holding the full chamber pot.)

SPALLANZANI: Leave then.

HOUSEKEEPER: I am sick of it.

SPALLANZANI: I can make my own porridge.

HOUSEKEEPER: I ask very little.

(HOUSEKEEPER exits with chamber pot. Pause. SPALLANZANI sets to work. Loud frog croak. Cuts a swath of taffeta. Begins to pin a paper pattern to the taffeta, but pricks his finger.)

SPALLANZANI: Bah!

(SPALLANZANI impulsively crumples up paper pattern violently. Beat. Then begins to retch. Looks about for chamber pot. He cannot find it.)

SPALLANZANI: You stole my chamber pot ... *(Opens door and calls out.)* You stole my chamber pot! You stole my chamber pot! You stole my chamber pot!

(Great amount of stomping, HOUSEKEEPER opens door, flings in now-empty chamber pot. SPALLANZANI grabs pot, waits for it, then vomits convulsively. HOUSEKEEPER lingers at door due to begrudging compassion. It can be seen that she wears a traveling smock or is carrying a bag, though still empty.)

SPALLANZANI: *(Through retches.)* How did you come to be ... How did you come to be ... *(Pause.)* I'm asking you a question!
HOUSEKEEPER: Be what?
SPALLANZANI: Be what?
HOUSEKEEPER: You mean your Housekeeper?
SPALLANZANI: Human! I mean Human! This! You once were not, and now you're here ...
HOUSEKEEPER: Yes I am here, but soon in Pavia.
SPALLANZANI: Do you have any idea how you came to be?
HOUSEKEEPER: I know the answer but I will not say.
SPALLANZANI: I know, you are thinking of sexual intercourse, but I am talking about the mechanism behind sexual intercourse that creates life.
HOUSEKEEPER: I am leaving.
SPALLANZANI: I am trying to explain why I've been up every night in tears for over a week, in tears, I'm trying to explain why I

purchased a bolt of fine taffeta, and you said you will quit my service if I do not—

HOUSEKEEPER: And you must drag sex into all of it?

SPALLANZANI: No, Sex drags *us* into all of it. Drags us. And here we are. And I'll say it now—I'd rather we split in two and have done with all this coming together, but there's nothing to be done.

HOUSEKEEPER: But as the church says, "there is pleasure too, at coming together, which God in his mercy arranged for."

SPALLANZANI: Pleasure? To hell with pleasure! It only distracts from the issues that truly matter. How much better if God had made the act excruciating, so that each couple would have to pause in the middle of sex if only to ask, "why again are we doing this?" Why indeed! That is how it would be if I were God.

HOUSEKEEPER: You would be an unpopular God.

SPALLANZANI: So be it.

HOUSEKEEPER: I would not worship you.

SPALLANZANI: And why not?! When have you ever been with a man?

HOUSEKEEPER: If you do not explain to me what a bolt of taffeta has to do with this, I swear to you I will return to Pavia within the hour.

SPALLANZANI: *(Derisively.)* Within the hour.

HOUSEKEEPER: *(Earnest to point of tears.)* I mean it. I mean it. I mean it.

(Pause.)

SPALLANZANI: Come here . . . *(Pause.)* Come here! *(He holds up a vial.)* This is a liquid, like water is a liquid, like wine is a liquid, like milk is a liquid. But this liquid, in the womb of a woman, creates life.

HOUSEKEEPER: Semen.

SPALLANZANI: Yes, and I want to discover exactly what it is in semen that initiates life, and where it is—in the watery part, or in the denser part containing the worms.

HOUSEKEEPER: Worms?

SPALLANZANI: *(With vial.)* Believe it or not, there are thousands of spermatick worms swimming about in here . . . Some even think these worms are essential to reproduction.

HOUSEKEEPER: But you don't?

SPALLANZANI: I don't Housekeeper, no. Parasites are found everywhere, in our blood, our intestines, and I think these spermatick worms are merely parasites that have taken up home in my testes. It doesn't make sense that we would come from worms.

HOUSEKEEPER: I think it makes much sense.

SPALLANZANI: But look—so many sperm are found in semen that it would mean an incredible waste of potential life, and it is not conceivable that a God would allow such waste.

HOUSEKEEPER: I think I've never heard anything more conceivable.

SPALLANZANI: You are very cynical, Housekeeper.

HOUSEKEEPER: And you, what are you?

SPALLANZANI: Don't change the subject. I'm working with frogs because I like frogs, and they're a damn sight easier to work with than humans. Not to mention that with *frogs* I can use artificial insemination. I can paint the semen onto the eggs directly! No one has thought of that before!

HOUSEKEEPER: Not even Reaumur?

SPALLANZANI: Reaumur? One fine day when Reaumur figures out where his nose is, he'll at long last take one of his digits . . . and shove it up a nostril. That's our Reaumur.

HOUSEKEEPER: And then he will publish his findings.

SPALLANZANI: Exactly. Exactly.

HOUSEKEEPER: *(Again impatient.)* But what does this have to do with a bolt of taffeta.

SPALLANZANI: I'm telling you!

HOUSEKEEPER: You're not telling me!

SPALLANZANI: It comes down to this. There is no point in experimenting with frogs if I can't afterward apply what I've learned to humans. Right?

HOUSEKEEPER: But frogs are not humans.

SPALLANZANI: The difference is trivial! *(Sudden profound weariness.)* No . . . I can't . . . It's too much . . .

HOUSEKEEPER: *(Taking it personally.)* I will listen.
SPALLANZANI: No, it's not you, it's . . . I need something to drink.
　　(Now panicked.) I need something to drink! Quickly!

*(HOUSEKEEPER pours water from pitcher into a cup. He drinks.
Pause. Grabs chamber pot, or bowl of unfinished porridge, and
throws water up.)*

HOUSEKEEPER: Do you feel better?
SPALLANZANI: I truly am dying.
HOUSEKEEPER: Even puppies vomit more than you.
SPALLANZANI: Puppies? *(On soapbox.)* To hell with puppies!
HOUSEKEEPER: *(Disapproving.)* Signore.
SPALLANZANI: *(Now contrite after outburst.)* Where was I.
HOUSEKEEPER: You think frogs and humans are the same, which I
　　can't understand.
SPALLANZANI: No, you can, you can, stop pretending you're thick
　　and just *try* . . . There are those who believe that unlike a
　　human, a frog does not need semen to fertilize its egg. So if I'm
　　going to work with frogs, and by god, I want to work with frogs,
　　I first have to prove, once and for all, that semen is required,
　　that the frogs *can't go it alone* . . . that they, in that, are like
　　human beings . . . Now . . . how do I do that?
HOUSEKEEPER: How.
SPALLANZANI: Well this very issue came up at a party I went to—
HOUSEKEEPER: You?
SPALLANZANI: Yes. Don't interrupt. I was at a party . . .
HOUSEKEEPER: Where?
SPALLANZANI: It was a ball at a chateau.
HOUSEKEEPER: Really?
SPALLANZANI: Yes, there's no reason to be so surprised. I was at a
　　party—
HOUSEKEEPER: When was this?
SPALLANZANI: Not long ago.
HOUSEKEEPER: How long?
SPALLANZANI: It was . . . fifty years ago . . . I was new to Paris, I
　　barely knew the language, but yes, damn it, I was at a party.

HOUSEKEEPER: Fine.

SPALLANZANI: Fine! And I met a fellow scientist by the duck pond, and the frogs were quite loud and it was in casting back to events of that night . . . A scientist, a mishap involving a bodily function, and his damp clothing . . . that I had a revelation.

HOUSEKEEPER: I am ready.

SPALLANZANI: *(Containing excitement.)* All right . . . Housekeeper . . . can you think of a situation in which a man and a woman has sexual intercourse . . . stay here, stay here . . . the man remains in the woman until he ejaculates . . . and yet they both can be utterly assured there will be no pregnancy?

(Pause.)

HOUSEKEEPER: *(Clearly uncomfortable.)* When a man uses . . . When the man's . . . semen . . . . is contained.

SPALLANZANI: *(Nearly embracing her, near tears.)* Yes. Exactly! Exactly! And therefore none of the frog eggs should develop if the frogs mate while each male frog is wearing . . . a pair of tight-fitting taffeta pants! and that is why I am determined to make twenty-nine pairs of tight-fitting taffeta pants as soon as possible, and that is why I have been up these miserable sleepless nights, being occupied in the unforseeably difficult task of constructing twenty-nine very small pairs of tight-fitting taffeta pants, for frogs.

(Pause.)

HOUSEKEEPER: Ah.

(Pause. She turns to leave.)

SPALLANZANI: Where are you going?

HOUSEKEEPER: Pavia!

SPALLANZANI: Good God, haven't I just done what you asked?!

HOUSEKEEPER: *(With fury.)* So I am to come in every morning and be . . . and be mocked by these frogs fashionably dressed—

SPALLANZANI: This isn't about fashion, it's about Life, Life—
HOUSEKEEPER: It's about loyal service.
SPALLANZANI: Holy Christ you have not heard a word I've said—
HOUSEKEEPER: They will be wearing fabric meant for me—
SPALLANZANI: *(Shrill.)* It was never meant for you. It was never meant for you!
HOUSEKEEPER: This . . . is meant for you.

(HOUSEKEEPER spits, exits, slamming the door.)

SPALLANZANI: Just tell me, what's the trick for pinning taffeta together? Why is it so damned slippery!

(The door is opened by the HOUSEKEEPER and slammed again. SPALLANZANI sets to work on pants. Sound of carriages on cobbles outside window. Frog croak. Exhalations and great curses of frustration. And outside the window)

STREET NOISES:
Knives to grind!
Buy a bird cage!
Knives to grind!
Have your boots cleaned!
Dust o! Dust o!
Buy a door mat!
Onions fine onions!
Sprats alive!
Sprats alive o!
SPALLANZANI: *(Derisively.)* Sprats . . .

(Thunderstorm. A miserable example of pants is completed. Holds it up for inspection. Pulls each end of waist to test durability. It splits down the middle. Lights begin to fade. Takes match to candle. He listens to church bells ring.)

SPALLANZANI: And there's the day. Done. Damn it to Hell.

(He shoves several of his materials off desk. HOUSEKEEPER enters.)

SPALLANZANI: Why haven't you left yet.

HOUSEKEEPER: I have found a coach that will take me as far as Milan for a reasonable price. It leaves tomorrow morning.

SPALLANZANI: I have no traveling money for you.

HOUSEKEEPER: And I would be a fool to expect any. There is a man here who wants to see you.

SPALLANZANI: Where?

HOUSEKEEPER: At the front door.

SPALLANZANI: Why didn't you say so? Who is he?

(HOUSEKEEPER shrugs.)

SPALLANZANI: What does he want?

HOUSEKEEPER: To see you.

SPALLANZANI: About what?

HOUSEKEEPER: *(Shrugs.)* He seems upset.

SPALLANZANI: Well I'm working.

HOUSEKEEPER: What should I tell him?

SPALLANZANI: That I'm busy.

HOUSEKEEPER: I will tell him you are busy with your pants and can't see anyone for a few days.

SPALLANZANI: Don't tell him that.

HOUSEKEEPER: I will tell him that.

SPALLANZANI: Fine. Fine! Send him in.

(Pause. CONDORCET, secretary of the Royal Academy, rushes in, shuts door behind him, pale, panicked, wild-eyed, drenched, and wearing women's clothing. Gown, wig, makeup ill-applied. He is missing a shoe, his articles are in disarray. Heavy French accent.)

CONDORCET: Lazarro, thank God!

SPALLANZANI: What is this?

CONDORCET: Please, you must hide me! Immediately!

SPALLANZANI: Jean? Is that you?

CONDORCET: Yes, it is I, Jean Condorcet. Your friend.

SPALLANZANI: I thought you were in hiding.

CONDORCET: My hiding place has been discovered. Someone leaked. No matter. Praise be to God I made it here. I am nearly collapsed with exhaustion.

SPALLANZANI: *(Calling out from door.)* Housekeeper, get a drink for this man! A disguise, that was quick thinking.

CONDORCET: It was the work of panicked minutes, it is a most ill-fit.

SPALLANZANI: No, it is convincing.

CONDORCET: It is not *too* attractive, I trust. I do not wish to call any attention to myself if I am to escape the city.

SPALLANZÁNI: No, be assured, you are not too attractive.

CONDORCET: In the downpour, through Paris, first here then there, always one step ahead of the gendarmes, seeking asylum with old friends, but all my old friends—half have been arrested already, and the other half cast me back out on the street. These shoes make things impossible.

SPALLANZANI: But the gendarmes—they will not follow you here, will they?

CONDORCET: Yes, they might! That is why you must hide me, or they will arrest you too for harboring me.

SPALLANZANI: Arrest me? But I am Italian!

CONDORCET: Please, I fear for my life . . .

SPALLANZANI: But I have no place to hide you.

CONDORCET: Anywhere! I just need a few days. Don't you have a cellar?

SPALLANZANI: This is the cellar! I am very poor. But look, is it wise to even stay in the city?

CONDORCET: It's true, my only hope is to flee Paris, for if I am caught it is surely the guillotine which I will never allow, which is why I have this . . .

SPALLANZANI: What is it?

CONDORCET: Arsenic.

SPALLANZANI: *(Looking into eyes.)* No man . . . no . . .

CONDORCET: I won't suffer execution . . . *(Pulling out of bosom a large bundle of papers tied with string.)* but look, I'll leave Paris, but first a day of rest, and time to pass on this manuscript to some former member of the Academy sympathetic to the cause.

SPALLANZANI: What do you mean, "former member"?

CONDORCET: The National Convention has disbanded the Royal Academy of Sciences.

SPALLANZANI: They can't!

CONDORCET: Hah, can't they now. They have. "An elitist institution" they called it and snip snap. But we will go on, we must.

SPALLANZANI: What is the manuscript?

CONDORCET: Oh Lazarro, it is the culmination of my life's work! I completed it while in hiding. I was to hand the work off to a man tonight in fact, but I was flushed out before I could meet him.

SPALLANZANI: The topic, is it mathematics?

CONDORCET: No, it is a Sketch for a Historical Picture of the Progress of the Human Mind!

SPALLANZANI: (Agape.) You say there is progress?

CONDORCET: (Solemnly.) I know there is, Lazarro, I know there is. And you do too. In the 10th epoch, there will be equality among the classes and people will improve physically, intellectually, morally . . . (Reads from work solemnly, much dignity in his muddied gown.) "I picture posterity and how welcome is this picture of the human race, freed from all its chains—

SPALLANZANI: (Hearing a distant knock.) Ssh.

CONDORCET: —released from the domination of chance, advancing with a firm and sure step in the path of truth, virtue—"

SPALLANZANI: Ssh!

(Distant knock on front door.)

CONDORCET: Did you hear that?

SPALLANZANI: Yes!

CONDORCET: It was a knock on the door!

SPALLANZANI: The gendarmes!

CONDORCET: Lazarro, what can I do?!

SPALLANZANI: Get out.

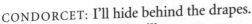
CONDORCET: I'll hide behind the drapes.
SPALLANZANI: No they'll see you.
CONDORCET: Then what can I do?
SPALLANZANI: You can get out. Try the window.
CONDORCET: It's too small. What about under your desk!
SPALLANZANI: No no, there are frogs underneath, they will be
    crushed—

*(Pause. CONDORCET looks at the vial of poison in his hand.
Looks at SPALLANZANI.)*

SPALLANZANI: No . . . no . . . Put it away . . .

(A knock on the door. HOUSEKEEPER enters.)

HOUSEKEEPER: There is a man here who wants to see you.
SPALLANZANI: Just one?
HOUSEKEEPER: Yes.
SPALLANZANI: Did he say who he is?
HOUSEKEEPER: *(Shrugs.)* He is old.
SPALLANZANI: What does he want?
HOUSEKEEPER: To see you.
SPALLANZANI: About what?
HOUSEKEEPER: I couldn't care less.
SPALLANZANI: Housekeeper! Is he armed?
HOUSEKEEPER: I will send him in.

(She exits.)

SPALLANZANI: No, wait!

*(An elderly man enters. Quite frail, appalling condition.
Coughing wretchedly. It is JACQUES DE VAUCANSON, scientist.
Pronounced French accent. Approaching a senile parody of his Act
I self.)*

VAUCANSON: Monsieur Spallanzani?

SPALLANZANI: Yes.

VAUCANSON: My pardons for disturbing you at such a late hour. I—Oh! And you have company . . .

(VAUCANSON winks and nudges knowingly for he has noticed a female form hiding not very well.)

CONDORCET: Jacques?

VAUCANSON: *(Flirting.)* Do I know you?

CONDORCET: It is I!

VAUCANSON: Madam?

CONDORCET: No!

VAUCANSON: *(Amazement.)* Jean?

SPALLANZANI: *(To CONDORCET.)* Is he one of us?

VAUCANSON: I have been all over Paris in search of you.

CONDORCET: *(To SPALLANZANI.)* This is Jacques de Vaucanson, he is the man I was to give my manuscript to tonight.

VAUCANSON: *(To CONDORCET.)* Yes, but I heard you had to flee.

SPALLANZANI: *(Calling out from door.)* Housekeeper! A drink for this man! Monsieur Vaucanson, it is an honor to meet such an eminent scientist.

VAUCANSON: The honor is mine.

SPALLANZANI: I am no scientist. I have one last series of experiments and even that I see now I shall be forced to abandon. But how old you are! I beg your pardon but was there no one better suited for such a grueling assignment?

VAUCANSON: *(Making an unwitting mockery of Act I.)* I'm worn out, it's true. But we must push on. If we do not strive, then what can posterity hope for?!

SPALLANZANI: But how did you know to come here?

VAUCANSON: I received a tip from one of the gendarmes who knew Jean was headed in this general direction.

SPALLANZANI: *(Panicked.)* They knew?! Then they will wind up here, surely!

VAUCANSON: *(To CONDORCET.)* A disguise, that was quick thinking.

CONDORCET: It was the work of panicked minutes, it is most ill-fitting and the rain made a shambles of it.

VAUCANSON: No, it looks fine.

CONDORCET: It is not *too* attractive, I hope.

SPALLANZANI: It's not.

VAUCANSON: I am not so sure.

SPALLANZANI: You need to get out.

CONDORCET: For an attractive lady alone on the outskirts of the city might arouse suspicion. Ideally, I should appear past my prime.

VAUCANSON: Perhaps even a washerwoman.

CONDORCET: You must help me!

(HOUSEKEEPER enters with water.)

VAUCANSON: You can't be too careful. Perhaps you should swap clothing with his Housekeeper, her clothes seem more down-at-the-heels.

HOUSEKEEPER: *(Indignant.)* There is nothing wrong with them.

CONDORCET: *(To VAUCANSON.)* Yes, perhaps you are right. We will change immediately.

HOUSEKEEPER: Change?

SPALLANZANI: Yes, exchange dresses with the man.

HOUSEKEEPER: But I am not of a mind.

VAUCANSON: Give him your smock, quickly!

SPALLANZANI: Damn it woman, this is a great man! His life is on the line!

HOUSEKEEPER: Signore, you wish to take the very dress from my body. I am sorry but no, I cannot allow it. I am after all in your service no longer.

CONDORCET: *(Desperate, near tears.)* Please! Please!

HOUSEKEEPER: No. Jean-Marie Condorcet. Mathematician, philosopher, supporter of the Revolution, and member of the revolutionary Legislative Assembly and Convention. Fleeing the city dressed as a woman, you will be discovered in a country inn outside of Paris and arrested. Two months later, at the age of fifty-one, you will be found dead in your cell, officially from exhaustion, though more likely from your vial of poison.

(*HOUSEKEEPER exits. Pause.*)

SPALLANZANI: (*Having heard only the HOUSEKEEPER's "No."*) Well, so be it.

VAUCANSON: You look fine without the smock.

SPALLANZANI: This is the manuscript.

VAUCANSON: (*Reading.*) "Man will not always be corrupted by greed, fear and envy. He will one day be restored to the rights and dignity of his nature!"

CONDORCET: (*Overlapping, reciting from memory.*) "He will one day be restored to the rights and dignity of his nature!"

SPALLANZANI: You can't stay here.

CONDORCET: But friend, you are my last hope.

SPALLANZANI: But of course I'm not. At the very least, take a room in a country inn, you will surely be safer there than here. Go now, quickly, before they gain any more ground.

CONDORCET: But—

SPALLANZANI: No, this is for the best, I'm thinking of you.

CONDORCET: If we but had your Housekeeper's smock—

SPALLANZANI: Forget the smock—

CONDORCET: But—

SPALLANZANI: Hang the smock! Here, drink this. Now you must go.

CONDORCET: Thank you. I should like to have stayed, I am very tired. But perhaps you are right.

SPALLANZANI: Good then. Farewell.

CONDORCET: (*Reluctant to leave.*) I'm off.

VAUCANSON: Safe passage.

CONDORCET: (*Still reluctant.*) Farewell.

SPALLANZANI: Godspeed.

CONDORCET: Thank you.

VAUCANSON: Good luck my friend.

CONDORCET: We'll meet again.

SPALLANZANI: Of course.

CONDORCET: (*Still reluctant.*) Farewell!

VAUCANSON: Au revoir.

(Beat.)

CONDORCET: *(Still reluctant.)* I'm off.
SPALLANZANI: Au revoir.
VAUCANSON: Au revoir.

(CONDORCET reluctantly exits. And as VAUCANSON is about to exit:)

SPALLANZANI: And you, Jacques de Vaucanson.
VAUCANSON: We have met before.
SPALLANZANI: Your clockwork duck will survive you.
VAUCANSON: Its parts were more durable than my own.
SPALLANZANI: It will be exhibited by Bontems, the famous maker of the mechanical singing birds. The duck will end up in the cabinet of curiosities of a certain Mr. Gassner of Karkov in the Ukraine. This cabinet, and the duck with it, will burn to ashes in 1879, the same year Albert Einstein was born, Cetewayo, king of the Zulus, was deposed, and Robert Louis Stevenson wrote *Travels with a Donkey.*
VAUCANSON: And you, Lazarro Spallanzani, will die of a urinary tract infection in Pavia. Your corpse will fall into the hands of your rival, Reaumur, who will remove your penis and testicles out of maliciousness and put them on display in a jar at the university museum, where they will stay for over two hundred years.
SPALLANZANI: That is most upsetting. Goddamn Reaumur.
VAUCANSON: Reaumur's corpse will be seized after his death by your colleagues, who will decapitate him and place his head in a jar, and for over two hundred years his head will sit on a shelf next to your testicles.
SPALLANZANI: The result of our struggles is meaningless.
VAUCANSON: Yet the struggles themselves are noble—
SPALLANZANI: Life is a difficult movement of the bowels. If we persevere, it is because we haven't a choice. Call that noble.
VAUCANSON: And yet . . .
SPALLANZANI: *(Conceding.)* And yet . . .
VAUCANSON: *(Decisively.)* And yet.

SPALLANZANI: Yes. Yes . . . Now get out. Out. Out.

(SPALLANZANI kicks VAUCANSON to the door, hurls him out door and he slams it shut. Gathers materials still on floor. Places them back on desk. Sits down. Shoves materials off of desk. Knock on door. HOUSEKEEPER enters with bowl.)

HOUSEKEEPER: They are all gone?

SPALLANZANI: We still might get a call from soldiers come to arrest me . . .

HOUSEKEEPER: I will tell them you are busy with your pants.

SPALLANZANI: That man's dress was far nicer than yours. Why didn't you swap when you had the chance?

HOUSEKEEPER: It was not a dress for housekeeping.

SPALLANZANI: I thought you were done with housekeeping.

HOUSEKEEPER: I am done housekeeping for you, but the dress still is no good. I am not returning to Pavia for the balls and banquets, am I . . .

SPALLANZANI: You are returning to glimpse once more the Ticino River from the old town where once you sat with your lover when you were young and comely.

HOUSEKEEPER: I couldn't give a curse for the foul Ticino.

SPALLANZANI: Perhaps you've never glimpsed it with a lover. *(Pause.)* Perhaps you never had a lover.

HOUSEKEEPER: Eat.

SPALLANZANI: Ah, porridge. I shall miss your cooking.

(HOUSEKEEPER meanwhile picking up the materials lying on the floor, stifles a snicker.)

SPALLANZANI: What was that?

HOUSEKEEPER: My pardons, Signore. A sneeze.

SPALLANZANI: A sneeze indeed. What is it? You did something to the porridge? As a last gesture of frustration you have spit in it.

HOUSEKEEPER: No. It is nothing.

SPALLANZANI: *(Seeing her with materials in hand.)* Or is it my patterns?

HOUSEKEEPER: No.

SPALLANZANI: Yes it is. I know that little smugness of yours.

HOUSEKEEPER: Have any of your frogs been fitted out yet in your pants?

SPALLANZANI: I have to make them first don't I.

HOUSEKEEPER: *(Pointing to pattern.)* How will you get their feet through so small a space at the bottom of the leg?

SPALLANZANI: Eh

HOUSEKEEPER: Frogs have large feet.

SPALLANZANI: I know they have large feet.

HOUSEKEEPER: I suppose you'll just push.

SPALLANZANI: Yes, I'll just push, it won't be difficult. *(Pause.)* The pants must be tight!

HOUSEKEEPER: Good luck then.

SPALLANZANI: They must be tight!

HOUSEKEEPER: Fine.

SPALLANZANI: There can be no leakage! *(Broods.)* But I see your point. But I cannot contrive another way. A hook and eye perhaps?

(HOUSEKEEPER stifles another snicker.)

SPALLANZANI: *(Fed up, pushes bowl off desk.)* I am not hungry. Take this. Get out. *(She picks up bowl and makes to leave.)* I suppose you have a better way?

HOUSEKEEPER: No.

SPALLANZANI: You do.

HOUSEKEEPER: I can't think of anything.

SPALLANZANI: Well then stay out of it.

HOUSEKEEPER: A drawstring perhaps.

(HOUSEKEEPER exits.)

SPALLANZANI: A drawstring? How? Come back here!

HOUSEKEEPER: At the bottom of each leg. The pants legs can be quite baggy, but then pulled in at the ankle and kept there with a knot.

SPALLANZANI: But the string might fall off.

HOUSEKEEPER: Do you know nothing? You would keep it there by sewing it into a hem of course.

SPALLANZANI: A hem?

(Pause. Blank face of SPALLANZANI. She hastily grabs fabric on desk and demonstrates—)

HOUSEKEEPER: You see, and you turn it over, with the string, then sew it shut, but leave an opening for the string to dangle out.

(She makes to exit again.)

SPALLANZANI: What sort of string?

HOUSEKEEPER: For something so small, it would do with strong thread.

SPALLANZANI: I have strong thread.

HOUSEKEEPER: It stinks in here.

(HOUSEKEEPER begins to exit.)

SPALLANZANI: I am not using all the taffeta . . . I won't be needing the entire bolt.

HOUSEKEEPER: Oh with the way you sew you will . . .

SPALLANZANI: There is a chance.

HOUSEKEEPER: What do I care?

SPALLANZANI: You can have what is left.

HOUSEKEEPER: I will be in Pavia long before you are finished.

SPALLANZANI: If you assisted me, the pants could be completed sooner and you would have all that remained to take with you.

HOUSEKEEPER: Why are you in such a rush?

SPALLANZANI: I am near death.

HOUSEKEEPER: It stinks in here.

SPALLANZANI: Stop saying that. Will you or will you not? There's a good seven hours before dawn, twenty-nine pairs of pants divided by two fourteen and a half by seven hours, a little more than two pairs an hour per person.

HOUSEKEEPER: It can't be done.

SPALLANZANI: It can!

HOUSEKEEPER: Why should I help you?

SPALLANZANI: I told you. For the taffeta.

HOUSEKEEPER: Do you think my life is ruled by fabric?

SPALLANZANI: *(Agape.)* Isn't it?

HOUSEKEEPER: *(With bit of relish.)* But you need my help.

SPALLANZANI: Yes I need your help. And . . . more than that . . .

HOUSEKEEPER: I'm listening.

SPALLANZANI: Well I don't think you'll credit it but . . . it's true—

HOUSEKEEPER: Tell me . . .

SPALLANZANI: Well . . . damn it . . . after forty-one years . . . you owe me.

HOUSEKEEPER: I owe you?!

SPALLANZANI: Well find your own reason then!

HOUSEKEEPER: I owe you?!

SPALLANZANI: I said find your own reason—

HOUSEKEEPER: I don't know why you bother at all!

SPALLANZANI: What do you mean? With what?

HOUSEKEEPER: This! Your work—

SPALLANZANI: *(Exasperated.)* Why? I told you why.

HOUSEKEEPER: Did you?

SPALLANZANI: Why does anyone do anything?!

HOUSEKEEPER: *(Sincere.)* Why *does* anyone do anything?

(Long pause.)

SPALLANZANI: *(Feebly.)* . . . why . . .

HOUSEKEEPER: Why have I persisted in cleaning your chamber pot every day for all these years.

SPALLANZANI: *(Beginning to cough.)* It is crucial, a clean chamber pot . . . And no doubt you have a nurturing personality. You could not live alone. You would shrivel.

HOUSEKEEPER: You would shrivel.

SPALLANZANI: *(Continuing coughing fit, trying not to call attention that he is doubled over.)* I? No, no . . . I can live alone.

HOUSEKEEPER: I don't think so.

SPALLANZANI: Are you going to help me with my pants or not?

(Pause. And the HOUSEKEEPER at last relents and crosses to the table.)

SPALLANZANI: There we are! The Great Nurturer.
HOUSEKEEPER: Enough of that.
SPALLANZANI: We can try at least.

(Pleased, SPALLANZANI shows her a seat. HOUSEKEEPER picks up needle and thread.)

HOUSEKEEPER: And all for semen.
SPALLANZANI: As soon as I acquired my first microscope sixty years ago, it was the first thing I examined, and it shall be my last . . .
HOUSEKEEPER: What did you do?
SPALLANZANI: What do you mean.
HOUSEKEEPER: When you first acquired your microscope. Where did you obtain the semen? Did you have frogs even then?
SPALLANZANI: You have so little imagination that you cannot construe where and how I might have obtained some semen?
HOUSEKEEPER: It's not sold in shops.
SPALLANZANI: Are you baiting me?
HOUSEKEEPER: I am sincere.
SPALLANZANI: I will tell you plainly then that I manipulated my own privatees in a fashion thereby obtaining a sample.
HOUSEKEEPER: *(Shocked and intrigued.)* Did you? What do you mean, "manipulated"?
SPALLANZANI: Forget it.
HOUSEKEEPER: Does it have something to do with masturbation?
SPALLANZANI: *(Impatiently.)* Yes, it has everything to do with it.
HOUSEKEEPER: *(Still more shocked and intrigued.)* Really? And where did you commit this sin?
SPALLANZANI: Sin indeed.
HOUSEKEEPER: In Pavia?
SPALLANZANI: Yes in Pavia.

HOUSEKEEPER: Have you masturbated here in Paris?

SPALLANZANI: Enough of this.

HOUSEKEEPER: Have you masturbated in this room?

SPALLANZANI: I said enough.

HOUSEKEEPER: *(Suddenly aware of the chair she is in.)* Do you sit down when you do it?

SPALLANZANI: Good God woman, have you never done it?!

(HOUSEKEEPER, without a word, puts down sewing materials and makes to exit.)

SPALLANZANI: Where are you going?

HOUSEKEEPER: I am leaving.

SPALLANZANI: Are you making tea?

HOUSEKEEPER: No.

SPALLANZANI: You're coming back aren't you? *(Realizing.)* You're not pretending to have modesty!

HOUSEKEEPER: I do have modesty.

SPALLANZANI: Housekeeper, tell me truthfully, you've never had a lover, have you?

HOUSEKEEPER: *(Lashing back.)* You, the Great Fornicator, do what you will, but I have my beliefs—

SPALLANZANI: Who are you calling the Great Fornicator?

HOUSEKEEPER: You are the Great Fornicator.

SPALLANZANI: Oh I see!

HOUSEKEEPER: Intercourse before marriage is wrong—

SPALLANZANI: Yes—

HOUSEKEEPER: —and afterso its purpose is for making children! I am not ashamed of my virginity!

SPALLANZANI: But I've said the same thing all along!

(Pause. HOUSEKEEPER intrigued.)

HOUSEKEEPER: And yet you've never married . . . *(Silence from SPALLANZANI.)* You Signore have never been with a woman?

SPALLANZANI: No I have not.

HOUSEKEEPER: Not one?

SPALLANZANI: No.
HOUSEKEEPER: In all your life?
SPALLANZANI: Let's just drop it.
HOUSEKEEPER: So all these years—
SPALLANZANI: Yes.
HOUSEKEEPER: *(A statement.)* So.

(A brief moment between them.)

SPALLANZANI: Yes. *(Beat.)* Yes.
HOUSEKEEPER: Why? Why no lover?
SPALLANZANI: I was busy . . . Or because no one would have me . . . or no, I refused and I refuse to have sex for mere pleasure's sake, and I refuse to procreate if I don't know why I even exist . . .
HOUSEKEEPER: Were you never attracted to a woman?
SPALLANZANI: If I copulated out of blind attraction, if I didn't think about what it all meant I'd be no different and no better than Johann Carl Wilcke over there.
HOUSEKEEPER: Over where?
SPALLANZANI: There. That one.
HOUSEKEEPER: *(Touched, actually.)* You have named your frogs.
SPALLANZANI: Yes, after great men of our age.
HOUSEKEEPER: Who is Wilcke?
SPALLANZANI: He discovered the concept of specific heat—the amount of heat required to raise the temperature of a unit mass one degree.
HOUSEKEEPER: *(Intrigued, pointing to another frog.)* And who is that?
SPALLANZANI: That one with the spots is Antoine Lavoisier. Among other accomplishments, he revolutionized the language of chemistry.
HOUSEKEEPER: And that croaking one there?
SPALLANZANI: William Herschel. His was the largest reflecting telescope ever built and with it he discovered Uranus, the first planet to be revealed in over two thousand years. And this hopping bastard here is Francis Glisson, who explained how the gall bladder discharges bile only when it is needed. And there,

Andreas Marggraaf, and there, Anders Celsius and Johannes Kepler and Joseph Black and Henry Cavendish and Allesandro Volta and Jan Ingen-Housz and Claude Berthollet. Each one has a story and we will make pants for them all!

HOUSEKEEPER: And Lazarro Spallanzani. You too deserve pants. For your work in casting doubt on the theory of spontaneous generation, and for your development of artificial insemination, you will be known as one of the great experimentalists of the eighteenth century. But due to elements you could not have foreseen, you will still conclude wrongly that spermatick worms are only worms and have no part in reproduction. You will never know that you got it wrong. You will not survive to see the year 1875, when Wilhelm Hertwig will be the first to observe the fecundation of an egg by sperm—that we are fertilized by what you call worms, just as worms turn us in our graves to dust. *(Finishing a pair of pants.)* There. That is one.

SPALLANZANI: Fine. Shall we have a fitting? Who shall it be?

HOUSEKEEPER: Who is this one?

SPALLANZANI: That is Francis Hauksbee, producer of a useful electrostatic generator.

HOUSEKEEPER: Are there any women?

SPALLANZANI: Have you not heard a word I've said? We are putting pants on *male* frogs—

HOUSEKEEPER: But you could still name one after a woman.

SPALLANZANI: No. That's too confusing. And no women scientists come to mind—

HOUSEKEEPER: You mentioned once a . . . Chamanet.

SPALLANZANI: Chatelet? Gabrielle du Chatelet?

HOUSEKEEPER: Yes, what about her?

SPALLANZANI: No. We're using Hauksbee. Get back to work.

(A pronounced sigh of resignation from HOUSEKEEPER.)

SPALLANZANI: I said no.

HOUSEKEEPER: Fine.

SPALLANZANI: All right, look, all the twenty-nine female frogs, every one can be named Gabrielle du Chatelet. If I remember correctly, she died in childbirth. Now if our trousers fail, she'll give birth to 3,000 progeny.

HOUSEKEEPER: That's fine.

SPALLANZANI: *(Having fitted pants.)* Well, there's one fitted frog.

HOUSEKEEPER: So you will stay in Paris till you die?

SPALLANZANI: It is not a long wait.

HOUSEKEEPER: You should return to Pavia.

SPALLANZANI: With you? That's a horrible idea. But perhaps.

HOUSEKEEPER: There's no reason to stay.

SPALLANZANI: Sssh! Listen . . . *(Cricket chirp.)* And you said there were no crickets in the city!

(Cricket chirp and frog croak up to unnaturally high levels as lights dim. We hear birdsong. SPALLANZANI awakes.)

SPALLANZANI: Birds? . . . Those are birds . . . robins I think . . . *(Realizing.)* Oh Christ, I fell asleep! Housekeeper? . . . Housekeeper?! *(We hear only a gentle, or actually rather pronounced, snoring from HOUSEKEEPER, who is asleep in chair.)* It will soon be dawn and what have I to show for it? Yes, go on, snooze on and abandon me . . . *(He then notices a collection of small pants near her. He holds up pants and counts them as lights slowly rise. Birdsong heard.)* One, two, three . . . eight, ten . . . one two three four . . . twenty . . . twenty-six, twenty-seven, twenty-eight, plus one on Hauksbee . . . twenty-nine . . . she did it, the old cow, twenty-nine pairs of tight-fitting taffeta pants . . . *(SPALLANZANI finds an old blanket and gently drapes it over sleeping HOUSEKEEPER. Tucks it to chin. Kisses her.)* . . . dark now . . . dark now . . . but soon dawn will come, and even now, the dawn chorus . . . and then the street cries . . . the fresh fish and old chairs to mend. *(Pause.)* And kettles to mend. And sprats alive o! . . . sprats alive . . . *(Derisively.)* Sprats . . . *(Shrugging.)* Well . . . there is that at least . . . they are alive . . . *(Relishing.)* Sprats . . . alive . . . o! . . . *(A trial run.)* . . . Spallanzani alive o . . . *(Shouting.)* Spallanzani alive o! *(His shout however is cut short by a truly violent coughing fit. HOUSEKEEPER stirs in sleep. And he, resigned, exhausted, awed.)* . . . Well let it. Let it

begin then. Let it. Let the day become . . . beguile . . . bewilder
. . . benumb . . . bedim . . . and then . . . beget . . . then beget . . .
yet . . . another . . .

(Music louder, and in growing light, CHATELET revealed.)

CHATELET: *(Sung.)*
    Awake my Paris . . .
    Stir from thy slumberings
    The worlds you now strive in
    Shall be snuffed and forgotten
    come the dawn . . .
    Bid farewell and return
    To this one Dream we share . . .
    Paris . . . Awake . . . Awake . . . Awake . . . Awake . . .

    (Stirring music continues through curtain call.)

Five Flights

by Adam Bock

No performance or reading of this work *Five Flights* in any medium may be given without express permission of the author. Inquiries regarding performance rights, publication, duplication of any kind should be addressed to: Val Day, Gersh Agency, 41 Madison Avenue, 33rd Floor, New York, NY 10010 (212) 634-8124

≫ BIOGRAPHY ≪

Adam Bock's play *Five Flights* was produced at San Francisco's Encore Theater for a five month extended run in 2002, after staged readings at the Magic Theater and Playwright's Horizons. It won the 2002 Will Glickman Award for best new play produced in the Bay Area, and was nominated for the American Theater Critics Award and the Elizabeth Osborn Award. It was named in the *San Francisco Chronicle*'s and *Oakland Tribune*'s Top Ten Theatrical Events and the *Chronicle*'s Top Ten Cultural Events for 2002.

Shotgun Players' production of *Swimming in the Shallows* won the 2000 Bay Area Theater Critic Circle Awards for Best Production, Best Ensemble, and Best Original Script. *Swimming* was a Clauder Competition award winner, a Weissberger Award nominee, and has been produced in Boston, London, and the Edinburgh Fringe Festival. The play had a recent staged reading at New York Theater Workshop, and was produced at the Kitchen Theater in Ithaca, New York, and at the Red Barn Theater in Key West, Florida, in 2003.

Another play, *The Typographer's Dream*, was workshopped by New York City's Clubbed Thumb in 2002, had a staged reading at the Courtyard in London, and was showcased by Clubbed Thumb at HERE. His newest play, *Thursday*, received its first workshop by Clubbed Thumb at the Ohio in 2002, was read publicly at Playwrights Horizons, and will be produced in September 2003 by Encore Theater, with a grant from the NEA.

He is a Shotgun Players Artistic Associate, and a member of the Soho Rep Writer/Director Lab, and the MCC Writer's Coalition. He is currently at work on a commission from Playwrights Horizons.

⇛ PRODUCTION HISTORY ⇚

Five Flights by Adam Bock
Produced by Encore Theatre Company
January 17–June 8, 2002
Showing at The Thick House
Directed by Kent Nicholson

Cast

Jane	Dawn-Elin Fraser
Andre	Kevin Karrick
Olivia	Alexis Lezin
Tom	Craig Neibaur
Adele	Lisa Steindler
Ed	Liam Vincent

Designers and Technical Staff

Sets	James Faerron
Costumes	Julie Phanstie
Lights	David Szlasa
Sound	Drew Yerys
Stage Manager	Kathryn Clark
Publicity	Shawn Ferrayra
Photographer	James Faerron

Encore Theatre Company

Encore Theatre Company is a professional ensemble dedicated to the production of affordable, innovative, intimately staged theatre, with a particular focus on dramatic works that foster social awareness and affirm the diversity of human experience. Encore presents art that clarifies issues, inspires fellowship, and encourages a sense of community and hope in ourselves and our audiences.

Encore Theatre Company celebrated our fifteenth anniversary as a passionate, professional theater ensemble in the year 2001. Since 1986 Encore has been firing up Bay Area stages, creating innovative, immediate and critically applauded contemporary theater in intimate settings, and sharing a spirited dialogue with our theater-loving patrons.

Originally a showcase for experimental work by alumni and associates of American Conservatory Theater, Encore Theatre Company has claimed our own distinct identity within the Bay Area theater community over the years. From our first success, Arthur Schnitzler's *La Ronde* (Critic's Choice, *San Francisco Chronicle*), to our first in the Thick House, Lynne Alvarez's *Hidden Parts*, critics have hailed our work as "daring," "provocative," "compelling," and "dynamic." Leigh Fondakowski's *I Think I Like Girls*, was extended twice due to a sell-out run and was applauded as "bracingly honest, gently confrontational, ruefully funny and deeply moving" by Robert Hurwitt of the *San Francisco Chronicle*.

The range of our work is as notable as our accolades. 1999's *Simpatico*, a West Coast Premiere by Sam Shepard, brought us sold-out houses, several Dean Goodman awards, and a Critic's Choice in the *San Francisco Bay Guardian*. In 1998 we sold out the Magic Theatre with a "strong, timeless" (*San Francisco Examiner*) production of Pulitzer Prize winner Lanford Wilson's classic *Balm in Gilead*, winning us "Best Ensemble, 1998" in the *San Francisco Bay Guardian*. From 1989's four-month run of Stephen Sondheim's *Marry Me A Little*, which then toured by invitation to L.A.'s Coronet

Theatre, to Anthony Clarvoe's *Let's Play Two*, which ran four months at the Cable Car Theatre in 1994, Encore productions have been well received by audiences and critics alike.

While World Premieres and West Coast Premieres have dominated our repertoire, rarely produced classics such as Shakespeare's *Pericles* (Dramalogue Award, 1990) have livened the mix. Our *Uncle Vanya*, by Anton Chekhov and adapted by David Mamet, was hailed as "exquisite" by the *San Jose Mercury News* in 1992. Reviewers applaud our premieres. 1991 saw two *San Francisco Chronicle* Critic's Choice awards going to Encore for Howard Korder's *Search and Destroy* and Arthur Kopit's *Road to Nirvana*. In 1995, Katy Hickman's smash one-woman comedy *Meteor Girl* gave us such a highly successful run it was later remounted as a coproduction with the Magic Theatre. Our work has run the gamut artistically, but critically and commercially, it has succeeded in winning consistent raves throughout the years.

—Lisa Steindler
Artistic Director
Encore Theatre Company
2003

⇛ SETTING AND CHARACTERS ⇚

Characters

```
ED . . . . . . . . . . . . . . . . . . 36 years old
OLIVIA . . . . . . . . . . . . . 42 years old
JANE . . . . . . . . . . . . . . . 39 years old
ADELE . . . . . . . . . . . . . 39 years old
TOM . . . . . . . . . . . . . . . 32 years old
ANDRE . . . . . . . . . . . . . 28 years old
```

Setting

A bare stage, except for a long white wall that cuts the center of the stage from stage left to stage right. Can be sat on, stood upon, walked behind. Perhaps white benches.

1. The Narrative

(*ED enters. He is carrying a landscape model. Trees, an aviary, two tiny human figurines to scale. He puts it on a stand, tilted so the audience can see it. Like an aerial shot.*)

ED: Here is the landscape of this story. This white building here. Is an aviary. My father built it. It's a birdhouse, but it's the size of a real house, it's a house for birds, for as many birds as you could imagine, he didn't want my mother to be lonely. Not my mother exactly. Her soul really. He built it to house the soul of my mother.

This is the glass roof he put on it, so she could look up at the sky. These're trees he planted, so she wouldn't miss the seasons as they went by. He planted cherry and then apple, red maple, pine. This is a stream he diverted, so she could watch the water move and so she could remember flying. All of this was him asking her to stay.

Now. It stands empty. My father's dead. My mother's soul has flown away. The glass in the windows is breaking. Wind. Tree limbs. They don't care. They don't care, they have no reverence for the sorrow that built this place. (*Points to figurines.*) This is Olivia. She's my sister Adele's best friend. (*Lights up on OLIVIA.*) And this. This is my brother Bobby's wife. Jane. Look at the shoes. (*Lights up on JANE.*) They're arguing.

(*ED exits.*)

JANE: He left the aviary to us. To all three of us, actually. Well I mean to the three kids, to Adele and of course to Ed and to Bobby. Which means in some ways to me. Well. To me, really, also, since what is mine is Bobby's and what is Bobby's is mine.

OLIVIA: He said he doesn't care what happens to it.

JANE: Ed said that?

OLIVIA: No Bobby did.

JANE: Bobby never said that.

OLIVIA: He said he didn't care.

JANE: Oh no Bobby cares.

OLIVIA: That's what he said.

JANE: Why you care what happens to it?

OLIVIA: I'm helping Adele. Decide. What to do.

JANE: Adele should decide for herself.

OLIVIA: She asked me. As a friend. To help her.

JANE: The will said "Three agreeing would be best. But two can decide." Three being Adele and Ed and Bobby. Not Adele and Ed and Bobby and Olivia.

OLIVIA: Or Jane.

JANE: Two being Bobby and Adele. Or Bobby and Ed.

OLIVIA: Or Adele and Ed. Since Bobby doesn't care.

JANE: Oh. Bobby cares. A lot.

OLIVIA: He told Adele "Take it." "I don't want the old thing." "I hate that place." "I hate the smell."

JANE: Bobby loved his mother. He loves this place.

OLIVIA: Bobby doesn't love this place. Adele told me he said "Take it. Take it!"

JANE: When did he say this?

OLIVIA: Adele said "He was so loud." "Take it!" she said he said.

JANE: When did he supposedly say this?

OLIVIA: After the funeral. When they were alone. In the dining room.

JANE: He was upset.

OLIVIA: Of course he was upset. But Jane. That doesn't mean he was lying.

JANE: That was the wrong time to talk to him. He was upset. She shouldn't have been talking to him about things like that at a time like that.

OLIVIA: It sounds like that's what Bobby wants.

JANE: No.

OLIVIA: Doesn't it?

JANE: That's not what Bobby wants.

OLIVIA: That's not what you want.

JANE: Okay. (*Long pause.*) Because what I want. (*Long pause.*) Is what Bobby wants. (*Pause.*) Too. (*Long pause.*) That's how we work. (*Pause.*) Bobby thinks we should sell it.

OLIVIA: You want to sell it?

JANE: It's worth a lot of money. Someone should build something reasonable out here. Houses or. Condos or. Something useful. Something new. Something clean. Something clean someone new could use.

OLIVIA: I want to build out here.

JANE: This land would be perfect for a house.

OLIVIA: I want to rebuild out here.

JANE: It's so close to town, but with air and trees. It's attractive. People are attracted to this spot.

OLIVIA: This is a holy place.

JANE: Someone could work magic out here.

OLIVIA: This isn't a place to develop. This is a place that already is.

JANE: Olivia. It's an old aviary. It's crumbling. Look at the paint. Look at the broken glass. The wood is splitting. It's covered in birdshit. It's unsafe. The birds are all gone. The plants are all dead. It's done.

OLIVIA: It's not done.

JANE: It is.

OLIVIA: It's not done

JANE: It's old.

OLIVIA: It's tired. It needs care.

JANE: It's not holy.

OLIVIA: It's still awake.

JANE: Its back is broken. It's done.

OLIVIA: Your heart is broken that's what's broken. (*Pause.*) Adele's father loved this place. So he got old. So he let some of it fall down. So. We shouldn't tear the rest of it down. We should push it back up.

JANE: I'm not interested in your holy-roller stuff.

OLIVIA: That's where the pulpit going to be.

JANE: Oh. Is that what Adele wants?

OLIVIA: No. That's what I want. Adele wants it over there. People will sit here. On pleasant days, on benches, under the trees. The birds will come back. We'll need a parking lot.

JANE: A parking lot?

OLIVIA: Big enough for our church.

JANE: Your church for the birds.

OLIVIA: You'd have house and house and house

JANE: No. I'd have one nice new house.

OLIVIA: And house and car and house and house

JANE: Maybe two. Something clean.

OLIVIA: I want. A church that would soar. For the glory of.

JANE: It's ridiculous. A waste. Of space. And of listening.

OLIVIA: Ridiculous is thinking the spirit doesn't matter. Jane.

JANE: Oh the spirit matters. Olivia. But I'm quite sure that what you're describing would house a spirit completely unlike any I would ever care for.

ED: (*Enters.*) It's beautiful out here.

JANE: It is, isn't it Ed.

ED: Be pretty to live out here.

JANE: Wouldn't it though.

ED: Still. Be a shame if it got packed with houses.

OLIVIA: Wouldn't it. Though.

ED: It's hard to figure out what to do.

OLIVIA: I've had some thoughts.

JANE: I've had some thoughts too.

OLIVIA: What we might be able to do.

JANE: With the land.

OLIVIA: And the aviary.

ED: I guess it's something Adele and Bobby and I'll just have to figure out, hmm. (*Pause.*) I think we should keep it. (*Long pause.*)

OLIVIA: That sounds good.

ED: Keep the land. Let the old place crumble, just sort of fade away. Shall we go? (*OLIVIA and JANE exit.*) Okay. Here we are. Different place. New moment. Same story. Adele! Come here and help me with this. (*ADELE enters. She helps ED with a banner. It is on five-foot poles. It's awkward.*) I made it too big.

(*Unfurls the banner. It reads: THE CHURCH OF THE FIFTH DAY.*)

ADELE: You think it's too big?

ED: It's way too big.

ADELE: Oh no no no. It's good.

ED: You don't think it's too big? It's gaudy huh.

ADELE: No no it's not gaudy.

ED: Gaudy's good Adele.

ADELE: Oh then yeah It's gaudy!

ED: You like it?

ADELE: Oh yeah.

ED: You really like it?

ADELE: I do yeah.

ED: I kind of like it too.

ADELE: It's great.

ED: Think it's gaudy enough?

ADELE: Yeah.

ED: Think she'll like it?

ADELE: Oh no yeah.

ED: Really?

(*ADELE nods.*)

ED: I'm glad you like it.

ADELE: Will you stay?

ED: For what?

ADELE: To help us?

ED: Well. I don't really. Believe all this.

ADELE: You could stay to visit. With me.

ED: Oh well then yeah I'll stay.

ADELE: Good. (*Pause.*) You don't have to tell her. You don't believe.

ED: Have you told her?

ADELE: (*Laughs.*) No. No.

ED: It's too big.

ADELE: No.

ED: I don't think she'll like it.

OLIVIA: (*Enters.*) Like what? That's great. That's great. Did you make that Ed? That's beautiful. That? I love that.

ED: Adele asked me to.

OLIVIA: You did? Adele. That's great. Look how big it is! It's perfect. It'll go right behind me. This is going to be. This is going to be. Something. Today. Today's the start of something. Really. Really really. Really good. Great. Whole. Large. Holy. I can feel it. Holy. (*Pause.*) I'm a little nervous.

ADELE: Well.

OLIVIA: Of course. That makes sense. (*To ED.*) This is the first time I've ever done this in public. Not practicing. For real.

ED: Well.

OLIVIA: Makes a lot of sense. That's great. I love that banner. THE CHURCH OF THE FIFTH DAY. That says it. I'm going to get the box. And the brick. The banner and the box and the brick and we're all set.

(*She exits.*)

(*Long pause. ED and ADELE hold the banner.*)

ED: She's a little nervous.

OLIVIA: (*Off.*) I'm nervous but I'm confident. (*OLIVIA enters with soapbox. In the soapbox are pamphlets and a brick. She puts the pamphlets on the ground, puts the brick on them, and flips the box.*) The truth makes you confident. Telling the truth shouldn't be hard. It's a generous act. Right?

ADELE: Right.

OLIVIA: That's right. (*Gets up on the box.*) The first day of the Church of the Fifth Day. Please help me tell the truth. (*Pause.*) And on the Fifth Day he made the creatures of the air! God made the creatures of the air!

Imagine:

On the fifth day

All of the birds opening their wings for the first time in a great stretch and up and flying up and all of them appearing all and calling each other the first great sound of rapture in the sky floating up through air and over water and up through trees all calling to find brother and lover and family

Imagine:

On the fifth day

The loon laughing that laugh across the water for the first time and imagine his astonishment at the sound and the hummingbird flying up down and then backwards! and up down and into flowers Oh sweet and Oh and on great wings and small and all and all across the blue blue sky

This is where we live now! they call. This is where we live! This is

(Birds descend and cover OLIVIA. She disappears from sight, wrens, pigeons, ducks, parrots perhaps, hawks. We see wings and the flash of eyes and beaks. Then, all at once they lift and fly off.)

ADELE: Oh.

ED: Oh. Olivia. Are you all right. Is she all right? That was.

OLIVIA: That. Was.

ADELE: That was.

OLIVIA: That was something. Hey! That was something!

ADELE: Something!

OLIVIA: (*Laughs.*) Whoa! (*Laughs.*) I saw him. Inside all of that. I saw him and he was smiling. He. Was. Smiling.

ADELE: Hey!

OLIVIA: We're on track. That was really it!

ED: Of course the rest of that week we went back. To that exact spot. The next day (*ED, ADELE and OLIVIA look up. Thunder.*) it rained. The day after that (*ED, ADELE and OLIVIA look up. Thunder.*) it rained. The day after that (*ED, ADELE and OLIVIA look up. Thunder.*) it rained. The day after that— (*ED, ADELE and OLIVIA look up.*) It looks like rain Olivia.

OLIVIA: I don't think so.

ED: It kind of does.

OLIVIA: You. Come here. Yeah. You. (*TOM enters.*) What's your name?

TOM: Tom.

OLIVIA: Hi Tom. This is Ed. Hold the banner with him. Adele, you come with me.

(TOM takes ADELE 's place holding the banner. ADELE and OLIVIA exit.)

(*Long pause.*)

TOM: I have a bird.

(*Long pause.*)

(*Thunder. Hard rain. They're soaked.*)

ED: Oh blast. Blast. This is going to get ruined.

TOM: Quick, come to my place, it's just over here.

ED: Blast this blasted goddamned too-big goddamned banner.

TOM: Just there. Here it is. We can get dry. Come on in.

ED: Thanks.

TOM: Take off your shirt I'll get you a towel. (*ED does. TOM exits. Comes back with a towel and a dry shirt.*) Here.

ED: Thanks. A lot. (*They kiss.*) Then we did what guys do after they get caught in the rain, and run into one of their apartments and take off their shirts and kiss.

TOM: (*Showing ED photographs.*) This is my mom and dad. That's me. That's. There. That's my brother. That's. My mom again. And me. That's my dad.

ED: No that's a lie. Actually we just had sex. No that's a lie. We didn't even kiss. I thought about it. When I was looking around his apartment. Which was frigging huge.

TOM: Maybe. Ah. Can I.

ED: I think it's stopped raining.

TOM: Do you want something to drink?

(*Pause.*)

ED: Yeah look. It has. They're probably wondering where I am. I'm going to get going.

TOM: Don't take that. Take my shirt. It's dry.

ED: Sure? You want to trade?

TOM: Sure.

(*Pause.*)

ED: Okay. You keep mine. Thanks.
TOM: Okay.
ED: Okay. Bye. Thanks. Okay.

(*ED exits.*)

TOM: You forgot your banner! Ed! (*ADELE enters.*) Ed forgot your banner. Yesterday. He forgot this. He around?
ADELE: No.
TOM: I wanted to give it back to him.

(*OLIVIA enters.*)

OLIVIA : You brought the banner. Just in time to help us to close up shop! Brick and pamphlets in the box. And now banner. Hup. All packed there we are. Done! What a good day this was!
TOM: Is Ed around?
OLIVIA: He's supposed to pick us up with the van. Adele you have everything of yours?
ADELE: I do.
OLIVIA: I guess let's just wait then.
TOM: Is he coming soon?
OLIVIA: Who?
TOM: Ed.
OLIVIA: Oh yeah. I think so. He said he would.
TOM: So you're just going to wait?
OLIVIA: Over here.
TOM: Until he comes?
OLIVIA: Yup.
TOM: How'd you do all this?
OLIVIA: All what?
TOM: This. Church of the Fifth Day.
OLIVIA: That's quite a story. Right Adele?
ADELE: Sure is.
OLIVIA: That's right it is.

(*Long pause.*)

TOM: Really?
OLIVIA: Yup.

(*Pause.*)

TOM: So? How did you?
OLIVIA: What?
TOM: Do it?
OLIVIA: Okay. One day, when I was practicing preaching, outside, it rained. And I thought "We're gonna need a church. With a roof." And a miracle happened. Because that very day, Adele said to me—
ADELE: My father is dead.

(*Long pause.*)

OLIVIA: Now. In order to understand why I knew this was a miracle, we have to go back in time.
  Imagine:
  Two years ago, on the fifth day of my semiannual fast, which also happened to be on Cinco de Mayo, the fifth of May, which is the fifth month of the year, I was wandering through the basement stacks of the Rochambeau library. Just
  I was lightheaded. Well because I was fasting. I was lightheaded. I was discouraged. I had a low-paying job. My car was. My Visa bill was. I felt.
  I was in the basement of a library.
  So there I was. In the basement. Just reading. Here and there. And I opened a journal. With an article. About a medieval aviary. Not a building aviary. But a book aviary. A medieval book. Written by monks. Which explained everything. In the form of stories about birds. The vulture devours corpses like a sinner delights in carnal knowledge. And. The sparrow is an inconstant and restless bird. Like a faithless man flying from God. And

ADELE: The red feet of the dove is the blood of martyrs.

OLIVIA: Right. And. Suddenly a flashing insight cut through my lightheadedness and despair.

    I realized the bird is God revealing all. On the fifth day of the fifth month of my fortieth year and forty is five times five plus five and five and five, I realized that the fifth day of creation is really the holiest of holy days. Not the sixth, not the seventh, but the fifth. The day God created birds.

    And I felt a deep calm. I had a message to share. I went to work. With the number five and flocks of birds flying around in my head. I went to my low-paying job but so what I don't care. I was working at the paint department at Adler's. So what.

    That was the day I met Adele.

ADELE: I needed paint.

OLIVIA: She needed peacock blue paint.

ADELE: That's right.

OLIVIA: Whoever needs peacock blue paint? No one. She comes in for peacock blue paint. I got quiet.

ADELE: I was painting.

OLIVIA: Her father's aviary.

TOM: You were painting a book?

OLIVIA: Not a book aviary. His aviary aviary. It's a birdhouse. Only house-sized.

TOM: Oh.

OLIVIA: She said aviary. I got really quiet.

ADELE: On Church Road.

OLIVIA: Church Road! She said that. AWK! I fainted.

ADELE: She did.

TOM: You did?

OLIVIA: I did.

ADELE: She fainted!

OLIVIA: Made that sound. AWK!

ADELE: She did!

OLIVIA: And fainted!

ADELE: She did!

OLIVIA: This dramatic response naturally enchanted Adele

ADELE: It did!

OLIVIA: She returned the next day with coffee

ADELE: With two cups.

OLIVIA: And an order for more paint.

ADELE: Eggshell white.

OLIVIA: AWK! I fainted again.

ADELE: Ha!

OLIVIA: Of course we became friends. We went out. For coffee. I was always talking about the Fifth Day. Adele was studying electrical something at Where was that?

ADELE: Wampanaog Polytech.

OLIVIA: She's not a great electrician.

ADELE: No.

TOM: No?

OLIVIA: No.

ADELE: No.

OLIVIA: With her, when something is supposed to hum, it often zaps.

ADELE: Ha.

OLIVIA: And when it's supposed to zap, there can be smoke.

TOM: Really.

ADELE: Um.

OLIVIA: But. She is a great listener.

ADELE: Olivia.

OLIVIA: You are.

ADELE: Okay.

OLIVIA: She is. Not a good listener. More than good. Listening is a rare and difficult art. It takes stamina and generosity and a quick and responsive mind.

ADELE: Olivia.

OLIVIA: Adele is the Stradivarius of listeners, an ox, a silent rock of Gibraltar, with a crystal ear as they say.

TOM: Really.

OLIVIA: Her? She's been listening her whole life. You can tell. She's been listening to everything. Every day. To her mother. To gossip. In church. To drunks. To liars. To the radio. She doesn't care who she listens to. And she's heard a lot.

ADELE: If you listen, people will talk.

OLIVIA: So one day, when I finally really understood my theory of the soul, on that day when I told Adele

ADELE: The soul is a bird we keep in our heart.

OLIVIA: She burst into tears. (*Long pause.*) Now. In order to understand why, we have to go farther back. To Adele's childhood. Adele's mother died when she was

ADELE: eleven

OLIVIA: eleven. Right. Her father was

ADELE: inconsolable

OLIVIA: Right. He was

ADELE: inconsolable

OLIVIA: Right. He

ADELE: was (*Long pause.*) When um

When my mother died my father was inconsolable. He was He sat us in the living room on the couch. Me. Bobby. Ed. He couldn't. Look us in the eye. He couldn't stop. He walked around the house. In his socks. Room to room. Looking everywhere. For her.

The day of the funeral, we pulled up in front of the church, my father got out of the car, came around to open the car door for us, we got out, me, Bobby, Ed, he took me and Ed by the hand, we walked up the walkway to the church, Bobby was behind us, when suddenly (*ADELE blows a breath.*) the lightest flapping, a little little small small brown bird, a little small wren-like bird, maybe a wren, my guess I guess is a wren, landed on my father's hand, on his hand, my father looked into the wren's eyes, and he whispered—"this bird is my wife's soul," because I was listening I heard "this bird is my wife's soul"

(*ADELE breathes in.*) We sat in the front row pew during the funeral, me, Bobby, Ed, my father, crying, all of us in tears except my father, he was smiling, during the sermon the minister lost his place because he noticed the wren, flapping against the cloth of my father's suit-jacket pocket, my father was smiling and patting it, we went straight home, we barely talked to anyone, my aunt had to talk to everyone in the line waiting with consolations because my father just walked us right by them, me, Bobby, Ed, my father got us home, into the kitchen and he put the bird under a soup pot.

(*Pause.*) Then he ran upstairs to Bobby's room, dumped Bobby's records, dumped them, dumped them right out of his Georgia Peach record crate, right out onto the floor, brought the crate down into the kitchen, turned the crate over, got the bird out from under the soup pot and put it under the crate, he looked outside, into the backyard, at the doghouse, pulled the dog out into the front yard, tied the dog to the lilac bush, lifted up the doghouse, carried it into the kitchen, made a screen door for it, scratched "Mom" on it, put the bird in it. The bird went from pocket to soup pot to record crate to doghouse. The bird looked through the screen door at my father. My father looked back at the bird. The bird looked. My father looked. We watched. Me. Bobby. Ed. For a long time.

"That's not going to work," my father said.

He took Ed and sat him next to him at the kitchen table. "Ed, I'm going to build Mom a house but until then, she's going to stay in your room." Ed said that startled him because he had a thought he thought Oh great How am I going to sleep with Mom flying around and then he had another thought he thought Oh great I'm gonna have to put on my underwear in the morning with Mom tilting her head and looking at me and she's got new beady black eyes.

"We're going to put you in Bobby's room on the cot," my father said. "That's not fair!" That was Bobby yelling—"He's just a kid and that bird isn't Mom anyway that's just a dumb bird" my father slapped Bobby hard. Across his face. I ran and stood on the stairs. My father looked at me and I didn't cry.

So now my Mom is in Ed's room: And Ed was in Bobby's room, where Bobby'd only let him have as much stuff as he could stuff under the cot. Everything else anything that stuck out went out the window. Then Ed would have to run down the stairs out into the garden to get it before it got soaked by the sprinkler. And then he'd have to sneak it back into his room and put it back where it had been in the first place. My Mom made him nervous, 'cause the curtains were shut and the light was dim and he said she had a habit of flying low. So after a while Ed would make me come with him into his room with him where we'd sit in the dim light, me visiting Mom and Ed visiting his stuff. I'd sit on the edge of Ed's desk chair, remembering to sit up straight because this was my mother after all and my mother was very concerned about good posture. Sometimes I sat and I talked to her and sometimes I sat and I didn't have anything to say to her, and she'd hop and hop, hop hop hop hop, around the room, ending up under the bureau, and sometimes she looked so disinterested in what I was saying that I'd think, maybe Dad made a mistake, maybe this isn't Mom, but maybe it is just a bird, just a dumb bird like Bobby muttered every night, "just a dumb bird and Dad is even dumber than the bird thinking the dumb bird is Mom."

(*Long pause.*) My father built the aviary, I helped. (*Long pause.*) It was a long job that took a very long time because my father wanted it just right. I helped him do most of the wiring which was where I first got interested in electrical appliances, an interest which is still with me today. (*ZAP.*)

My father was very patient. We built it on an empty lot my father and mother had bought for their vacation/retirement home-to-be. "So she retired a little early" my father would say. "Who can blame her, she worked hard for a long long time. She couldn't wait to get out here" he'd say. Sometimes he'd look upset and say "I should have built this for her years ago, I shouldn't of made her wait" and he'd cry. But mostly he was pretty happy hammering.

When we finished, we brought my Mom there. I was happy to see her there because she seemed happy. And Ed was happy she was out of his room and Bobby was happy Ed was out of his room and so all in all it seemed like everyone was pretty happy.

Then my father came up with the thought that it would be a good idea to collect the other souls of various dead people from the area who were just flapping around any which way anywhere. It wasn't odd to see me and my father walking around the woods or down near the river, he'd found this big swimming pool net and I'd see one "there there Dad there get her get her get her" and woosh he would, get her, and I'd say

"Good catch Dad" and we'd bring Mrs. Fontaine or Mr. Leary or whoever it was flapping in the net and put'm into the aviary with Mom. My father would sit in there. Sometimes the squawking was loud.

Every now and then one of the other birds would die. Which was confusing. But my father would just smile and talk about the will of God. And that's how it went for a very long time. But then one day the wren died. Which was very. Confusing.

(*Very long pause.*) After that my father got pale. A bunch of windowpanes got broken one night. The other birds either flew away or died. Most of the plants dried up. Or were cut down. My father just sat in there. I'd try and spruce it up every now and then but he wasn't really interested. That was. For a whole bunch of years. Up until just. And then of course

(*Pause.*) Then. (*Pause.*) So. (*Pause.*) So back when (*Pause.*) Back when Olivia said

OLIVIA: (*Long pause. She looks at ADELE. Long pause.*) The soul is a bird we keep in our heart.

ADELE: I remembered

OLIVIA: (*Pause. She looks at ADELE.*) Her father saying "This bird is my wife's soul" and she knew I understood.

ADELE: Right.

OLIVIA: And this is why when I said "We need a church. With a roof." And Adele said "My father is dead" I knew a miracle had occurred. Because as sad as Adele is and as sad as I am for Adele, in a quiet backroom of my mind I think

Peacock blue paint and the basement of a library and Adele's mother and a tiny wren and five and five and five and five fives it all adds up. The aviary is going to be our Church of the Fifth Day! The time is here. I had asked and I had received.

ED: (*Enters.*) Course you haven't got it yet.

ADELE: Ed!

OLIVIA: Hi Ed.

ED: Because Bobby might have something to say about it.

OLIVIA: True.

ED: Jane might have something to say.

OLIVIA: True.

ED: I might have something to say.

OLIVIA: True.

TOM: Hi Ed.

ED: This everything?

ADELE: Yup.

ED: Okay. Let's get out of here. Shall we?

OLIVIA: Let's go.

ADELE: Okay. See ya Tom.

TOM: Okay. (*ED, ADELE and OLIVIA exit. ADELE reenters to get the banner.*) He forgot it again.

ADELE: Thanks. (*She exits with the banner.*)

TOM: Course I went back the next day.

(*He sits. ADELE enters. She carries pamphlets. She sits. They sit waiting. Long pause.*)

ADELE: I get tired. A bit. Of handing out pamphlets.

TOM: It's hard work.

ADELE: It's more the people staring at me.

TOM: It's hard to get used to people staring.

ADELE: They read them. Then they stare at me. (*Long pause.*) Olivia writes them.

TOM: She does a good job.

ADELE: She does. (*Pause.*) I don't really understand them.

TOM: They are hard to understand.

ADELE: Do you believe her?

TOM: I have a bird.

ADELE: I don't. Have a bird. But she understands why not. You know. Because of my Mom.

TOM: Right.

ADELE: I believe her.

TOM: You do.

ADELE: Because she believes. That's enough for me. (*JANE enters.*) Hey Jane!

JANE: Is that Olivia? Who are all those people around her?

ADELE: They came to listen to her.

JANE: She gives speeches out here in the park?

ADELE: Loads of people're showing up every day.

JANE: I want to talk to you and Ed about this aviary mess. Is Ed here?

TOM: Not yet.

JANE: I'm Jane.

ADELE: Oh yeah sorry this is Tom.

JANE: Hello Tom.

TOM: You're Ed's sister-in-law.

JANE: And Adele's.

TOM: Well hey then Jane.

JANE: Okay. Is Ed coming by because we really have things to discuss. About the aviary. I finally had a chance to really talk to Bobby about it. We were at the ballet last night. I talked to him about the possibility

TOM: You went to the ballet?

JANE: Yes.

TOM: I love the ballet. I mean. The ballet.

JANE: Have you seen this one?

TOM: Of course. Oh yeah of course. I'll go and see it a couple of times. I love the ballet. Man I. I'm a hockey player you know so I love it, it's the same in a way, the movement, it's the same, I mean you take Russian nineteenth-century ballet, it's just like a hockey game, it's got five acts, Russian ballet—five acts, act one, narrative it's the story told from beginning to end, act two's a vision, act three is mad scenes, act four the conclusion, act five, a frivolous dance. Now hockey—the game is like the first act of the ballet when the story is told, it's the narrative, the hockey game itself. Then the second act, that's the moment of when it's over, in your mind's eye there's that moment, that critical goal, that incredible, amazing save, or the penalty, that something that was the defining moment that brought us here, it's like act two in the ballet, that moment is a vision. Act three, we won euphoria, or act three, we lost despair, madness, act four, the interviews, the commentary, the coaches' recap, it's all over it's all wrapped up this is what happened this and this and then act five I have to go dance because I'm so fired up I couldn't go to bed. I gotta go dance. I gotta keep moving. I love the ballet.

JANE: You're a hockey player?

TOM: Oh. Yeah. Yeah. I am.

JANE: Professional?

TOM: Well. Yeah.

JANE: Do you play for us?

TOM: I do.

JANE: My husband Bobby would die to meet you. I would love you to meet Bobby. He hates the ballet. He loves hockey. I can't wait to tell him you love the ballet.

ED: (*Enters.*) So Olivia's over there talking to three of her new you know disciples you know Adele the one the sack of flour with the droopy eyes

ADELE: Martie

ED: Hey Jane hey Tom

TOM: Hi Ed

ED: Hi yeah Martie so Olivia's talking to Martie and

This Martie was in the park the day all the birds came flying down and covered Olivia and so was this other one Ron he's the one who changed his last name to Dove rhymes with love and so was the third her name's Dolores so Olivia and Martie and Ron Dove rhymes with love they're all trying to talk Dolores off the emotional ledge because Dolores used to be a sous-chef at this fancy restaurant and she used to serve duck all the time, she used to stew'm fry'm grill'm roast'm, she pan-broiled them! She ate the redemption, she keeps saying that. "I ate the redemption I ate the redemption."

I know I know I know Adele. It's not funny. It's a little funny. I know. It's not funny. How's everyone doing?

ADELE: You shouldn't make fun.

ED: No I know I know. I know.

ADELE: They all look up to Olivia.

ED: Absolutely. Hey Jane.

JANE: Ed we need to talk about the aviary and what we're going to do.

ED: Yeah. Okay sure.

JANE: Will you excuse us Tom?

ED: He can stay.

JANE: It's personal Ed.
TOM: Oh sure. Of course.
ED: What's the big deal?
JANE: It's nothing personal Tom. But.
TOM: No.
JANE: It was nice meeting you.
TOM: I'll just. See you later. Adele. Ed.
ED: Okay.
ADELE: Bye Tom.

(*TOM exits.*)

JANE: Ed. It's personal. I mean
ED: Yeah okay okay so
ADELE: He's a hockey player.
ED: Who is?
ADELE: Tom.
ED: He is?
ADELE: Yeah.
ED: Professional?
ADELE: Yeah.
ED: Really.
ADELE: Yeah.
JANE: Ed. The aviary.
ED: Does he play for us?
ADELE: Yeah.
ED: Really.
JANE: Adele.
ED: Huh.
JANE: Augh!
ED: What.
ADELE: What Jane?
ED: So what do you think we should do with the aviary?
OLIVIA: (*Enters.*) Oh man oh man. They're driving me nuts those
    three. Jane. It's unbearable. The monotony. The aggravation.
    The pure tedium of a congregation. I never realized that just
    because I start my own church I have to have people in it.

JANE: That's kind of the point though isn't it.

OLIVIA: Of course but Well just because the church I'm starting might seem odd to some people, I am looking at you Jane, it doesn't seem fair that all its members should have to automatically be odd.

JANE: It seems odd to expect them not to be.

ADELE: Jane.

JANE: Well really Adele. It's a bird religion.

ADELE: So?

JANE: These are all bird people.

OLIVIA: She's right.

ADELE: She's not right.

OLIVIA: With Martie it's her mother, her father, her brother, that weird forklift exhaust pipe thing I don't even.

ADELE: Well.

OLIVIA: I don't What am I even supposed to say to that? Her brother. The forklift. The exhaust pipe. What am I supposed to say?

ADELE: Well.

OLIVIA: I don't even want to tell Ron where the study class is, in case he shows up.

ADELE: Well.

OLIVIA: and Dolores

ADELE: Yeah.

OLIVIA: She's daffy.

ADELE: Well.

OLIVIA: She is. I don't even.

ED: Tom's a hockey player.

ADELE: He's a hockey player.

OLIVIA: He is?

ED: Yeah.

OLIVIA: Professional?

ED: Yeah.

OLIVIA: Really. Does he play for us?

ADELE: Yeah.

OLIVIA: Really.

JANE: Oh good God.

ED: It's kind of interesting he didn't tell us, isn't it.

JANE: Tell us what?

ED: That he's a hockey player.

JANE: Ed.

ADELE: Yeah.

ED: And that he plays professional hockey.

ADELE: Yeah.

JANE: Ed.

ED: And.

ADELE: He plays for us.

ED: Yeah.

ADELE: I know.

ED: I just think he would have said something earlier.

ADELE: Most people would have.

ED: You should have seen his apartment.

ADELE: When'd you see his apartment?

ED: It was huge. There was this whopping huge statue of something in his hallway. Had to be this big. I thought he must be a lawyer. I never thought he was a professional hockey player.

JANE: Ed.

ED: I like that though. It was modest. Not to tell us.

JANE: He seems very nice.

ED: You make that sound bad.

JANE: I'm sure he's a very good hockey player.

ADELE: I like him.

ED: You do?

ADELE: Yes I do.

OLIVIA: I like him too.

ADELE: He has a bird.

OLIVIA: He's normal.

ED: He's a normal bird person.

OLIVIA: Which means it's possible.

ED: To be a normal bird person.

JANE: Bobby and I think we should sell it.

ADELE: Sell what?

JANE: The aviary.

ED: I thought Bobby doesn't care.

JANE: Bobby cares! Bobby cares! Bobby cares! (*Pause.*) I just have to

say I'm not sure a banner and some pamphlets and a congre-
gation with one normal hockey-playing bird person and the
rest weird and faith in a half-baked bird/fantasy/miracle/birds
coming down and covering you thing constitutes a real church.
Ed, Adele I'll call you.

(*She exits.*)

(*Pause.*)

OLIVIA: You know what'll make this a real church?
ED: Then Olivia had a terrifying idea.
OLIVIA: We'll have a bake sale. That'll show her who has a real church.

(*OLIVIA, ADELE and ED exit. TOM and ANDRE enter off the
ice. They've just finished hockey practice. They are suited up and
sweaty. During this scene they take off their skates and uniforms.
In the middle of the scene they shower in fast motion, like a film
speeded up. They dress into their street clothes.*)

ANDRE: You know what I think? I think you should just kiss him.
TOM: I should just kiss him.
ANDRE: Yeah. Yeah absolutely. That's what I did with Jeanine. I just
        kissed her. Course we were both shit-faced and already fucking
        naked in bed. But she seemed to like it. She told me afterwards
        that it was the kiss that did it.
TOM: Yeah?
ANDRE: Yeah absolutely. Course I'm from Lithuania.
TOM: So?
ANDRE: You know Lithuanians.
TOM: They're from Lithuania.
ANDRE: We know how to kiss.
TOM: That's what Jeanine says.
ANDRE: That's right. I can't be making any promises for you.
TOM: Yeah. Like you could do it and I couldn't.
ANDRE: That's funny I don't see your guy up in the wives' box. I see
        Jeanine. I don't see this Ed guy.

TOM: Yeah okay.

ANDRE: That's funny I see Jeanine, she's got a wedding ring on her finger that she's still showing everyone. I don't see this Ed guy, not with any no even friendship ring or I'm your boyfriend ring he's waving around.

TOM: You're right.

ANDRE: He has no ring.

TOM: No he doesn't.

ANDRE: Fact, I don't even see this Ed guy. He's probably at some other hockey game. Someone else's probably been kissing him.

TOM: Oh that's what you think huh.

ANDRE: That's funny I see Jeanine she's got a belly out to here, makes it hard for her to sit through the whole game without peeing every five minutes. Someone's been kissing her.

TOM: That's right. I wonder who?

ANDRE: That's not funny.

TOM: That's not funny?

ANDRE: No.

TOM: Okay okay.

ANDRE: You're talking about my wife.

TOM: Okay okay you're right.

ANDRE: My wife who's pregnant with my kid.

TOM: I was joking.

ANDRE: That's not funny. Cause she would kick your ass! Hah!

TOM: You better believe she would!

ANDRE: She'd come running down the stands swinging at you, she heard you making fun of me. Hah! I don't see Ed standing anywhere near here ready to take a swing at her for you! Hah!

TOM: Okay okay.

ANDRE: What are you scared of?

TOM: What?

ANDRE: What are you scared of?

TOM: Nothing.

ANDRE: With this Ed guy.

TOM: Nothing.

ANDRE: What?

TOM: With other guys I'm not. But with him. I don't know how to talk to him. I start. I want to start and say something. I. It. I don't know the right. I've never known how to. And.

ANDRE: You afraid he's not going to like you?

TOM: (*Pause.*)

ANDRE: If he doesn't like you he's a dope.

TOM: He's not a dope.

ANDRE: Hey all I'm saying.

TOM: I'm the dope There's nothing stupider than being in love.

ANDRE: What?

TOM: It makes me think too much. I can't speak because I can't speak fast enough to keep up with my mind. I think about him, then I think about how I can never know what he's thinking about me, does he think about me? what if he doesn't think about me? then I think Don't think! because I think—I don't want to think that. So I just stand there and look at him. Then I think he must think I'm a freak. (*Pause.*)

ANDRE: Oh boy.

TOM: I gave him an orange the other day. He shared it with everyone. He gave a piece to just anyone. (*Pause.*)

ANDRE: What are you doing tonight?

TOM: Want to go to a bake sale?

ANDRE: A bake sale?

TOM: Yeah.

ANDRE: With rice crispy treats and shit?

TOM: Yeah.

ANDRE: Fuck yeah. I'm totally in. I just gotta call Jeanine at home let her know. Lemme call her lemme call her. (*Takes out his cell phone.*) Baby Hey baby. How's it going? (*Long pause.*) Hey baby, was there a guy named Ed up in the wives' booth at the last game?

TOM: Oh funny guy.

ANDRE: She says she doesn't know any Ed guy. So baby Tom invited me out. Tonight. To a bake sale. I know! You okay with that? (*Pause.*) Hey Tom, where's it at?

TOM: Tell her church.

ANDRE: Yeah.

TOM: No really.

ANDRE: Okay. (*To Jeanine.*) He says church. Yeah. Yeah! (*Pause.*)

What? Nah Tom wouldn't shit you. (*To TOM.*) She thinks you're shitting her! (*To Jeanine.*) Yeah me too. You know that. (*Pause.*) I won't be too long. Okay. (*Hangs up. Pause.*) I love that fucking woman.

TOM: You should.

ANDRE: I do.

TOM: She's a hot shit.

ANDRE: I know. (*Pause.*) I was down near the bus station today.

TOM: Yeah?

ANDRE: So I saw this little kid, little you know, maybe three maybe four. With his mom and his grandma, they're all waiting for the bus, this little kid's looking up into the sky, his chin's up like this, he's screaming his head off in Spanish he's yelling and laughing yelling more and laughing, his mom and his grandma are laughing and smiling at the rest of us, I'm thinking How come they're not telling him to shut up and be polite you know because he is screaming. A lot. And loud. So I look at the mother, she smiles at me and looks a little embarrassed because she should be, but she says to me, we can't stop him because he's praying. He's shouting up to God.

The kid's a total fucking hot shit. He knows already that as long as he's shouting up to God, he can be as noisy as he wants. There's his grandma laughing at him screaming! Hey God hey God hey God hey God in Spanish! I was laughing and I got upset.

TOM: You got upset?

ANDRE: Yeah.

TOM: Why?

ANDRE: I got upset because my kid he's going to be a hot shit like that little kid. I know it.

TOM: You bet he is.

ANDRE: I got upset because what if I'm not good enough to him? (*Pause.*)

TOM: You will be.

ANDRE: You know? (*Pause.*) Are we going or what?

TOM: Yeah let's go. (*They exit.*)

ED: (*Enters. He has a rice crispy square. He has just come out of the bake sale.*) There is something truly disturbing about a bake sale.

(*TOM and ANDRE enter.*)

TOM: Hey Ed.

ED: Hey.

TOM: This is my friend Andre. This is Ed.

ANDRE: Oh. Ed. Is that a rice crispy treat?

ED: It is.

ANDRE: I am headed into heaven. (*To TOM.*) You coming?

TOM: You going back in?

ED: Naw. It's a little crazy in there.

TOM: I'm going to wait outside for a bit.

ANDRE: I'm going to get me a nice rice crispy treat. I'm going to get me a whole plate of'm. Made by a nice little old church lady from your church. (*Exits.*)

ED: He doesn't know what he's getting himself into.

TOM: No.

ED: It's kind of weird in there.

TOM: Yeah?

ED: It's a bake sale with a bird theme. A bake sale on its own is kinda. Add cookies shaped like pelicans. And. Ostriches. And. (*Long pause.*)

TOM: Yeah. (*Long pause.*)

ED: Add Olivia.

TOM: She's okay.

ED: No yeah okay. She is. (*Pause.*) She's actually kinda (*Shakes hand.*)

TOM: Nice night.

ED: Yeah. (*Pause.*)

TOM: (*Pause.*)

ED: She wants to use my Dad's aviary as the foundation of her church. My sister Adele is all for it. My sister-in-law Jane is adamantly against it. My brother Bobby doesn't care.

TOM: What do you want to do with it?

ED: What do you mean?

TOM: Do you want to give it to her?

ED: No. No. No. I want it to crumble down back into the ground. I'm tired of the thing. (*Pause.*) It was my Dad's.

TOM: That's what Adele said.

ED: Yeah. She and him. They were very close. And. He was a good guy. He was a really. But. I just didn't really. I wasn't invited. In, with them. (*Pause.*) What do you think we should do with it?

TOM: Oh. (*Pause.*)

ANDRE: (*Enters.*) Did you kiss him?

TOM: No.

ANDRE: Oh. (*Exits back into bake sale.*)

TOM: I want to take you to the ballet.

ED: You what?

TOM: I'd like to take you out.

ED: To the ballet.

TOM: Yeah.

ED: Like on a date?

TOM: Maybe you and your sister.

ED: Oh. Me and Adele.

TOM: And Andre. He'd probably want to go too.

ED: You want to take all of us. To the ballet.

TOM: (*Long pause.*)

ED: Sounds fun. All of us. Going together. To the ballet.

TOM: (*Kisses him. They kiss. And kiss. And kiss. And kiss. And kiss. And lean back.*)

ED: Huh. (*They kiss. And kiss.*) The ballet'd be fun.

TOM: (*Kisses him.*)

(*ANDRE and ADELE enter.*)

ANDRE: Shit Tom you heard this woman Olivia?

TOM: Yeah.

ANDRE: She's unbelievable! That bird thing that happened?

TOM: Yeah.

ANDRE: That's fucking unbelievable. They should be telling the goddamn Pope.

TOM: Yeah.

ANDRE: A whole bunch of people in there saw it! She saw it! Didn't you Adele!

ADELE: I did!

ANDRE: Olivia gave me this thing to read every morning. If I read it

I'm going to be scoring better! All these birds came fucking What? What? What.

TOM: Nothing. What?

ANDRE: You ready to go?

TOM: Are you?

ANDRE: You want to go? Okay.

TOM: I didn't say I wanted to go but if you want to.

ANDRE: Yeah we can go if you want to.

TOM: Oh yeah okay. I guess we can. Go. Okay.

ANDRE: Okay then.

TOM: Now?

ANDRE: Want to go now? Okay.

TOM: If that's what you want.

ANDRE: Okay.

TOM: Okay then.

ANDRE: Okay.

TOM: I'll call you about the ballet.

ANDRE: You going to call him about the ballet?

TOM: Yeah.

ANDRE: Okay.

TOM: Yeah.

ANDRE: Okay then.

TOM: Let's go Andre.

ANDRE: The ballet!

ED: You're coming too.

ANDRE: I am?

ED: That's what Tom says.

ANDRE: The three of us're going to the ballet!

TOM: Let's go Andre.

ANDRE: We should take Adele too then!

ED: Oh she's coming.

ANDRE: She is!

ADELE: I am?

ANDRE: Everybody's going!

TOM: Andre.

ANDRE: That'll do it!

TOM: Andre.

ANDRE: Good job.

ED: See ya Tom. (*TOM and ANDRE exit.*) What?

(*Pause.*)

(*TOM reenters and kisses ED. Kisses ED again. Exits.*)

ED: What?

ADELE: Nothing. (*Exits.*)

ED: Jane has a thing or two to say about the aviary.

JANE: (*Enters.*) One. It's a hazard. Two. It's an eyesore. (*Jane exits.*)

ED: Olivia has her own opinion.

OLIVIA: (*Enters.*) Some people think affairs of this material world are more important than affairs of the spirit. Some people are very deluded. (*OLIVIA exits.*)

ED: Jane has a thing or two to say about Olivia.

JANE: (*Enters.*) One. Someone might think that just because another certain someone in my family, okay Adele, just because this other second certain someone is easily led, that this first someone can get whatever she wants.

Two. And the first someone might think that no one else in my family is watching and no one else knows what is going on. (*Pause.*)

Three, that first someone is very mistaken. (*JANE exits.*)

ED: Olivia whispered in my ear:

OLIVIA: (*Enters.*) Who will remember your mother after the aviary is gone? Who will remember your father?

ED: Jane is stubborn.

JANE: (*Enters.*) It's an eyesore! It's a heap of dirty wood! He used to sit in the middle of it hunched over and crying. Why would you want to remember your father like that?

OLIVIA: It would be a celebration of their lives.

JANE: Someone might want to check her ambition at the door.

OLIVIA: Someone else might want to think about whether she is being blinded by greed.

JANE: Okay that's enough.

ED: This is Olivia. She's my sister Adele's best friend. And this. This

is my brother Bobby's wife. Jane. The shoes. They're fighting.
(*ED exits.*)

JANE: This is not about greed.

OLIVIA: I don't know Jane.

JANE: This is about how we should use an aviary and a parcel of land that was left to my husband and his sister and his brother by their father.

OLIVIA: Adele and Ed both agree that the church is a good idea.

JANE: They don't both agree about that.

OLIVIA: They do.

JANE: I've talked to Ed. He hasn't agreed to anything.

OLIVIA: He was there when I called them. When the birds came down.

JANE: And?

OLIVIA: I was inside that whirlwind of feathers and wings.

JANE: And so?

OLIVIA: I heard the voice of God Jane.

JANE: You did.

OLIVIA: Ed was there when I heard Him.

JANE: You heard a voice.

OLIVIA: It was His voice.

JANE: You think it was God's voice.

OLIVIA: Oh it was.

JANE: Fine. How about this. I don't care about your spiritual experience.

OLIVIA: Oh.

JANE: Period. It has no meaning for me. Birds flapping down around you, the voice of God calling you. It doesn't. I don't. That's not how I.

OLIVIA: Jane. How can I convince you? If you won't

JANE: Maybe you can't convince me.

OLIVIA: I can't accept that.

JANE: There's your problem.

OLIVIA: I can't

JANE: There are people who won't be convinced.

OLIVIA: Those people

JANE: Some won't be.

OLIVIA: That's what prayer's for.

JANE: Do you hear how rude how pushy that is?

OLIVIA: What?

JANE: We're going to just pray right through your disinterest.

OLIVIA: All I want Jane all I pray for is for you to have

JANE: For you to use it, this spiritual experience, this whatever, for you to use it as the basis of an argument to get me to grant you moral. Anything. So that you can get what you want, even if you think it's what's supposed to. Doesn't resonate with me. That. Doesn't. No.

OLIVIA: I'm sorry to hear that.

JANE: Olivia.

OLIVIA: It's a shame.

JANE: What's a shame?

OLIVIA: It's discouraging. When people can't see. When it's right there boom in front of us.

JANE: Don't.

OLIVIA: Don't what?

JANE: Don't.

OLIVIA: I'm sorry you

JANE: I won't let you choose my God for me Olivia.

OLIVIA: Jane.

JANE: No matter how strongly you believe your God is the God. The only God the God the God.

OLIVIA: It makes me sad

JANE: I see my God every day.

OLIVIA: Then you have to understand.

JANE: The one you heard, the one you're talking about right now

OLIVIA: God.

JANE: No. Not God. Not. God. Your God. Your. God. There's a difference.

OLIVIA: You're being very picky. Jane.

JANE: My God? My God. I see my God in the order that we can sometimes. Sometimes see. In the world. I see my God in the quiet and unadorned cleanliness that we sometimes we rarely but we sometimes sometimes even if it's rarely we can achieve. In a hedge that has been clipped and trimmed well. For example. A hedge. That.

OLIVIA: A hedge.

JANE: That someone has cared for. That someone has taken the time to. This splash of birds that you

You wanting to build and To cover over this green piece of land with a parking lot and garbage cans so your people can come and

No.

OLIVIA: Jane. I did hear His voice. I did. Jane. There're people gathering around me who can hear that truth from me. Adele. Adele can hear it. She believes me.

JANE: Adele used to follow her father around trying to catch people's souls in a big net.

OLIVIA: Jane. More important than

It's important no it's necessary for people to believe in something or when they believe in something it's important it's necessary for them to be allowed to live in that belief.

JANE: I can agree with that.

OLIVIA: Well there. I knew if you just listened.

JANE: However. Olivia. There is one thing I can't abide. And that's when someone thinks they've made a big discovery oh oh oh and suddenly I have to live in that belief with them. You and your birds? That. On my little plot of land, and it's mine and Bobby's too, I'm not having it.

OLIVIA: Jane.

JANE: Olivia.

(*JANE exits.*)

OLIVIA: (*Following her offstage.*) Jane.

(*ED, TOM, ADELE and ANDRE enter. They are all four at the ballet. During this scene, they arrive and take their seats facing the audience—as if the audience is the stage where the ballet is happening. They sit, read their programs, look behind them to see who is there.*)

TOM: We're over here. Excuse me. Pardon me.

ANDRE: These are good seats. You go next Ed.
ED: Sure?
ANDRE: Yeah yeah.
ED: Okay. Excuse me.
TOM: You okay? These okay?
ED: They're great.
ANDRE: I did that.
ADELE: You did?
ANDRE: Yup. I told him just to kiss him.
ADELE: And he did?
ANDRE: I said kiss him.
ADELE: And that's what got them together?
ANDRE: Yeah I said kiss him and he did. And now look.
ADELE: That was good advice.
ANDRE: It was, wasn't it. After you.
ADELE: Oh thank you.
ANDRE: Certainly.
ADELE: Excuse me.
ANDRE: Excuse me.
TOM: I hope you like this.
ED: This place is beautiful.
TOM: Isn't it?
ANDRE: Look. Look.
ADELE: What.
ANDRE: Look at that woman's hair.
ADELE: Where?
ANDRE: There. Don't look. Look. Don't laugh.
ADELE: Oh my gosh.
ANDRE: I used to have a neighbor. Back in Lithuania. Named Merta.
ADELE: Ed look.
ED: What
ADELE: That woman.
ANDRE: Her hair! Don't look. Look!
TOM: Andre.
ANDRE: What?
TOM: Andre.
ANDRE: Did you look at it?

ED: Tom.
TOM: Andre.
ED: You gotta look at it.
TOM: Andre.
ANDRE: This place is amazing. What are we going to see?

(*They all look at their programs.*)

ED: I think her husband's hair's a toupee.
ADELE: Sh.
ANDRE: Her hair is tilting.
ED: His is going to flap up.
ANDRE: Hers is definitely going to go over.
ADELE: Ed.
TOM: Andre
ED: Sh. Andre.
ADELE: Ed!
ED: Adele!
ANDRE: Okay okay I'm sorry. I shouldn't even have started it.
    (*Pause.*) Sorry Tom.
ADELE: Sorry Tom.
ED: Sorry Tom.

(*The orchestra warms up. There is the hush as the conductor
arrives. They applaud. The ballet begins. We watch their eyes
move in unison as they watch the ballet, their heads bobbing in
time to the music and the dancing. We see the ballet by watching
them watch it. This should be choreographed.*)

TOM: There is something so damn fucking Oh my God about falling
    in love.

(*The ballet is over. ADELE and ANDRE exit.*)

ED: Tom.
TOM: Yeah?
ED: That was beautiful.

TOM: Yeah.

ED: Tom?

TOM: Yeah?

ED: I'm not going to do this.

TOM: What?

ED: This.

TOM: What do you mean?

ED: I'm. I'm not going to

TOM: Okay. (*Pause.*) Why not?

ED: It's not you.

TOM: So. Why not?

ED: I was really in love. Before.

TOM: Uh huh.

ED: And it didn't work. And. I'm really. I was really. I'm broken by it. I wanted it more than. And I didn't. So why would I want. So you. Come and ask me. And. And so I'm afraid here it is offered to me again the chance that.

TOM: Well sure okay that makes (*Pause.*) I guess I'd be. But.

ED: So I think. What if love shows up again, hands in pockets, and what if it. What if it looks innocent. I don't want to take the chance. I don't want to. I don't want to. I don't want to.

TOM: Well don't you think

ED: Because you look innocent.

TOM: I'm not innocent. I mean.

ED: I don't want to.

TOM: Oh. Okay.

ED: I.

TOM: Shoot.

ED: I.

TOM: Oh um. You sure?

ED: Yeah.

TOM: Because, well because

ED: I don't want.

TOM: Okay sure sure sure. Sure. Okay. That's too bad. I. You're sure. That's too bad. That's.

(*TOM exits.*)

(*New scene. ADELE enters.*)

ED: I told him. No.
ADELE: Oh.
ED: I told him I wasn't going to
ADELE: When did you tell him?
ED: Last night. After the ballet.
ADELE: He must have been sad. It seemed like he liked you a lot.
ED: What's wrong?
ADELE: Nothing. No. Nothing.
ED: What?
ADELE: Nothing. That's too bad. I like Tom. I was hoping it was going to work.
ED: Well I'm just. I don't want to.
OLIVIA: (*Enters.*) Ron found a storefront in the city that will work perfectly for the Church. Andre's going to help me buy it. You can tell Jane we won't be needing the aviary.
ED: Okay.
OLIVIA: Okay. (*Picks up banner.*) Can I take this? (*Pause.*)
ED: Adele, can Olivia have the banner?
ADELE: Of course she can have it.
OLIVIA: Okay. Well.

(*OLIVIA exits.*)

ADELE: I think we should let the aviary just be there until it goes. I don't want Olivia to have it. I don't want anyone to have it. I'm not doing anything with it anymore. (*Pause.*) And I don't want to be in her church anymore. I don't believe her.
ED: Okay. (*Pause.*) And that's what we let it do. We let it crumble to the ground. (*Pause.*) That's where our story ends. That's what happened. (*Long pause.*) Now. In order to understand why it happened that way we have to go back in time in our story.

2. A Vision

(*OLIVIA enters. We see the moment when the birds came down and surrounded her, but this time from her perspective, without the birds, from inside. In slow motion. Loud flapping. She is terrified.*)

(*OLIVIA pulls down a shade/presentation tool with a diagram of a bird on it. She has a pointer. ADELE and ANDRE sit before her.*)

OLIVIA: In the Church of the Fifth Day we take as our guide the bird. (*ANDRE raises his hand.*) Yes Andre?

ANDRE: Should I write this down?

OLIVIA: No it's in the
Look on the first page of the pamphlet. At the top. See "In the Church of the Fifth Day we take as our guide the bird"?

ANDRE: Oh oh oh yeah okay Got it.

OLIVIA: In each of our hearts lives a bird called the soul. Man has always tried to capture and to tame and to own this bird.

ANDRE: Huh. Did you know that?

ADELE: Kind of.

ANDRE: Huh. I didn't know that. You excited about seeing the ballet tonight?

ADELE: Oh I am.

OLIVIA: Andre.

ANDRE: I'm listening. I'm listening.

OLIVIA: The nun imprisons the bird in a chaste marriage. The rabbi tries to sing and to argue it to sleep. The Protestant builds it a cage of stone and gold. The Buddhist winks and hopes—boink—the bird won't be there anymore.

ANDRE: Huh. Did you know that?

ADELE: Um.

OLIVIA: We want to let the bird fly free. On the Fifth Day God created the bird to be a constant reminder of his love. Not so we could use it as target practice.

ANDRE: Olivia?

OLIVIA: Yes Andre?

ANDRE: Not even hunters?

OLIVIA: No.

ANDRE: Oh. Not even hunters in the woods?

OLIVIA: No. No.

ANDRE: Oh. Are chickens birds? I mean technically?

OLIVIA: Yes. Of course. Chickens are birds.

ANDRE: I mean they're not fowl? And so maybe exempt?

OLIVIA: Chickens are definitely birds.

ANDRE: Because I eat a lot of chicken. That's probably not.

OLIVIA: No.

ANDRE: Oh. Huh. See the thing is I really (*Pause.*) like chicken. But.

OLIVIA: Andre. Don't worry about the whole chicken thing. It's confusing it confuses the

It's not whether or not you eat

I'm trying to teach you about a path of faith.

ANDRE: Huh.

OLIVIA: God created birds as a reminder to have faith.

ANDRE: Huh.

OLIVIA: When we see them it's a reminder.

ANDRE: From God.

OLIVIA: To have faith.

ANDRE: Huh.

OLIVIA: Faith works like this: We're lost.

ANDRE: Okay.

OLIVIA: Like?

ANDRE: We're not where we're supposed to be?

OLIVIA: Right!

ANDRE: We're late?

OLIVIA: Okay.

ANDRE: Something's smacked us in the head we've fallen down we don't know what the fuck's going on.

OLIVIA: We're lost.

ANDRE: Right.

OLIVIA: Now we can do one of two things. We can despair or we can have faith.

ANDRE: Huh.

OLIVIA: I'm telling you not to despair. I'm telling you to have faith.

ANDRE: Okay.

OLIVIA: I'm telling you to follow me as I continue to have faith.

ANDRE: Okay.

OLIVIA: I'm telling you that I was in despair and then suddenly I had a sense of relief a sense that God would relieve me of this despair if I would only let him

well

lead me. And so I started listening and now I know I know I know that I'm going to be okay.

ANDRE: Really.

OLIVIA: Really.

ADELE: Really.

OLIVIA: Really.

ANDRE: I want that.

(OLIVIA smiles.)

ANDRE: That's what I want. I'd give up chicken for that.

OLIVIA: It was terrifying when the birds It is terrifying to see the Really to see to know that God exists. That He does love us. That love is all. It was terrifying. But it was also so I had such a sense of When I realized that there is help.

ANDRE: And you think he'll help me?

OLIVIA: God wants everybody. You love him, he'll help you.

ANDRE: Is that what you're doing?

ADELE: I'm trying.

ANDRE: Huh. Is it hard?

ADELE: I kind of think it's hard.

OLIVIA: But it's worth it.

ADELE: It is.

ANDRE: And you get all this from that bird.

OLIVIA: It's what the bird reminds me to remember.

ANDRE: I scored two goals last night.

OLIVIA: See? It's already working.

ANDRE: (Pause.) We should tell people.

OLIVIA: Yes we should.

(*They exit.*)

JANE: (*Enters. Points at bird picture.*) This is a pewee. A western wood pewee. It's generally indistinguishable from an eastern wood pewee, except when you happen to hear its voice. And even then, when you hear a harsh, slightly descending peeer or a clear whistling pee-yer then it sounds just like the eastern pewee and it's still very hard to tell which one is which. But the western? In the early morning and at dusk it'll sing tswee-tee-teet mixed with peeer. Sometimes it'll go chip. Then you know it's the western pewee. It never goes pee-a-wee. That would be the eastern pewee and that's not this bird here.

You can also tell it's not the eastern pewee because it doesn't have a black tip on its mandible.

I don't think we should shoot them either.

3. The Mad Scenes

ED: My sister-in-law Jane can be quite determined.
JANE: It's a PEWEE!
ED: Let me stop this for a second. (*JANE stands still. ED talks to the audience.*) My sister-in-law Jane was a very particular child. She was extremely neat and precise. Things needed to be just so and often they weren't. There is a story of her sweeping the autumn leaves off the sidewalk back up on to the lawn and back under the various trees they had fallen out of. And another of a house that she walked by on her way to school, every day she stared at the ground as she walked by it, because it had been painted a certain unsatisfying shade of yellow.

She's a scientist. Her dissertation and lifework have centered on the habits of the damselflies of New England. They're like dragonflies but smaller and less significant. American rubyspots and Ebony jewelwings, swamp spreadwings, skimming bluets. I've been at more than one unnerving dinner party where Jane has described the heart-shaped coupling of the male and female damselfly in rigorous, clinical detail.

I've wondered if her resistance to Olivia comes from the fact that birds eat damselflies.

JANE: All that aside Ed, it's still a PEWEE.

ED: Let me just continue this for a moment longer. (*JANE stands still. ED talks to the audience.*) My sister-in-law Jane lives her life according to the rules. The dishes should be done in the evening before going to bed. The word fuck should only be used very late at night with your husband while enjoying a good glass of scotch. Women who marry after forty should wear silver gray suits instead of wedding dresses. Lights on a Christmas tree should be white.

Olivia is chaotic.

When this story is all said and done, Jane will return to her husband my brother Bobby, her children Alison, Andrew, and Alex, and her house. To her job and her books and her circle of satisfying friends and neighbors. She will continue to study her little flying (*Makes hand gesture.*)

Twelve years from now, she will keel over dead at a barbecue while making stuffed mushrooms. My brother Bobby will be inconsolable.

JANE: Ed. (*Pause.*) It's a pewee.

ED: Yeah.

JANE: But to Olivia it's a symbol. It's a call to action. Action that will lead to asphalt and an aviary cathedral, and to the formation of a doctrine, and of course doctrine leads to a lack of imagination and a lack of imagination leads to a feeling of scarcity because we can't imagine the world any other way, all we can hope for is the small world we already see, and as a result all we feel is scarcity and then of course we have the urge to purchase things, to try and fill ourselves up, so what this bird as symbol leads us to is a feeling of overwhelming scarcity, to the feeling of scarcity that is the basic fuel of consumerism.

That's the problem with symbolism. It presents us with answers. It stops us from thinking. That's the problem with doctrine. It stops us from thinking. That's the problem with

telling others what to think. It stops them from thinking. That's
   my problem with Olivia. It's maddening!

ED: What is?

JANE: It is. It's maddening! It's infuriating!

ED: What?

JANE: She'll continue to spout this birdish nonsense and the faithful
   will tromp after her, faithfully flattening everything in their
   way! Who's going to clean up after her spiritual mess? She's like
   those movie supercops crashing cars and blowing up buses in
   order to catch the criminal! Who sweeps up the glass? Who
   cleans up? (*Pause.*) Oh Ed.

ED: What Jane.

JANE: I'm so tired.

ED: You seem a little worked up.

JANE: We're all making our little piles of, and leaving them just anywhere, and it just adds up, layer after layer covering
      Seeing it exhausts me.

ED: I understand that.

JANE: And it will be impossible to stop her. Because it is simply easier to just follow someone.

ED: They're comforted.

JANE: I just think if we
      What if we just put a nice house where the aviary
      I see the piles we leave and I think Oh it would nice to tidy
   that up, I could tidy that up. A small house would be tidy.

ED: I'd like to see tendrils of ivy rip the wood apart.

JANE: Really.

ED: I want to see it crack and split. To see the wood shredded and
   torn, the nails bent and rusted and dangerous, shards of glass
   scratching

JANE: Ed.

ED: to watch the land pull the building down. To watch it bury it
   while it still breathes. Under the heavy dead weight of earth. To
   see it disappear.

JANE: Oh.

ED: To have it erased completely. To have no memory of it.

JANE: No Ed. That would be too

ED: That's what I want to happen.

JANE: Ed. That would be irresponsible.

ED: We could let the land rest.

JANE: That would be wasteful. Ed.

ED: Fine. Fine. Fine. Whatever. You and Olivia aren't that different Jane. She's messier.

JANE: We're nothing alike.

ED: You both want what you want.

JANE: We want very different things though.

ED: She wants to leave her mark on the world. You want to tidy it up. You both want the world to look just like the way you want it to look.

JANE: Don't you?

ED: No.

JANE: Everyone does.

ED: In this world, where my father doesn't, where I'm not listened to (*Pause.*) I only have a few small weapons Jane. I have sweetness and I have politeness and a mean word here and there that might cut and a look and a joke but my strongest weapon? My strongest weapon is not caring.

JANE: That's.

ED: That's the truth.

JANE: You don't care?

ED: I don't. I want to live a paler life. One that's too loud attracts too much attention.

(*They exit.*)

(*ADELE and OLIVIA enter.*)

ADELE: Olivia?

OLIVIA: Yes Adele?

ADELE: Love is really the most important thing, isn't it.

OLIVIA: It is.

ADELE: Of all.

OLIVIA: It definitely is. (*ADELE kisses OLIVIA. Pause.*) No no no that's not okay. That's not love.

(*Pause.* OLIVIA *turns and walks offstage.* ADELE *stands. Pause.* ADELE *stands.* ADELE *stands.*)

4. The Conclusion

(ED *enters.*)

ADELE: I think we should let the aviary just be there until it goes. I don't want Olivia to have it. I don't want anyone to have it. I'm not doing anything with it anymore.

ED: So we let the aviary crumble to the ground. (*Pause.*) That's where our story ends. That's what happened. That's why it happened the way it did. (*Pause.*) What?

ADELE: Nothing. No.

(*Lights start to go down.*)

5. A Little Dance

(TOM *enters. This scene is very quiet and direct.* ADELE *sits slightly to the side.*)

TOM: Hey.
ED: Hey.
TOM: Can I talk to you?
ED: Sure. Okay.
TOM: Just for a minute. Do you mind?
ED: No. No.
TOM: I've been thinking
ED: Um
TOM: About what you said to me
ED: I'm sorry about that
TOM: No. No. You said
ED: I'm sorry I was
TOM: No you said what

what you needed to say and I think
I think I understand it I mean
Can I talk to you I mean can I tell you

ED: Sure.

TOM: I know you're not going to. I got that. I understand. I got that. But I like you. And even if. I like you so

ED: (*Pause.*) Okay.

TOM: It's just I. I love hockey. I love the ballet. It's. I love. Because of the movement. That's what it. Because when I move. I go back into my body. That's why I love hockey. It's why I love the gym. Same reason why I dance. Or when I have sex. Or. Cause I come back to myself. (*Long pause.*)

Like six months ago before I met you I went to a sex club for the first time. Right?

(*Smiles.*) You know? You ever been? And I and I remember thinking so why, I mean, I don't need, but for some reason I really wanted I mean I wanted to see it, I wanted to find out what it was like. So I went, over on Otis Street, paid my ten bucks, up the stairs, and it's two floors there, with men all different kinds of men, wandering around a maze, looking

It was like poetry or No it was like dance too, the men walk by each other sort of a little slow, silent, in this dim sort of, might murmur and might might trail a hand across my stomach to tell me that

And I remember I remember I remember smiling cause

I'd found another way to get back into. I found another place I could move.

I think rejection, rejection can be so strong, sometimes, from out there, I mean yeah, or from in here, or from other guys, or from them It's like the rejection bounces us out of our bodies. It bounces us out of our bodies. Right. And we have to find a way back in.

And I'm going to do anything, I'm going to, I'm
Cause that's. No.

What I can hear, what I hear from you, you don't want to be here. Something, or more than, and you. Right? You don't

I hear that. (ED's *head has been down during the end of this*

speech. He lifts it and looks at TOM.)
But I also. I also.
I just wanted to say to you, it's not okay to just give up. Just.

(*Lights down on them and up on* ADELE. *Dance music. She stands up, begins to move tentatively. Pause. Feathers fall like snow.*)

BLACKOUT

Delirium Palace
A Play of Rapture

by Gordon Dahlquist

No performance or reading of this work *Delirium Palace* in any medium may be given without express permission of the author. Inquiries regarding performance rights, publication, duplication of any kind should be addressed to: Pat McLaughlin, Beacon Artists Agency, 208 W. 30th Street, Rm. 401, NYC NY 10001, (212) 736-6630

➤ BIOGRAPHY ◀

Gordon Dahlquist is a native of the Pacific Northwest, where he worked for several years writing and directing plays. He also co-managed two theatre companies, and was the recipient of several regional arts grants. Since 1988 he has lived in New York. He is a member of New Dramatists, and a New York Theatre Workshop Usual Suspect.

Dahlquist's works include *Delirium Palace* (Evidence Room, Los Angeles), *The Secret Machine* (Twilight Theatre Company at Soho Rep), *Vortex Du Plaisir* (Ice Factory '99 Festival at the Ohio Theatre, WKCR's "Manhattan Theatre of the Air"), *Island Of Dogs* (4th Street Theatre), *Severity's Mistress* (Soho Rep Theatre, New York University, winner of Primary Stages' Bug & Bub award), *Mission Byzantium!* (American Globe Theater, NYTW's "Just Add Water Festival") and *Reticence* (the Horace Mann Theatre). He has written and directed several experimental films, including *Boise And Beyond* (selected for the San Francisco International Film Festival), *Requiem* (Seattle International Film Festival) and the feature-length *Rope of Blood* (Northwest Film and Video Festival).

He is a graduate of Reed College and Columbia University's School of the Arts.

⇛ PRODUCTION HISTORY ⇚

Delirium Palace by Gordon Dahlquist
Produced by Evidence Room
November 8-December 15, 2001
Directed by Bart DeLorenzo

Cast

IRENE .... Lauren Campedelli
PIERSON .... Christian Leffler
THACKARAY .... Leo Marks
DELPHINE .... Ames Ingham
CELESTE .... Ann Closs-Farley

Designers and Technical Staff

Assistant Director .... Adrian A. Cruz
Dramaturg .... Mead Hunter
Stage Manager .... Beth Mack
Set Designer .... Jason Adams
Costume Designer .... Candice Cain
Lighting Designer .... Rand Ryan
Sound Designer .... John Zalewski
Fight Choreographer .... Nick Offerman

Delirium Palace was part of the Hot Properties series, a collaboration of the Los Angeles County Arts Commission and A.S.K. Theater Projects. A major contribution from the James Irvine Foundation supported artists' fees and design elements for the production. *Delirium Palace* was developed in part with the support of A.S.K. Theater Projects.

Evidence Room

Evidence Room is both a performing arts center and a theater company comprised of actors, directors, and designers who have been working together for seven years. Our aim is to expand traditional ideas of theater and produce striking, unpredictable theater events designed to rouse a new generation of theatergoers. We are building a self-supporting arts institution where we offer performances, workshops, and educational opportunities in theater, dance, and music to the residents and youth of the city of Los Angeles.

In 1994, a group of Los Angeles actors, directors, and designers began meeting regularly to read classic and new plays amongst themselves as a kind of education. We would talk as theater artists about what we felt was missing in our community. We were interested in very contemporary theater and plays that spoke to our generation (the term of the moment was Gen X) and younger audiences. And we would talk about our interest in serious theater and genuine artistry and not the exuberant, slapdash free-for-all style that had become synonymous with many younger presentations. And we decided we weren't exclusively driven, like many theaters, to producing a nonstop diet of our own performances, but also wanted to present what we felt was the best or most important new work, regardless of its origin.

Out of these discussions, we decided to build a theater. Throughout 1994 we worked to raise start-up funds and began looking at raw spaces. We envisioned a theater that could accommodate many different styles of presentation and sought a building that had some history and resonance. In March 1995, this group incorporated under the name Evidence Room and found its first home, a 5,800 square-foot warehouse in an industrial area of Culver City. For several months our company cleaned and converted the space, negotiated with the city, attained our permits and created the largest and most versatile equity-waiver venue in the Los Angeles area. In May of that year we opened our first production, *SWELL*, a reworking of

Ferdinand Bruckner's *Krankheit der Jugend*. One week after it closed, we hosted our first coproduction, a collaboration with another of Los Angeles' most adventurous theaters. And thus began our complicated and busy history as a performance company and space.

Over the course of three years, we staged twelve company productions including Buchner's *Leonce and Lena*, Harry Kondoleon's *The Houseguests*, the American premiere of Simon Donald's *The Life of Stuff*, Constance Congdon's *Tales of the Lost Formicans*, Edward Bond's *Early Morning*, a contemporary adaptation of Racine's *Andromache*, and Keith Reddin's *Almost Blue*. We also hosted many other readings, workshops, benefits, classes, concerts, guest and coproductions. We presented more than twenty additional projects generated by outside arts organizations. We hosted benefits, symposiums, dance performances, art installations, and even an indoor carnival. In 1997 alone we produced over 170 nights of theater and events, attracting a large and varied audience from all over the Los Angeles area.

In 1998, the Culver City Redevelopment Agency offered us a new home, the landmark Ivy Substation building, in a more accessible location where we relocated and produced two additional seasons with even greater success. These productions—Naomi Wallace's *One Flea Spare*, Philip K. Dick's *Flow My Tears, the Policeman Said*, and Robert David MacDonald's adaptation of *No Orchids for Miss Blandish*—broke all our previous box office records and won many awards.

Interested in more control over our venue and wanting to produce more frequently, the company's Executive Directors, along with several private investors, put together resources to purchase and convert a new building into an affordable permanent home in which Evidence Room might forward its mission. These investors scoured Los Angeles and found a 10,000-square-foot former brassiere factory with high bow-truss ceilings, polished concrete floors, and two parking lots. We raised additional funds to support the set-up costs and opened our first production in the new space in May 2000, Charles L. Mee's *The Berlin Circle*. This production doubled all previous box office successes, expanded our audience and went on to win more local awards than any other show that year, including the

"Production of the Year" award given by *L.A. Weekly*.

The Berlin Circle was immediately followed by an acclaimed coproduction with the Fabulous Monsters of *Speed-Hedda*, a modern version of Ibsen's play, a guest residency by the internationally celebrated SITI company, and another award-sweeping production, Edward Bond's drama *Saved*. The year 2000 finished with a celebration of solo work with performances by Heather Woodbury and Tony Abatemarco alongside a remounting of *Saved*.

In 2001, we began the season hosting the award-winning revival of Zoo District's production of *Nosferatu* and our own well-received presentation of the L.A. premiere of Richard Greenberg's *Three Days of Rain*. In June, we premiered John Rafter Lee's new adaptation of Friedrich Schiller's classic tragedy *Don Carlos*. The acclaimed production sold out and played through the summer. In addition, we hosted several individual performers during this time: Heather Woodbury in her continuing series of pieces, *A Tale of Two Cities*, John Fleck in an early version of his new performance piece, *Mud in Your Eye*, and Broadway and television star Megan Mullally in a weekend of blistering fundraising concerts.

The SITI company enjoyed another residency with us this August as we prepared the September opening of another Charles Mee play, *The Imperialists at the Club Cave Canem*. This loosely structured event was a collaboration with Ken Roht's musical troupe Orphean Circus and played to large houses in the difficult weeks of that fall. In November 2001, the Mark Taper Forum produced its New Work Festival in our home while we opened the world premiere of Gordon Dahlquist's *Delirium Palace* at the John Anson Ford Theater as part of the Hot Properties series, a collaboration of A.S.K. Theater Projects and the L.A. County Arts Commission with funding from the James Irvine Foundation.

In 2002, we coproduced Padua Playwrights' World Premiere of John Steppling's *Dog Mouth* and hosted the Taper's Next Step series. Through the spring and summer we presented the L.A. premiere of David Edgar's expansive political drama *Pentecost*. We also opened two late-night cabaret-style events, *THE STRIP: a living comic book*, a comedy serial that featured many local writers and performers, and *Nothin' Beats Pussy*, John Fleck's latest performance piece. In the fall, we opened an ambitious three-play repertory of world-premiere plays, all comedies, all by L.A. writers, all about Hollywood, called *Hollywood Stories*. These included Michael Sargent's *Hollywood Burning*, Justin Tanner's *Hot Property*, and Peter J. Nieves *Cringe*. These played through the fall and reopened in slightly revised form for an encore presentation in 2003. We are currently preparing the world premiere of Kelly Stuart's domestic political comedy (*Mayhem.*)

We have received funding from several private foundations including A.S.K. Theatre Projects and the James Irvine Foundation as well as through agencies, the Los Angeles County Arts Commission, the Los Angeles Cultural Affairs Office, the California Arts Commission, and the National Endowment for the Arts. Over the past few years, in recognition of this work, Evidence Room has received 21 *BackStage West* Garland Awards, 11 *L.A. Weekly* Theater Awards (among 47 nominations), and many Critic's Pick's and year-end Top Tens, consistently more than any other Los Angeles theater of its size. *The Los Angeles Times* recently referred to our organization as L.A.'s most valuable rising theater.

—Bart DeLorenzo
Artistic Director
The Evidence Room
2003

❧ SETTING AND CHARACTERS ❧

Dramatis Personæ

IRENE . . . . a woman in her 30s
PIERSON . . . . a man in his 30s
THACKARAY . . . . a man in his 30s
DELPHINE . . . . a woman in her 30s
CELESTE . . . . a younger woman

The action of the play is intended to be precise, deliberate, extreme, and emblematic.

It is vastly preferable that *Delirium Palace* be played with a curtain. When the curtain is drawn, the actors can be visible in dim light, or simply in blackness until the lights are raised full, at the director's discretion. In Act II, the curtain should not be employed for the individual scene breaks.

The moments of violence in the play should be presented in as realistic a manner as is possible.

Impulses toward generating a universal field theory should be resisted.

— ACT I —

(*A wide, low, open, sparse white room: two doors, white with metal fixtures, a metal chair with white cushions, tiled floor. An inadequate number of fluorescent lights hang in fixtures from the ceiling, providing illumination both bleached and dim.*)

(*IRENE, in a white robe, bare feet, in the chair, smoking, tapping her ash to the floor.*)

(*Across the room, standing, in a suit, PIERSON. Near him on an industrial metal table, a metal briefcase.*)

(*IRENE inhales. Silence as she holds the smoke in. She exhales, looking away.*)

IRENE: It was the . . . the . . . the weirdest thing.

(*Slight pause.*)

I was in a hurry—of course—I was running away, from so much, but also, specifically, from very immediate, you know— an unexpected part of town—my shoes ridiculously wrong for the sidewalk—ancient, broken—cobblestones for fuck's sake— not that I could have known at the start of the day what I knew then, even as I was trying my damnedest to ignore its full significance, not that I could have prepared—can you ever prepare? And so when I found myself sitting in the street, trying to determine if my ankle was broken or just giving me sass, mad as hell, sobbing, in a state—and, all right, given everything, big picture, I can see now that it was a small state really—Andorra, Liechtenstein—I like a bit of drama: darkened street, shooting pain, approaching footsteps, shouts in a foreign language, shots

... shots? Or just my head hitting the road? And *anyway ... that* was when I saw the door. Which was red. Which was open. So I went in. And closed it behind me.

(*Slight pause.*)

So perhaps I wasn't ... really ... paying attention.

(*Slight pause.*)

What I'd like is a drink. Or a steak. Or to get fucked by someone who knows what he's doing. That's the kind of place I'm in. I'm an American. Perhaps you've read about our kind. Itchy.

(*Slight pause.*)

My name is Irene.

(*Slight pause.*)

I'm pretty sure about that. I'm a doctor.

(*Slight pause.*)

You're not smoking. Let me guess, you've just finished some celery juice.

(*Slight pause.*)

A red door—that's a bit much. I thought so at the time, up the stairs, hobbling—on guard—you have to be willing to—whatever—run, kill, react—live in the world. Live in the mother-fucking world—I said that to myself, up the stairs, the hall, the cement floor, all of it red. Please.

(*Slight pause.*)

PIERSON: And what did you hear?

(*Slight pause.*)

Tell me again . . . Irene. Is it? Irene? Is it?

(*Slight pause.*)

IRENE: Long hallway, fluorescent light, cement floor, everything red as a car accident—*Weekend* red if that registers with you—and in the air . . .

(*IRENE sighs, closes her eyes. Opens them.*)

Do you like films? Difficult films? "A modern vision of hell to rival Dante"? No?

(*Slight pause.*)

Chanting. Female—in Arabic? Malay?—louder as I walk, and when I finally round the corner, barefoot because I'm holding my shoes like the high heels are weapons: an open room, completely red, one table, a cassette player plugged into the wall. I turn it off. In the silence I notice how cold the floor is. All right?

(*Slight pause. IRENE smokes.*)

PIERSON: Are you feeling clear?

(*Slight pause.*)

Irene?
IRENE: Now or in the story?
PIERSON: The story is always now, Irene. That's why we tell it.
IRENE: I tell it.
PIERSON: Answer the question, Irene.

IRENE: I don't know what it means.

PIERSON: Despite everything, Irene, this *is* your life.

IRENE: Have you ever been hit with a high-heel shoe? In the head?

PIERSON: No.

IRENE: It's not as stupid as it sounds.

(*Slight pause.*)

On the far side of the red room, another door. I open it: an even larger room, this time completely white, full of people, kneeling. They're all wearing headphones, facing a wall with words on it, painted in red.

PIERSON: What words?

IRENE: I don't remember.

PIERSON: You've remembered before.

IRENE: Then what does it matter—if you know this—

PIERSON: Each time you remember new things, Irene.

IRENE: Like what?

PIERSON: The headphones.

IRENE: They *did* have headphones. And dark hair . . . are they Chinese? I don't remember what city I was in—if everyone is Chinese is that totally normal because I'm in Shanghai or is it a little strange or unsettling, because—I don't know—I'm in Denver or—or London—

PIERSON: Are the letters Chinese?

IRENE: No. They're . . . backwards. To be read in a mirror.

PIERSON: Really?

(*Slight pause.* PIERSON *walks to the table, turns the case so that* IRENE *can not see the contents and snaps open the lid. He looks back at her.*)

Cigarette?

IRENE: Thank you.

(PIERSON *removes a pack from the case, walks to her, offers it while keeping hold of the pack.* IRENE *takes one.* PIERSON *pock-*

ets the pack, offers a lighter. IRENE leans to his hand, lights up, leans back in the chair, PIERSON standing over her.)

PIERSON: Do you feel clear?
IRENE: About what?
PIERSON: The letters? Maybe it's a secret message.
IRENE: Maybe.
PIERSON: Do you have a mirror?
IRENE: No, I don't—look, I just keep—I'm—I'm going to start making things up—I don't know what city, I don't even know my last *name*—
PIERSON: Irene. Listen to me.

(PIERSON kneels in front of her, between her legs.)

IRENE: Yes?
PIERSON: You are the mirror. *Now.*

(PIERSON snaps his fingers. IRENE lolls in the chair, eyes open, head to the side, hand dangling, cigarette held loosely, still burning. Slight pause. PIERSON takes her pulse at her throat. He takes the cigarette, stands, smokes. He steps away from IRENE, looks at his watch.)

PIERSON: Let's continue, okay?

(IRENE replies, without moving, her voice even, without affect.)

IRENE: Uh huh.
PIERSON: Let's go further. Where were you?
IRENE: In a room.
PIERSON: Which room?
IRENE: White. I'm naked, in a robe, in a chair—
PIERSON: No, another room.
IRENE: My room, green linoleum, there's a cot—
PIERSON: *Another* room, Irene.
IRENE: There's a metal table, with a drain—

PIERSON: Stop! Continue, again. What is your name?
IRENE: Magdalena.

(*Slight pause.*)

PIERSON: Magdalena?
IRENE: Yes?
PIERSON: Irene?
IRENE: Yes?

(*Slight pause.*)

PIERSON: You're in a red room, with chanting. You stop the chant-
ing, and then you walk into a white room, with people in it, and
red letters.
IRENE: Everyone's listening to their instructions. I say something
they can't hear. One of them takes off their headphones, turns:
a woman with black hair.
PIERSON: Do you speak again?
IRENE: I'm in tears.
PIERSON: Does she speak?
IRENE: There are sounds from the dislodged headphones.
PIERSON: What does the woman say?
IRENE: Behind me someone's restarted the chanting, much loud-
er—it's deafening. The woman steps toward me. I can read her
lips—the word "injection"—
PIERSON: Stop.

(*PIERSON mops his face. He looks at his watch. He crosses to the
open case, removes a metal vacuum flask, unscrews the lid and
drinks from it, steadily. He replaces the flask, crosses back toward
IRENE, and abruptly staggers. PIERSON drops to his knees, holding his head in both hands. IRENE remains still.*)

IRENE: And at once everything is clear: the letters are painted on the
inside of a large two-way mirror. Beyond the letters is a new

room, also white, containing a man, in a suit. The letters tell him he's going to die.

(*PIERSON breathes heavily, remains on his knees.*)

The woman with dark hair reaches into her dress—a red dress, red silk, I think it's Chinese—and offers me a syringe. She indicates the man. She places her lips against my ear and whispers: *Magdalena.* My code name. I'm a professional killer.

(*PIERSON manages to snap his fingers. IRENE blinks, sits up, freezes.*)

PIERSON: Help me.

(*IRENE launches herself from the chair and kicks PIERSON across the face, knocking him sprawling. She rushes to the right-hand door. It is locked. She runs to the left-hand door. She opens it. PIERSON raises himself to one elbow and snaps his fingers. IRENE stops in the open doorway, lurches into the wall and slides to the floor, sitting. PIERSON drops to the floor, on his back, gasping, his nose bloody.*)

(*The outside surface of each of the two doors is painted a bright red.*)

(*THACKARAY enters from the right-hand door, in a suit and white lab coat. He closes the door behind him, stands, taking in the room. He crosses to the opposite door, closes it. THACKARAY kneels, takes IRENE's pulse at the throat, checking it against his watch. Satisfied, he rolls up his sleeve and pushes his middle finger into IRENE's mouth. After a moment she begins to suck on it, as if nursing, her expression blank. He consults his watch for a moment, then, satisfied, gently detaches her, pressing her forehead back with his other hand.*)

(*THACKARAY stands, goes to PIERSON, drags him into the chair, stands.*)

THACKARAY: Doctor Pierson?

PIERSON: Yes . . .

THACKARAY: Is there a problem?

PIERSON: No . . . it's just . . . a very demanding schedule.

THACKARAY: Is there a dosage problem?

PIERSON: No—I haven't slept—

THACKARAY: Why not?

PIERSON: I can take the dosage—I can take more, whatever's necessary—

THACKARAY: Why haven't you slept?

PIERSON: Dreams. O Christ—terrible dreams—

(*THACKARAY claps his hands together sharply. PIERSON lolls in the chair. THACKARAY lights a cigarette, takes his middle finger, pushes it into PIERSON's mouth. PIERSON sucks on it. THACKARAY smokes, looks at his watch.*)

(*DELPHINE enters through the left-hand door, wearing a red silk dress—Asian collar, sleeveless, slit up the thigh—and black heels. She has dark hair. She stands.*)

DELPHINE: Someone opened the door.

THACKARAY: I'm taking care of it.

DELPHINE: There's blood on her foot.

THACKARAY: As I say.

DELPHINE: What did he find out?

THACKARAY: I don't know yet.

DELPHINE: Then ask him.

(*Slight pause. THACKARAY detaches PIERSON, pressing his forehead back with his other hand, crushes his cigarette out on the floor.*)

THACKARAY: You ask him.

(*THACKARAY crosses to the briefcase, closes it, goes out through the right-hand door with it, closing the door behind him.*

(*DELPHINE closes her own door, walks to stand midway between PIERSON and IRENE. She claps her hands, PIERSON bursts into a coughing fit. DELPHINE speaks to PIERSON with an Italian accent.*)

DELPHINE: *Scusi, Dottore* . . .

PIERSON: Momentary lapse—full of confidence, enthusiasm— absolutely.

DELPHINE: Your unfortunate nose. Is it broken?

PIERSON: Nonsense—water under the bridge.

DELPHINE: (*Smiles.*) Blood under the bridge, yes? It is—the nose has a bridge, yes—it is clever?

(*PIERSON sniffs, smiles. Slight pause.*)

PIERSON: Did you—Mr. Thackaray was here—we spoke . . . did you—

DELPHINE: He had his finger in your mouth.

(*Slight pause. DELPHINE walks to PIERSON, extends her middle finger.*)

Like this—open up, *Dottore*—there—and, how is it—you *suck* on it. It is nice, yes?

(*PIERSON sucks on her finger. She smoothes his hair.*)

PIERSON: (*Mouth full.*) Very nice.

DELPHINE: It was something of a *turn-on* for me.

(*DELPHINE removes her hand, places the finger in her mouth, smiles.*)

PIERSON: Yes, certainly, perhaps—excuse me—but you say—I— Mr. Thackaray's—

DELPHINE: You don't remember?

PIERSON: I was hypnotized.

DELPHINE: You are not now?

PIERSON: I remember *now*.

DELPHINE: Will you keep remembering it? It is a thing I ask myself. In this place I dream like it is a river in my head—it is so difficult for me. Do you dream here? Does Mr. Thackaray dream? I know he dreams—I have walked past his door in the night. He was weeping. Can you believe it? After what he's done to you? Do you think she is pretty? Or do you think Mr. Thackaray is pretty? I know the way boys can behave. He is an animal-boy, yes? All boys are animal-boys, but he is a really big animal. The kind you have to shoot with a tranquilizer dart. (*Laughs.*) Then you *fix* them.

PIERSON: Someone is tampering with me, with my work—

DELPHINE: You take the medication—

PIERSON: Of course I take it, yet—yet what if *it* were subject to tampering—

DELPHINE: But we prepare the medication ourselves—

PIERSON: *You* prepare it. And you do take it as well—

DELPHINE: Of course.

(*Slight pause.*)

PIERSON: But—

DELPHINE: Should you be continuing with the patient?

PIERSON: Of course I should!

DELPHINE: Your nose is swelling.

PIERSON: *Signora*, this is my process—my expertise—I don't want to be rude, but I would like to try and get a little work done properly—make the morning worthwhile?

DELPHINE: Of course.

PIERSON: I would appreciate it very much.

DELPHINE: I will just sit on the table.

(*DELPHINE walks to the table, sits on it, crosses her legs, smiles. PIERSON stares at her, impassive, then turns to IRENE, snaps his fingers. IRENE blinks, sits straight, freezes, takes in the room. She orders her robe about her.*)

PIERSON: Would you like to sit in the chair?
IRENE: Thank you.

(*IRENE stands, wincing a little as she places weight on her foot, goes to the chair, sits.*)

PIERSON: Hurt yourself?
IRENE: Not really.
PIERSON: Cigarette?
IRENE: Thank you.

(*PIERSON walks to her, removes a pack from his jacket, offers it while keeping hold of the pack. IRENE takes one. PIERSON pockets the pack, offers a lighter. IRENE leans to his hand, lighting the cigarette.*)

PIERSON: Learn anything?
IRENE: Next time I'll step on your hands.

(*Slight pause. PIERSON walks behind her, so IRENE is facing DELPHINE. They make eye contact. DELPHINE smiles.*)

PIERSON: Continue?
IRENE: (*To DELPHINE.*) Who are you?
PIERSON: One of my students. You're not without interest, as an example.
IRENE: Of what?
PIERSON: For you to tell me, yes? Thus, where were we? Right, you were describing the woman who turned to you, in the white room with red letters. A woman in, what did you say, "a red dress, red silk, I think it's Chinese?"
IRENE: I don't remember saying that.
PIERSON: You also said "dark hair"—did you get a look at her shoes?
IRENE: *I don't remember.*
PIERSON: That's right, you were in tears.

(*Slight pause.*)

And are you feeling better now, or just cried out?

IRENE: I'm feeling clear.

PIERSON: Now you know where you are.

IRENE: Can I ask you a question?

PIERSON: Of course, Irene.

IRENE: Not you, her.

(*Slight pause.*)

PIERSON: That depends on the question. She's not really here—by rights she should be on the other side of a two-way mirror, but that room's being painted, so we're stuck. Unprofessional.

IRENE: Which do you think came first: "swift" the name of a bird or "swift" an adjective meaning fast? Do you see my point? One is a metaphor drawn from the other, but which way? I'd like to think the bird came first, that the adjective is richer than we give it credit—have you ever watched swifts fly? They fly all over the place—amazing—even if it's the opposite, it's curious, don't you think? And here we are, trapped without an OED. Victims of the modern age.

(*Slight pause.*)

PIERSON: That was an odd question.

IRENE: Sorry, it wasn't my question at all, I was just, you know, *musing*. My *question* is why your student isn't wearing any underwear.

PIERSON: Tightness of the dress, I suppose.

IRENE: Then why does she keep deliberately flashing me every time she crosses her legs?

PIERSON: Perhaps she's flashing me—I'm right behind you.

IRENE: You didn't even notice.

PIERSON: No. I didn't.

(*IRENE scoffs. Slight pause.*)

Now, of course, I'm pierced with regret.

IRENE: (*To DELPHINE.*) You know me.

PIERSON: Irene—

IRENE: (*To DELPHINE.*) Help me. I don't know what to believe—
I've disappeared down a goddamn rabbit hole—*please*—

(*PIERSON snaps his fingers, IRENE lolls, still, eyes open. Slight pause.*)

DELPHINE: She is so resilient.

PIERSON: *Signora*—

DELPHINE: You must have to do this all the time—the *snapping*—

PIERSON: This is why you should leave.

DELPHINE: I am supposed to wear it—

PIERSON: But to be effective, I . . . where's . . . where is my case?
Where is my case?

(*PIERSON stares at the empty tabletop.*)

He just took it upon himself to take my case.

DELPHINE: (*Laughs.*) Men like that should be *whipped*.

PIERSON: It's enough that I do it to her—that's my profession, I
know who she is, what she's done, I'm in to my elbows without
qualm—but, when it's being done to me, and granted, I know
what I am, what I've done, the smell of vain regret—and unlike
the lady, I know—or I flatter myself—where I am, how I am
subject, willingly—you can tell anyone who isn't listening in
already, but—but—surely—but—you must—don't you—
surely . . . do you—the dreams I have, sleep is my head held
underwater in an ice-cold bath—O Christ.

(*Slight pause.*)

I'm in a white room. There are mirrors. Women's voices, somewhere, singing—suddenly there's a table. A filled syringe—
something red. It just keeps going.

(*Slight pause.*)

Of course, my room is larger than her cell—there's a window—with a locked iron grille—carpet, AM radio, bathroom, full amenities, shampoo, baby oil, notepaper.

DELPHINE: The windows must be locked—it is a dangerous part of town—warehouses, sailors—

PIERSON: I'm saying as opposed to her room.

DELPHINE: Her room has no window at all.

PIERSON: What about your room?

DELPHINE: My room?

PIERSON: Yes, what is it like?

DELPHINE: (*Smiles.*) *Dottore*, you will turn my head.

(*Slight pause.*)

PIERSON: I woke up last night—did I wake up—have I ever woken up—convinced that if I just felt in the dark I would find my wrists bloody and my tongue burned to a stub. I seriously didn't know one way or the other, nor could I make a sound until I forced a finger into my mouth to confirm I was unharmed.

(*Slight pause.*)

I've *seen* the bruising on your arms—the handprints—

(*DELPHINE claps her hands together. PIERSON freezes, sinks gently to the floor, sprawling, eyes open. DELPHINE stands, looks to IRENE, paces. She digs a cigarette from PIERSON's pocket, lights it. She looks to the door, steps closer to IRENE, snaps her fingers. IRENE blinks, sits up, freezes. DELPHINE speaks normally, as before.*)

DELPHINE: Okay, concentrate. There isn't much time. Magdalena?

IRENE: What?

DELPHINE: *Irene?*

IRENE: You're confusing me—

DELPHINE: You'll tell them eventually, you can't help it—you won't even know what you've said.

IRENE: *Who are you?*

DELPHINE: Someone will be sent to silence you, before you can tell them. If you have told them you'll be killed, if you haven't told them no one will believe you—your only chance is to get away now—go now, Irene.

IRENE: Go where? Where am I? Where—where the fuck—

(*The right hand doorknob is turned. It's locked. They both turn to it. A knock.*)

DELPHINE: Fuck.

IRENE: Wait—

(DELPHINE *snaps her fingers.* IRENE *goes limp.* DELPHINE *steps quickly out of the left-hand door, closes it behind her.*)

(*The right-hand door is unlocked, opens.* THACKARAY *enters with* PIERSON's *case, replaces it on the tabletop. He goes to* IRENE, *takes her pulse at the neck, looks at his watch. He pushes his finger into her mouth, as before, watching* IRENE *as she nurses on his finger. After a moment,* THACKARAY *tears up, sniffs. He takes out a handkerchief, wipes his eyes, blows his nose. He detaches himself, wipes his finger, pockets the handkerchief. He clears his throat, then snaps his fingers.* IRENE *blinks, sits up, freezes.*)

IRENE: Where is she?

THACKARAY: Beg pardon?

IRENE: What happened?

THACKARAY: You've been having dreams.

(*Slight pause.*)

How do you feel? Irene—can I call you Irene? I'm one of the people who's been seeing you on a regular basis without your knowledge. I've examined you physically, watched videotapes of your sleep—whole nine yards.

(*Slight pause.*)

IRENE: More like four inches.
THACKARAY: My name is Thackaray.
IRENE: My name is Irene. I'm a doctor.
THACKARAY: Of what?

(*Slight pause.*)

Well, make a guess. Medical doctor? Psychologist? Ph.D.? Something vital to world culture, Doctor of Square Dancing, Doctor of Amazonian Gender Studies, Doctor of Primate Flattery?
IRENE: Why are you doing this?
THACKARAY: I'll tell you something. I was once asked a question by a small boy—a rather annoying, insistent creature—I dislike boys, I fight a general impulse to thrash them—a boy who demanded of me "what was the secret word?" He knew what it was, I didn't, and he *demanded* that I guess. I didn't want to—you can imagine—we went back and forth, and finally when I had clearly failed he announced, in triumph, with a *leer*, that the secret word, was, in fact, "*ape*". True story—can't make that kind of thing up. So I mention it, in terms of, you know—you must know—our work here. All of our work. With you.

(*Slight pause.*)

No work, no life—what in the world is left? Clarity?

(*Slight pause.*)

Anyway, I think that's exciting. Not everyone is disinterested, Irene, or cruel. Or only cruel. I can't speak for others. It's heart-breaking—you, in that chair, on your adventure—well, heart *wounding*. I'll get over it. And you'll remain, the dusty rose wallpaper in several small but precious rooms in my mind.
IRENE: Can I ask what is up with him, on the floor?

THACKARAY: Stress reducer.

(*THACKARAY snaps his fingers. He stands for a moment, rubs his face with both hands. He steps closer to* IRENE, *snaps his fingers. She blinks, flinches.*)

IRENE: Why are you doing this?
THACKARAY: Like I say, you break my heart.
IRENE: Almost.
THACKARAY: No, you do—I just wasn't able to be honest.
IRENE: Clear now?
THACKARAY: Now I feel shockingly clear.
IRENE: May I change the subject?
THACKARAY: If it's important.
IRENE: Well, it's about you.
THACKARAY: Super.
IRENE: Are you a doctor?
THACKARAY: O no.
IRENE: You've got the white coat.
THACKARAY: Yes—and he *is* a doctor and he doesn't! I'm a . . . well, I like to find the right word.
IRENE: Administrator?
THACKARAY: (*Chuckles.*) No . . .
IRENE: Supervisor?
THACKARAY: No!
IRENE: Technician? I mean, the coat—
THACKARAY: No, no, I just like to be clean. I can't tell you how often I wash my hands, even with the mildest soap my fingers are cracked and dry as Death Valley mud—any experience of *touch* is necessarily an experience of pain, which is, eventually—as I've worked at this—its own source of great pleasure.
IRENE: Wow.
THACKARAY: I'll agree, it's intense.
IRENE: It's deranged. You're a deranged fucking nutjob.

(*Slight pause.* THACKARAY *snaps his fingers.* IRENE *lolls.* THACKARAY *moves to her other side, closer to her. He snaps his fingers again. IRENE blinks, looks for him, turns, flinches.*)

THACKARAY: It's so easy to judge, isn't it?

IRENE: I was taught to speak my mind,

THACKARAY: Wouldn't say it's really working for you. Was someone here with you?

IRENE: Who?

THACKARAY: You mentioned a "she." Perhaps it was a dream. Or your daughter.

IRENE: What daughter?

THACKARAY: Whoops. Butterfingers me.

(*Slight pause.*)

Anyway.

(*Slight pause.*)

IRENE: What happened to that boy?

THACKARAY: What boy? When? Then? Later? (*Chuckles.*) Later still?

(*IRENE leaps out of the chair, clutching the robe around her, toward the table.*)

Hey. Hey hey hey—get back in the chair.

IRENE: You get in the fucking chair.

THACKARAY: You've been instructed— repeatedly. Are you always this vulgar?

IRENE: Look, just what is *up*? Are you going to hurt me? Rape me? I don't want to be raped.

THACKARAY: (*Snorts.*) That old chestnut.

(*Slight pause. IRENE seizes the briefcase and comes at THACKARAY, swinging. He reaches to intercept her and gets hit sharply across both hands with the case. He pulls back, hissing in pain, stuffing his hands into his armpits.*)

THACKARAY: Ow! Ow! Fuck! Jesus Christ . . .

(*IRENE runs to the right hand door: it's locked. THACKARAY tries to snap his fingers, can't. IRENE runs to the left door: it's also locked. IRENE turns to see THACKARAY still trying to snap his fingers, ineffectually. She raises the briefcase and runs at him. He claps his hands sharply and steps back. IRENE stops, unsure about the significance of this action.*)

(*PIERSON bursts into a coughing fit, struggles to a sitting position. THACKARAY tries to rush IRENE as she glances at PIERSON. She swings the case, catching him squarely on the head. The blow stops his momentum. He staggers back, clutching his forehead, and drops to his knees. She raises the case for another blow.*)

PIERSON: *Irene.*

(*PIERSON holds his hand out, ready to snap his fingers. IRENE pauses, case raised.*)

    Irene . . . let's take a moment . . . shall we?
IRENE: How do I get out of here?

(*THACKARAY lurches forward, reaching for IRENE with both hands. She darts back a step, raising the case higher, about to bring it down.*)

PIERSON: Stop it.

(*THACKARAY stops, glaring at IRENE. PIERSON climbs to his feet.*)

IRENE: I'll hit him.
PIERSON: Cave in his skull—save me the trouble.
IRENE: He works for you?
PIERSON: If you call what he does work.
IRENE: Then what about that—that clapping—

PIERSON: What clapping?

IRENE: Why were you on the floor?

PIERSON: Stress reducer.

(*Slight pause.*)

Hurry up, Irene.

IRENE: Why am I here?

PIERSON: Have you read the Bible, Irene?

IRENE: What?

THACKARAY: Have you read the Bible?

PIERSON: I am trying to help you.

IRENE: No. Not for a long time. Actually, not—not actually *read* it—
no. Never.

PIERSON: That's what I thought.

(*Slight pause. PIERSON removes index cards from his coat, clears
his throat, reads.*)

"As for me, I am filled with power, with the spirit of the Lord,
and with justice, to declare to Jacob his transgression and to
Israel his sin. Hear this, you rulers of the house of Jacob and
princes of the house of Israel, who abhor justice and pervert all
equity, who build Zion with blood and Jerusalem with wrong!
Its rulers give judgment for a bribe, its priests teach for a price,
its prophets give oracles for money; yet they lean upon the Lord
and say, 'Surely the Lord is with us! No harm shall come upon
us.' Therefore because of you Zion shall be plowed as a field;
Jerusalem shall become a heap of ruins, and the mountain of
the house a wooded height."

(*Slight pause.*)

When you first came to our attention, this little bit, this Micah
3:8-12, was the only thing we could get from your mouth. You'd
say nothing else for seven days.

(*Slight pause.*)

IRENE: I don't believe you.
THACKARAY: You shouldn't believe him. He doesn't care, Irene. I care—
PIERSON: (*To THACKARAY.*) Stop *talking*.

(*Slight pause.*)

How's your head?
THACKARAY: (*Scoffs.*) Whatever.

(*Slight pause.*)

IRENE: (*Indicating THACKARAY.*) He mentioned a . . . a daughter.
PIERSON: Did he?
IRENE: My daughter.
PIERSON: It's entirely possible—childbearing age—
THACKARAY: Generous hips—
IRENE: Tell me the truth! Jesus Christ!
PIERSON: No one's against you, Irene. We all want to help you out.
THACKARAY: Whatever the cost—to us, to you—
PIERSON: Sit in the chair, Irene. We can start fresh.

(*Slight pause. THACKARAY rolls back to squat on his heels. IRENE, flinches, raises the case. She looks to PIERSON, then back at THACKARAY.*)

(*The knob on the left-hand door is turned. The door is locked. Slight pause.*)

(*PIERSON digs into his pocket for a cigarette, lights it, drags deeply three times in succession. He drops the cigarette on the floor, steps on it, takes his pulse.*)

PIERSON: (*To IRENE, still holding the case.*) Arms tired?

(*PIERSON finishes with his pulse, walks to the left-hand door, opens it. No one is there. He closes the door, wipes his brow with a handkerchief.*)

PIERSON: (*Abruptly, vehement.*) The thing is, that is my case—full of my gear! We have work to do—and severe deadlines!

(*The right-hand door opens. DELPHINE enters, closes it behind her. She takes in the scene, speaks with the accent.*)

DELPHINE: Is there a problem?

(*THACKARAY rolls up to his feet in one movement and snatches the case from IRENE's grasp. She starts and steps away from him, toward the corner of the room. He drops the case on the floor, kicks it across to PIERSON, stands, facing IRENE.*)

(*PIERSON stops the case with his foot, glances at DELPHINE, kneels, snaps it open. He removes the flask, opens it and, still kneeling, drinks at length. He wipes his chin with a handkerchief. He replaces the flask, removes a cigarette, lights it, stands.*)

PIERSON: Cigarette, Irene?

(*PIERSON bursts into a coughing fit. In the midst of it, he motions to THACKARAY, indicating IRENE. The fit continues, PIERSON dropping to his knees. THACKARAY moves decisively toward her, catches her hands and pins them behind her back, spinning her face to the wall. He then quickly wraps her in a bear hug, arms trapped, and marches her to the chair. IRENE kicks as he lifts her up. He drops her into it.*)

(*IRENE composes her robe. PIERSON remains on his knees, his coughing subsides.*)

DELPHINE: *Dottore . . . I* should like a cigarette.
PIERSON: By all means—help yourself.

(*PIERSON fumbles the pack from his pocket, offers a cigarette to* DELPHINE. *She bends over for a light, steps back, exhales. Slight pause.*)

IRENE: That's quite a cough.

(DELPHINE *rests a hand on* PIERSON'*s head, gently, stroking it, gazing at* IRENE.)

DELPHINE: She is pretty. Don't you think?
THACKARAY: Very pretty.
DELPHINE: She is a flower. In a place with no sunlight, she is our flower.
THACKARAY: A mourning lily. Should we call her Lily?
DELPHINE: What does she want to be called?
THACKARAY: She doesn't remember.
DELPHINE: She can decide.
THACKARAY: She could be wrong.
PIERSON: (*To* IRENE.) What about Magdalena?

(*Slight pause.*)

THACKARAY: Seriously?
IRENE: My name is Irene. I am a doctor. You are holding me against my will.
THACKARAY: We should call her *Pepper*.
DELPHINE: (*To* PIERSON.) Why Magdalena?
PIERSON: You don't fancy it?
DELPHINE: It seems, is it—"over the top"—
PIERSON: As opposed to *Pepper*?
THACKARAY: You can't deny she's spicy.

(*Slight pause.*)

IRENE: Does it mean anything?
PIERSON: Memory loss?
IRENE: The *name*, does the name mean anything—

DELPHINE: I was thinking "little gypsy girl"—

(*PIERSON stands.*)

PIERSON: It's a name from your past. Or your dreams. Or perhaps both. A person calling you "Magdalena" would be from your past, or with knowledge of your past—or a person from your dreams, or with knowledge of your dreams, or a person with any combination of these, including all of these, provoking you into some act of confession, or revelation, or simply toying with your present state of ignorance, and all of this—any of this—with the best intentions or with the worst, the most frivolous or the most grave.

(*Slight pause.*)

IRENE: (*Indicating THACKARAY.*) He called me that. When you were on the floor.
DELPHINE: You were on the floor?
THACKARAY: Apparently he's under stress.
DELPHINE: But—the deadline—
PIERSON: I am well aware of the deadline—
THACKARAY: (*Chuckling.*) And I never called her—
PIERSON: You shouldn't have been talking to her at all. I am the only one authorized—
DELPHINE: But you're not making progress.
THACKARAY: It's obvious to everyone.
DELPHINE: And we'll all be punished.
THACKARAY: I never said a word.

(*Slight pause.*)

Irene's a *mixer.*
PIERSON: Listen, will you—both of you—your own tasks, pressing as well, yes, I'm sure, I know that this, her—we're all—depending— we all know—we all know—know absolutely—know—

(*PIERSON stops abruptly. He snatches* DELPHINE's *cigarette from her mouth—inhales deeply, three times, crushes it on the floor.*)

I mean—honestly—what the hell are you two doing here? This is my time, my room—it's my head on the plate—so get the bloody hell out of my sight—and her sight—before I pull my own head off and force the pieces down your throats. Okay?

(*Slight pause.*)

THACKARAY: You're the boss.
DELPHINE: At once, *Dottore. Scusi.*

(THACKARAY *walks to the right-hand door, exits.* DELPHINE *walks to the left-hand door, opens it, pauses, looks to* PIERSON.)

Ciao.

(DELPHINE *exits.* PIERSON *exhales, chuckles thinly.*)

PIERSON: Christ almighty—right? What a morning. What a day—is it day? What's next—insects laying eggs in my brain? Enough. What about you? Irene—is it? Irene? is it?—can you say how you feel? Can you?

(*Slight pause.*)

Take a breath. Can you tell me what's in your mind? Forget about this room—this room is nonsense, it in itself won't help you at all—you've figured that out. What's important . . . Irene . . . dear . . . is what's in your mind.

(*Slight pause.*)

Can you tell me the first thing you remember? The earliest thing. I want you to describe it.

(*Slight pause.*)

I can promise you're not leaving until you do.

(*Slight pause.*)

IRENE: Well . . . it was the . . . the . . . the weirdest thing.

(*Pause. IRENE shifts her position, speaks.*)

It's a dream. A daydream—I was . . . waiting . . . I don't know where—an elevator . . . a closet—someplace small . . . and then I was thinking of the sea, and the idea . . . or dream—that the sea is alive, and aware in a way we can't understand, except I— and only I—was on a ferry boat, dark Northern waters, churning, densely grey, almost black, swelling up to me, looking over the rail, each swell splitting into white foam at its height—the realization that I was being watched, that these splits of white were in fact the eyes of the sea—innumerable eyes—opening and disappearing across the planet, constantly in communication—as cold as the stars, a gaze penetrating me utterly.

(*Slight pause.*)

And then through me, like my body was flayed into air.

(*Slight pause.*)

And so . . . elevator, climbing, a very tall building, hotel, night— suddenly, strangely, thinking of the sea. And—the inner surface of the elevator door is polished metal. I can see myself.

PIERSON: How do you look?

IRENE: I don't know—fabulous. Red dress, red silk, Chinese, slit up the thigh, high collar, black heels, hair perfect. In one hand is a handbag, in the other . . . in the other . . . is a scalpel. The handle is wrapped with electrical tape, so I can get a good grip.

(*Slight pause.*)

PIERSON: What happened next?
IRENE: I don't know. That's all—the elevator, the sea, the mirror.
PIERSON: Were you frightened?
IRENE: Do you want me to be?
PIERSON: It's not about me.
IRENE: Well it's not about "me" either if I can't remember anything.
PIERSON: Don't be difficult. Look, you were doing very well—
IRENE: I was making it up.
PIERSON: No you weren't.
IRENE: Nothing I have *ever* told you is true—
PIERSON: Don't tell me that—*I won't have it*—

(*PIERSON snaps his fingers. IRENE lolls, eyes open, head to the side. PIERSON abruptly walks to the right-hand door, yanks it open, looks out—no one. He closes the door, turns back to IRENE. PIERSON takes out a cigarette, hesitates, sticks it into his mouth, hesitates, looks back to the door, throws the cigarette to the floor, steps on it.*)

PIERSON: Let's continue, okay?
IRENE: Uh huh.
PIERSON: You're in an elevator. In a red dress. In a reflection.
IRENE: All right.
PIERSON: What's in your hand?
IRENE: It's a scalpel. I'm a doctor. My name is Irene.
PIERSON: Who is Magdalena?
IRENE: Who are you?
PIERSON: I'm your Doctor.
IRENE: I'm the Doctor, Doctor.

(*Slight pause.*)

PIERSON: What's in your bag?
IRENE: Makeup. Drugs. Birth control. Crap.
PIERSON: Where are you going?

IRENE: I'm going up.

(*IRENE chuckles.*)

PIERSON: Yes?
IRENE: I've come from another room where I've had sex. I've gone
   down, and now I'm going up.
PIERSON: I see.
IRENE: (*Chuckles.*) Down and up.
PIERSON: Who did you have sex with?
IRENE: O . . . who knows?

(*Slight pause.*)

PIERSON: Let's continue.
IRENE: When the elevator opens, the hallway is red, red carpet, red
   wallpaper. There's music from an open suite. Chanting women.
   Inside, everything is white. I kick off my shoes at the door.
PIERSON: Why?
IRENE: You can't kill a person in heels. Not with a scalpel. What kind
   of doctor are you?

(*The left-hand door opens several inches, DELPHINE poking her
head in.*)

DELPHINE: Ah, *scusi*—*Dottore* Pierson—
PIERSON: No, not now! I am in the midst—*a very delicate*—
DELPHINE: Someone's arrived.
PIERSON: What? But we haven't finished!

(*PIERSON sputters, stands. DELPHINE inches carefully into the
room, waits.*)

Then that's it. That's it—meet the challenge—embrace the
whipping—

(*PIERSON strides to the door, sees* DELPHINE *is not moving after him, stops.*)

Signora?

DELPHINE: We cannot leave her like so—where Mr. Thackaray can come in—yes?

(*Slight pause.*)

PIERSON: You're right. I'll stay—I'll *continue*—

DELPHINE: No, but someone—

PIERSON: I'm a working man, not a pincushion! I keep getting interrupted!

(*Slight pause.*)

You're my only ally.

(*Slight pause.*)

And, all right—who's exactly arrived?

DELPHINE: A young woman.

PIERSON: And she's come for, for—for our subject—the subject of—our—

DELPHINE: Evidently.

PIERSON: And why? Exactly? I mean, what have you done?

DELPHINE: What do you think I've done? She's been drugged, gagged, stripped, and strapped to the table in examination room nine.

(*Slight pause.*)

PIERSON: Ah. For some reason—what was I thinking—what else?

(*Slight pause.* PIERSON *giggles.*)

It's these dreams I expect—the strangest things. You'll watch her—room nine—and I'm expected?

DELPHINE: *Si, Dottore.*
PIERSON: Excellent.

(*PIERSON strides through the open door. As he just passes through* DELPHINE *claps her hands.* PIERSON *freezes, crumples to the floor, his feet sticking through the threshold.* DELPHINE *sighs, stands. She turns to* IRENE, *snaps her fingers.* IRENE *blinks, sits straight, freezes, takes in the room.* DELPHINE *speaks without the accent.*)

DELPHINE: I've bought us some time—
IRENE: Who are you?
DELPHINE: I'm helping you—remember that, okay? Afterwards?
IRENE: After what? I'm sorry, I don't know anything—*anything*—what I know is something's happened—*to me*—and some cocksucker's going to pay for it!

(*IRENE stands.* DELPHINE *steps back.*)

What?
DELPHINE: You don't have to be—vulgar—
IRENE: And what is with this *snapping* shit—
DELPHINE: Well, you can get—I'm told—the biblical—kicking, gouging, throat-chopping—
IRENE: I'm a *doctor.*
DELPHINE: Hmm?

(*Slight pause.*)

Anyway—
IRENE: Aren't I?
DELPHINE: You'd know more than me.
IRENE: But I wouldn't.
DELPHINE: No, you would—I mean, I *don't* know—and if you've even got a hunch—
IRENE: Why are you wearing that dress?
DELPHINE: Good question, but right now—

IRENE: He told me I was telling him about a woman wearing that dress. I think I know you—

DELPHINE: You don't, really.

IRENE: I feel like I do.

DELPHINE: You know—huh—it's—if you want to escape—

IRENE: I want to understand.

(*The right-hand doorknob is turned. It's locked. They both turn to it. A knock.*)

DELPHINE: Fuck.

IRENE: Wait—

DELPHINE: No—

IRENE: *Yes.*

(*DELPHINE makes to snap her fingers. IRENE reaches out and seizes her hand. DELPHINE tries to snap with her other hand, IRENE takes hold of it as well. Holding both hands, IRENE spins her sharply, securing DELPHINE's arms behind her back. Another knock at the door. DELPHINE calls out, without the accent.*)

DELPHINE: Yes?

THACKARAY: (*Off.*) Dr. Pierson?

DELPHINE: Unavailable, I'm afraid.

THACKARAY: (*Off.*) Is he there?

DELPHINE: (*With the accent.*) *Scusi?*

(*IRENE edges DELPHINE back to the open left-hand door.*)

THACKARAY: (*Off.*) Look, is someone there?

DELPHINE: (*With the accent.*) *Si, si*, it is myself, the very busy *Dottore*, our subject—

THACKARAY: (*Off.*) Someone from outside! Look, do I need to kick it down?

(*THACKARAY works the lock savagely. He throws himself against the door: it shakes.*)

DELPHINE: (*With the accent.*) No one has arrived—

THACKARAY: (*Off.*) I'll break this door. I'll enjoy doing it—but you'll be responsible!

(*THACKARAY throws himself against the door; it shakes.*)

DELPHINE: (*Without the accent.*) A woman arrived, she's been put in examination room nine!

(*Slight pause. They stand in the doorway, over PIERSON, looking at the other door.*)

DELPHINE: (*Calling.*) So . . . that's all right then?

(*THACKARAY appears behind them in the left-hand door, slightly out of breath. They start, IRENE dragging DELPHINE away from the door, trying to place the chair between them and THACKARAY.*)

THACKARAY: Didn't hear you. Why not just go around—right? Hell of a way—out of breath.

(*He takes in PIERSON, the women, chuckles*)

You're having fun at my expense.

DELPHINE: The strangest thing happened. A woman has arrived. I have placed her in examination room nine—drugged, gagged, stripped, strapped. Off you go.

THACKARAY: (*Indicating PIERSON.*) Did you do this?

DELPHINE: Of course I didn't. She did. He called out for help, I came in—she's insane—

IRENE : I'll hurt her.

THACKARAY: Excellent. How? I'm curious.

IRENE: Pull her hair to start, I expect. Pull it out.

THACKARAY: Sure—who wouldn't?

(*Slight pause.*)

What about me?

IRENE: I'm assuming you'd want to watch—so, I'd pull her hair, slap her, maybe step on her ankle and use her crumpling as an excuse to shove us both a little closer to you, then I'd probably get more sexual, viciously twist a nipple—whatever I think you'd like best—and then I suppose I'd throw her into you, and in the moment it took you to deal with this I'd punch you in the throat—hard, accurately—and you'd be a wheezing mess at my nonexistent mercy.

THACKARAY: You are a doctor.

(*IRENE releases DELPHINE, shoving her away. DELPHINE rubs her hands, warily.*)

DELPHINE: Why did you do that?

THACKARAY: She's a tease.

IRENE: Where am I?

DELPHINE: We can't tell you.

IRENE: Come on. What city? What hemisphere?

DELPHINE: We can't tell you because we don't know.

(*Slight pause.*)

For sure. I mean, I've looked around—

THACKARAY: She has a window that opens.

DELPHINE: There are sailors—whispering—I've heard stories—

THACKARAY: So, there's the sea. Or a river.

(*Slight pause.*)

So it's not, you know, Denver. Madrid. Kyoto.

IRENE: I have no memory. Memories from my time *here* are piling up like dirt on my grave.

DELPHINE: We don't know—

IRENE: HOW CAN YOU NOT FUCKING KNOW?

(*Slight pause.*)

THACKARAY: Am I out of a loop here? Some girl thing?

DELPHINE: Pierson called out, I came in, she grabbed me—

THACKARAY: I didn't hear him.

DELPHINE: Then you weren't listening.

THACKARAY: If she was difficult he would have called *me*.

DELPHINE: It doesn't *matter*—he called, I came, he was on the floor, she grabbed me—

THACKARAY: No, that doesn't make sense.

DELPHINE: She was hurting me—

IRENE: What are you two talking about?

THACKARAY: We have to go. Someone's arrived—

DELPHINE: No one's arrived.

THACKARAY: What?

DELPHINE: I just said that, for you, I said that—I was freaking out—(*To IRENE.*) Look, could you do me a favor? Could you just sit down for a second? Because—shit—because I think I— we—

THACKARAY: What are you talking about?

DELPHINE: Just a fucking minute . . .

(*DELPHINE buries her face in her hands. She pulls them away, exhales, moves to the briefcase, kneels, opens it. She removes the flask, opens it, drinks at length, spilling over her chin. She wipes her face, replaces the flask. Still on the floor, she looks up at IRENE. IRENE walks to the chair, glances at THACKARAY, perches on the arm.*)

DELPHINE: I just—I think I have to—if no one else is—

THACKARAY: (*Low, to IRENE.*) She's quite fetching on her knees, don't you think?

IRENE: (*To DELPHINE.*) Your arms are bruised.

DELPHINE: (*Scoffs.*) You are a doctor.

IRENE: What are you drinking?

(*Slight pause.*)

THACKARAY: Prescription, helps us focus.

IRENE: (*To THACKARAY.*) Could you go away?
THACKARAY: (*Chuckles.*) You'd like that would you?
IRENE: (*To DELPHINE.*) I need to leave. I'm going to leave—
THACKARAY: (*Chuckles.*) Can't tell you how many times you've said that—
IRENE: (*To DELPHINE.*) I have so many questions—
THACKARAY: Why are you talking to her? (*To DELPHINE.*) Look, *Signora*, up, back to work—

(*IRENE swivels on her seat and drives a sharp rabbit punch into THACKARAY's throat. He gasps, grasps his throat and drops to his knees. IRENE shoves him over with her foot. He lays on the floor, wheezing.*)

(*IRENE rises, stands over DELPHINE, who doesn't look up.*)

IRENE: Are you coming with me or not?

(*Slight pause. DELPHINE shakes her head "no."*)

Then get the hell out of my dress.

BLACKOUT

— ACT II —

(*The same room, as before.* PIERSON *inert on the floor in the open left-hand doorway.* THACKARAY *on the floor, breathing softly, still, eyes open, having crawled some distance away from his former position.* DELPHINE, *on the floor, curled, unmoving, naked. Near her on the floor is a discarded dark wig.* DELPHINE *is blonde.*)

(*Draped over the chair, the white robe. The briefcase nowhere to be seen.*)

(CELESTE *walks carefully around the room. She wears a black silk dress—Asian collar, sleeveless, slit up the thigh. She holds a pair of black heels in one hand, and a scalpel in the other, the handle wrapped with black electrical tape.*)

(*She stops at the chair. She picks up the robe, holds it out, holds it to her face and breathes in deeply. She lowers the robe, continues walking, past* DELPHINE, *to the right-hand door. She opens it, pokes her head through, steps back, closes it. She drops her shoes, tucks the scalpel into her dress and sharply claps her hands.*)

(PIERSON *erupts into a coughing fit. He thrashes, gropes, his upper body in the darkness beyond the door. He pulls himself into a sitting position and then into the room, on his hands and knees. He takes in the others on the floor,* CELESTE.)

CELESTE: (*Brightly.*) Hiya.

(*Sharp blackout. Lights up.*)

(*PIERSON in the chair, wearing* DELPHINE's *wig, his eyes closed. Behind him,* CELESTE, *the index finger of her left hand in his mouth. He sucks on it. The white robe draped over* DELPHINE. *Neither she nor* THACKARAY *has moved.*)

CELESTE: It was just the . . . I don't know . . . the weirdest thing. Don't you think? You come to a place expecting one thing, and the more you allow yourself to think about it, what you find is almost always something totally else. Eventually you're thinking of things just to eliminate them as possibilities—so you know what *not* to be prepared for. It's a skill. You learn it or you don't—you become active in your own life or you don't. Don't you think?

(*PIERSON nods.*)

Anyway, I don't know how you feel about sailors. I don't claim to understand what you're doing in this neighborhood—everyone has secrets—but I think sailors are distinguished by having some fixed notion of "home" that they in fact have nothing to do with. And when they are home it's like they're wearing gasmasks, right? Even the enlightened sailor, throwing in the towel and calling the ship home, will become dislocated from the ship, assailed instead by insubstantial destinations-for-a-day: oceans, ports, drink, prostitution—until *these* things become home, which in turn lose *their* reality—it just goes on—and even if in my acquaintance sailors pack less brain than a chunk of kelp it seems somehow more honestly confronting the final facts of a consciousness both chained in place and utterly adrift within the realm of its own soul.

(*CELESTE removes her finger, wipes it on* PIERSON's *jacket, stands.*)

You know?
PIERSON: What is your name?

CELESTE: Temple. Celeste. Celestial Temple. Are you Dr. Pierson?
PIERSON: I am.
CELESTE: (*Singsong.*) I'm supposed to give you a message . . .
PIERSON: I tried to contain her, to establish a meaningful, codependent doctor-patient relationship.

(*Slight pause.*)

CELESTE: Well, that's your job.
PIERSON: But she was just—just so . . . *angry—bitter—angry and bitter—*

(*CELESTE laughs. She fluffs the wig, whispers in PIERSON's ear.*)

CELESTE: Well, that's hers.

(*Sharp blackout. Lights up.*)

(*CELESTE sits on the floor, DELPHINE's head buried in her lap. CELESTE idly strokes DELPHINE's hair. PIERSON in the chair, slumped, his voice even, without affect. THACKARAY is gone.*)

PIERSON: How long has it been since I've seen the sun? Am I in a warehouse, underground, in an enormous vessel—or the city of Dis, which has no sky. As if drama would provide relief.

(*Slight pause.*)

I tell him all of this. Instead of answering, he merely turns and exits through the door, which he doesn't close behind him. I wait. I get dressed—my clothes are gone, but the suit fits. I enter the next room. It's entirely white. On a table is a metal tray, on the metal tray syringes, in the syringes red fluid. Next to the tray is a photograph: a dressmaker's dummy wearing a sleeveless silk dress with an Asian collar.
CELESTE: What color?
PIERSON: Who knows? It's a black and white picture.

CELESTE: When do you realize they're watching you?

PIERSON: The photo has Chinese characters written on it with a black grease pencil. You only see them when you tilt your head. And notice the large red characters on the wall, a wall of mirrors.

CELESTE: What do the characters say?

PIERSON: Who knows? I'm not Chinese.

CELESTE: When do you try to wake up?

PIERSON: When I realize the door's been locked behind me. Then the chanting starts—deafening—of course it's a dream, I try to recall where I am—what city, the date, my occupation—nothing comes. I pinch myself, slap my forehead. Eventually—I know this is what they want—I pick up a syringe, roll up a sleeve—

CELESTE: Is that when you wake up?

PIERSON: It's when I wake up here. With needle marks all over my arms.

(*CELESTE leans down, coos into DELPHINE's ear.*)

(*Sharp blackout. Lights up.*)

(*CELESTE sits on the table. PIERSON slumped in the chair, as before. On the far side of the chair from CELESTE, DELPHINE paces, smokes. She wears the robe, feet bare.*)

CELESTE: Huh. Why do you think you got a window that opens?

DELPHINE: It opens four inches.

CELESTE: Sometimes four inches is enough.

(*DELPHINE scoffs, paces, smokes.*)

(*With an Italian accent.*) You do not answer the *question*, yes?

DELPHINE: I don't have an answer. I don't know.

CELESTE: You were trusted. You should feel proud. Did you press yourself against the gap, so they could stand on their toes and lick you?

(*Slight pause.*)

DELPHINE: Who exactly?
CELESTE: Sailors, I should think. Bargewomen. The odd passing mastiff.

(*Slight pause.*)

Still, you're a professional. Maybe not a *good* one.
DELPHINE: And not that I've been paid—
CELESTE: This isn't payment for what you've done?

(*Slight pause.*)

DELPHINE: It's a job. I interviewed—
CELESTE: (*Laughs.*) I love those! I love those interviews—I watch those tapes at night—where did you have to go?
DELPHINE: Doctor's office.
CELESTE: (*Laughs.*) That one is the best!

(*Slight pause.*)

Come on! Okay, you fill out the forms, talk to someone, they look very serious, you fill out another form, talk to someone else, they look even *more* serious—then they tell you what, "it's a minor formality," and you're on the exam table?
DELPHINE: Uh huh.
CELESTE: And that rubber glove sound! *Snap!* I love that.

(*Slight pause.*)

Where'd you wake up?
DELPHINE: I woke up here.
CELESTE: No you didn't, Delphine.

(*Slight pause.*)

Listen. I may be asking questions, but your answers are for *you*.

(*Slight pause.*)

DELPHINE: In a hotel. On the bed, in a white robe. The phone rang. I woke up . . . I answered it. I hung up. A man called from the other room . . .

(*Slight pause.*)

Was I ready for champagne?

(*The right-hand door opens. THACKARAY enters with the brief-case. He looks to CELESTE, who nods, and closes the door behind him. He sets the case on the floor, kneels, opens the case, and removes several flasks. He tosses one to DELPHINE, who catches it awkwardly. He offers a second flask to CELESTE, who shakes her head "no." He drains it himself in a steady, deliberate series of swallows. He wipes his chin. He drops the empty flask back into the open case. Slight pause.*)

CELESTE: How's that? Feel better?

(*THACKARAY extends a hand, flat, tips it from side to side, a "so so" gesture.*)

DELPHINE: Can he talk?

(*THACKARAY drains a third flask, wipes his chin, drops it into the case.*)

   Can he talk?
THACKARAY: (*With extreme difficulty.*) Of course I can talk.
CELESTE: He's just been scarred by love.

(*Sharp blackout. Lights up.*)

(*CELESTE on the table, as before. THACKARAY sitting in the chair, smoking. PIERSON and DELPHINE are gone.*)

CELESTE: You shouldn't be doing that.
THACKARAY: Don't I know it? The tobacco user carries the reek of his vice every bit as much as the savage trails the stench of an unwiped rectum. Being inured to the stink is merely a measure of their lack of grace. Punishment will follow—unavoidable, relentless, total.

(*Slight pause.*)

How else?
CELESTE: Not the best for your throat.
THACKARAY: (*Scoffs.*) Whatever.

(*Slight pause.*)

He tried to talk to us of dreams. I should have acted then. But ... I think ... I ... prolonging it, her situation. There's so little pleasure in life. Have you learned that? How old are you? Your body's a deception.

(*Slight pause.*)

Isn't it? It is. Isn't it.

(*Slight pause. The right-hand door opens. PIERSON pokes his head into the room.*)

CELESTE: (*Sharply.*) No! Out!

(*Slight pause. PIERSON hovers.*)

PIERSON: Sorry—I was wondering—if—

(*CELESTE launches herself toward the door. She slams it shut on* PIERSON *with the flat of her hand. Slight pause. The door opens,* PIERSON *pokes through again.*)

Sorry—I—

(*CELESTE slams the door again—clearly bouncing it off his head. She leans her back against it, looking at* THACKARAY. *She smiles.*)

(*Sharp blackout. Lights up.*)

(*THACKARAY in the chair.* DELPHINE *stands in the open left-hand door.* CELESTE *sits on the floor in front of the closed right-hand door.*)

CELESTE: You always prepped the exam rooms.
DELPHINE: Yes.
CELESTE: And that *is* where you first saw her. Room nine.
DELPHINE: Yes.
CELESTE: Because that one has more outlets.
DELPHINE: Yes.
CELESTE: Dr. Pierson brought you in.
DELPHINE: Yes.
CELESTE: Was she awake?
DELPHINE: Yes.
CELESTE: She'd been injured?
DELPHINE: Yes.
CELESTE: And did she mention this . . . whatever . . .
DELPHINE: "Zion shall be plowed as a field"?
THACKARAY: Micah 3:8-12.
DELPHINE: No.
THACKARAY: Of course she mentioned it. She was possessed.
DELPHINE: They both said that, but I never heard the subject—
THACKARAY: Irene. Her name is Irene.
DELPHINE: Or Magdalena.
THACKARAY: She's a doctor.

DELPHINE: Of what?
CELESTE: Higher awareness? Moral authority? Tears?

(*Slight pause.*)

Why so mopey? A room, pharmaceuticals, three squares a day—
THACKARAY: *She's* the whiner.
CELESTE: Why is she here?
THACKARAY: She's a spy. But she's been left behind.
CELESTE: Poor expendable spy, huh?

(*Slight pause.*)

DELPHINE: I've walked by his door at night. He's inside bawling his goddamn eyes out. Can I go?
CELESTE: Sure.

(*DELPHINE marches out, shutting the left-hand door behind her.*)

THACKARAY: Told you.
CELESTE: You did.
THACKARAY: Butter wouldn't melt with that one, no matter where you put it.

(*Sharp blackout. Lights up.*)

(*PIERSON in the chair, slumped. CELESTE sits across his lap, her middle finger in his mouth. THACKARAY standing near the right-hand door, which is closed.*)

CELESTE: Do you want to do this? He's surprisingly vital.

(*THACKARAY scoffs. Slight pause.*)

And are you jealous of him or me?
THACKARAY: I'm hanging from a damned rope in the dark.

(*Slight pause.*)

How do you do that, without a watch?
CELESTE: I have excellent hearing.
THACKARAY: Beg pardon?
CELESTE: I can hear his heart.
THACKARAY: Bet that breaks the ice at parties.

(*CELESTE laughs. She removes her finger and wipes it on PIERSON's tie. She fluffs the wig, turns to THACKARAY. She pulls off the wig and throws it at THACKARAY. He does not move to catch it: the wig hits his chest and drops to the floor.*)

No thanks.
CELESTE: You'd be fetching . . .
THACKARAY: What do I need to do? Hunt her through the streets? Ritual self-criticism?
CELESTE: If you like.
THACKARAY: Is this a test?
CELESTE: Sure.

(*Slight pause.*)

I can hear your blood. Rushing.

(*Slight pause.*)

Did you ever think that she was only here to affect change in you?
THACKARAY: That's exactly what I thought all the time.

(*Slight pause.*)

Thrashing in ignorance. Fish in the bottom of a rowboat.

(*Slight pause.*)

What I've done is really only, merely—I'm prepared, mentally, I can do it. I've done it before.

(*Slight pause.*)

(*Indicating* PIERSON.) He's a grub. He's an aardvark's dinner. You see this. I'm your man, as I was hers. I mean that as a compliment.

(*Slight pause.*)

If you could just tell me—

(CELESTE *hops off* PIERSON's *lap and walks to* THACKARAY. *He drops to his knees. She stands over him, claps her hands.* PIERSON *erupts into a coughing fit, thrashes in the chair, blinking.* THACKARAY *claps his hand.* PIERSON *slumps.*)

THACKARAY: Please—

(CELESTE *claps her hands sharply.* PIERSON *erupts into a coughing fit. He thrashes for a moment in the chair, blinking. He takes in the others.* CELESTE *inserts her middle finger into* THACKARAY's *mouth. He sucks on it. One by one she inserts her other fingers, then her thumb, then her fist.* THACKARAY *gags, remains on his knees.*)

(*Sharp blackout. Lights up.*)

(CELESTE *sitting on the table.* THACKARAY *in the chair, smoking, rubbing his eyes.*)

CELESTE: Tell me about the time on the ship.
THACKARAY: What time?
CELESTE: I'll be very good.

(*Slight pause.*)

THACKARAY: A sea voyage is like nothing else. A sea voyage when you never glimpse the ocean is something else again. This is my idea of how most individuals navigate their lives.

CELESTE: That's gloomy.

THACKARAY: I spent the first half of the crossing well below, on the move—storerooms, steerage, engines—until I received my signal. That sounds dramatic—like some secret society—all I'm saying is that there are omens of many kinds, and I pay attention to them. I slipped into the laundry—you'd be amazed what people leave in their pockets. It was night, and I climbed—now in a white dinner jacket—staircases, corridors, how many oval doors, the casino, displays of food, displays in general—a final deck of staterooms, to one of which I had a key.

(*Slight pause.*)

When I reach the stateroom door, it's ajar. When I enter, I see blood on the carpet—footprints—bare footprints, small, a woman's foot. The carpet's still wet, but the room is silent. To my right is a first-aid kit, on the wall. I break it open—nothing beats a good medical kit for instruments of mayhem—but the only thing inside is a small cassette player. I push "play." This chanting rises up—female, foreign tongues . . . like an army behind my advance.

(*Slight pause.*)

Around the corner is the bar—champagne bottles, toppled ice bucket, broken glass—across is the bed, unmade, filthy, as if someone had been tied there for days, and beyond that the bathroom, where the light is on and the water's running. In the sink are the soaked contents of the medical kit. I pick up a syringe—it's full of something red—and raise it like a weapon as I pull aside the shower curtain.

(*Slight pause.*)

Details are like pitons on a cliff face. If our day is a cliff face. Our life. If you could just get these facts between your jaws you could somehow snap their necks—rabbits to a greyhound—it's dog thought, instead of . . . instead—face it, simply, on a ship, on a greater force pushing through the darkness.

(*Slight pause.*)

We are not this force. We're ignorant passengers.

(*Slight pause.*)

Have you heard, she mentioned a daughter?

(*Slight pause.*)

No work worth doing is ever done. No amount of water washes that truth.

(*Slight pause.*)

He should have given her to me.
CELESTE: What would you have done?
THACKARAY: She would have talked. About what she didn't think she knew. But I know she does. Everyone knows.
CELESTE: Knows what?

(*Slight pause.*)

Okay.

(*Slight pause.*)

What do *you* know?
THACKARAY: Why should I tell you?
CELESTE: I think you know.
THACKARAY: Not precisely.

(*CELESTE laughs.*)

THACKARAY: But I know who you might be.

(*CELESTE laughs.*)

THACKARAY: But I don't . . . I mean, I don't know what . . . what that will actually feel like.

(*CELESTE laughs. She hops off the table. THACKARAY sits up straight, gripping the arms of the chair. CELESTE reaches into her dress, holds her hand there, teasing him.*)

THACKARAY: Whatever.

(*Sharp blackout. Lights up.*)

(*CELESTE, alone, on the table, idly swinging her legs. The chair is stained with blood. DELPHINE enters through the left-hand door, leading PIERSON, still in the wig.*)

PIERSON: I don't understand why there hasn't been contact—we ought to be swarming with operatives, ferreting out the scent—*suivez la piste*, right?

(*DELPHINE stops, seeing the blood. She turns to CELESTE. PIERSON looks to CELESTE, then back to the chair, then away.*)

As I say . . . they send no one . . .

(*DELPHINE steps to the chair. She covers her mouth with her hand. She rushes to the right-hand door. It's locked. She turns to CELESTE, who smiles. DELPHINE rushes out the left-hand door. Slight pause.*)

CELESTE: (*Whispers.*) Your student seems a little on edge.
PIERSON: (*Whispers.*) She's a sensitive young woman.

(*Sharp blackout. Lights up.*)

(*CELESTE reclines on the table. DELPHINE sits in the chair, leaning forward, head in hands. PIERSON stands several feet away, wearing the wig, behind the chair.*)

PIERSON: Or . . . hypothetically . . . if you've done something that haunts you—terrible, even unimaginable. At times you can't believe it's even happened—indeed, it may seem part of a stranger's life story. The question is whether you'd do it again, given the chance, given the circs.

(*Slight pause.*)

We all have our habits . . . ghosts . . . the well-worn circuits of rage and desire . . .

(*Slight pause.*)

You think you've been weak. You've given in to urges that aren't flattering. Well, we're all weak. And we're all subject. That's another thing. There are two things. Look at a labyrinth from above—do you see a maze of paths, or a maze of walls?

DELPHINE: I'd like a cigarette.

PIERSON: By all means!

(*He steps close to her, removes a pack from his pocket and shakes one from the pack. DELPHINE takes it, waits as he fishes out a lighter, leans into the light.*)

You should lean back.

DELPHINE: I don't want to lean back.

PIERSON: You will eventually.

DELPHINE: Eventually isn't now.

PIERSON: It may as well be.

(*Slight pause.*)

(*To CELESTE.*) She does this accent quite well, for an Italian.

DELPHINE: (*With the accent.*) *Grazie, grazie Dottore, bravo, bravo, molto grazie grazie grazie.*

(*Slight pause.*)

PIERSON: Yes. And I'm reminded—apropos boots—of what our subject once said, a question in the absence of an Oxford English Dictionary, as to which definition of the word "talent" had come first—that of a monetary unit or that of a particular ability.

DELPHINE: Didn't know, did you?

PIERSON: But I appreciated the question. Is our notion of money— of value—based on uniquely human traits, or do we character- ize our own natures by an arbitrary token of metal? It had nothing to do with what we were talking about—

CELESTE: What were you talking about?

PIERSON: It overlaps maliciously. She was not happy here.

DELPHINE: There was no reason she should have been.

PIERSON: What an insight! As you're a real barn-burner yourself, mind like a whip, all that, maybe you'd care to tell us what you think we ought to have done here instead. (*To CELESTE.*) I'm sorry she's gone. I'm sorry I've been weak. I have been weak, made mistakes. I've misjudged so many things—this facility, the dosage, my sleep, the really crushing inability to sleep—

DELPHINE: I had to kick your door to wake you.

PIERSON: But I did not get any *rest*. I have had no rest. The dreams—

DELPHINE: Not again—

PIERSON: She's had them too—

DELPHINE: No I haven't—

PIERSON: We both heard her—Thackaray and I, in the hall— Thackaray—I—

(*Slight pause.*)

He could tell you.

(*Slight pause.*)

If I may ask, what would you call this section of town? The district name?

CELESTE: Well *I* call it Magdalenaville.

PIERSON: Ah. And the, uh, language? I have an AM radio—it's quite garbled—

CELESTE: Local dialect.

PIERSON: Of . . . ?

CELESTE: Normal mix—Italian, Chinese, Sanskrit. And English. Can't get away from English.

PIERSON: Of course that makes it easier for us. To blend in.

CELESTE: Should you continue?

PIERSON: Absolutely. Thank you. Thus—yes—*Signora*, though you may be assailed with feelings of inadequacy, dire consequences, blood on your hands—and well you may, who shall not be whipped with scorpions!—but you're a lovely young woman, all you need to be is frank. Think of what we've been through together—

CELESTE: Like when she arrived. All that excitement!

(*Slight pause. PIERSON turns to CELESTE.*)

PIERSON: Do you think we'll receive a new subject any time soon? Because we may have learned where we went wrong. What we can do to succeed. I can't speak for her. I never could.

CELESTE: That's not what I've asked you do, Doctor.

(*CELESTE claps her hands sharply. PIERSON slumps to the floor. DELPHINE looks over to him, then back to CELESTE.*)

Your turn.

(*Sharp blackout. Lights up.*)

(*DELPHINE leaning back in the chair. CELESTE stands behind her, with her middle finger in DELPHINE's mouth. Behind them, on the floor where he fell, PIERSON.*)

CELESTE: Okay, the first rule is you can't bite my finger. The second rule is you have to nod yes or no, really fast. No thinking. Okay?

(*DELPHINE nods "yes."*)

CELESTE: Super. Your name is Delphine?

(*DELPHINE nods "yes."*)

CELESTE: But they used to call you "Francesca"?

(*DELPHINE nods "yes."*)

CELESTE: And you hated this?

(*DELPHINE nods "yes."*)

CELESTE: Because it's a stupid name?

(*DELPHINE nods "yes."*)

CELESTE: And at the time, you wished those people were dead?

(*DELPHINE nods "yes."*)

CELESTE: Did you kill them?

(*DELPHINE nods "no." CELESTE smacks her head sharply with her other hand.*)

CELESTE: Did you make them unhappy?

(*DELPHINE nods "yes."*)

CELESTE: Did you drive them to the grave with a willful cascade of betrayal, thoughtlessness and neglect?

(*DELPHINE nods "yes."*)

CELESTE: Do you know why you'd do this to people you loved?

(*DELPHINE nods "no."*)

CELESTE: Do you know why you do it to yourself?

(*DELPHINE nods "no."*)

CELESTE: Do you know why you're here?

(*DELPHINE hesitates. CELESTE smacks her head sharply with her other hand.*)

CELESTE: It is because having money means freedom to do other things?

(*DELPHINE nods "yes."*)

CELESTE: Things that aren't your life so far?

(*DELPHINE nods "yes."*)

CELESTE: Things that aren't your job?

(*DELPHINE nods "yes."*)

CELESTE: Though this job takes all your time?

(*DELPHINE nods "yes."*)

CELESTE: And all your life?

(*DELPHINE hesitates. DELPHINE quickly nods "no."*)

CELESTE: Do you miss wearing that dress?

(*DELPHINE nods "yes."*)

CELESTE: Without it you feel naked?

(*DELPHINE nods "yes."*)

CELESTE: You feel like Francesca?

(*DELPHINE nods "yes."*)

CELESTE: Would Francesca have done what you've done? In examination room nine?

(*DELPHINE nods "no."*)

CELESTE: Then why would you feel like Francesca just because you've failed and lost your way? Because you've tried to help people who you've also harmed? Because you've sabotaged the very efforts you hoped would deliver some future freedom? Because you don't know what you ought to choose, or even what choices remain?

(*DELPHINE hesitates. DELPHINE nods "yes."*)

CELESTE: Okay.

(*Slight pause.*)

What is your life?

(*DELPHINE hesitates. CELESTE smacks her head sharply with her other hand.*)

CELESTE: That's a yes or no question. Answer it.

(*DELPHINE hesitates. CELESTE smacks her head sharply with her other hand.*)

CELESTE: Answer it or pay the penalty, Delphine!

(*DELPHINE nods "yes." Slight pause. CELESTE smoothes DELPHINE's hair where the blows have ruffled it, and removes her finger. She wipes it off on the collar of the robe, and places her hand against DELPHINE's cheek.*)

CELESTE: You're running a little cold.

(*Sharp blackout. Lights up.*)

(*CELESTE squatting on the seat of the chair. DELPHINE stands near the table, with a cigarette in one hand, the other hand over her eyes. Behind CELESTE, on the floor where he fell, PIERSON.*)

DELPHINE: She was sick, delirious, God knows what she was saying.
CELESTE: (*Indicating PIERSON.*) What did he say about it?
DELPHINE: He didn't talk to me about anything unless I, you know, got it out of him. He was freaking out as much as anyone—the whole mess is his fucking fault—he could have told me to do something, and then I would have—
CELESTE: But he didn't tell you to talk to her, did he?
DELPHINE: She said a lot of things—he didn't follow up on them—
CELESTE: That you were aware of.
DELPHINE: I can only respond to what I'm aware of—
CELESTE: Where you aware of Thackaray?
DELPHINE: Aware of what?

(*CELESTE stares at her. DELPHINE smokes, runs her hands through her hair.*)

I'll tell you what you want to know as soon as you tell me what that is!

CELESTE: Huh.

(*Slight pause.*)

DELPHINE: Because what was happening to me—I was a part of it, like I was drugged—I am being drugged, I know that—but I'd wake up exhausted, like I'd been swimming . . . like . . . like I didn't really notice that I was in a totally different situation . . . like my body knew it . . . but I didn't. Like in an earthquake. Have you been in an earthquake?

CELESTE: Uh huh.

DELPHINE: Then you know. The start of an earthquake, things start to shake, but your brain tries to explain it through normal options—it's the washing machine making more noise than normal, it's a jackhammer, it's someone stomping around upstairs with boots on . . . but there is no upstairs. But your mind accepts that before it accepts the truth.

(*Slight pause.*)

CELESTE: So, if I told you about an innocent woman, suffering from amnesia, mistakenly attacked?

DELPHINE: Do me the favor of not *toying* with me. If she's nothing why are you here?

CELESTE: I didn't say she was nothing.

DELPHINE: Everything that happened to her, even if she didn't remember it, it had to take a toll, right? It took a toll on me— but *she* kept going—she was so . . . resilient, like a . . . I don't know—

CELESTE: She-wolf? Cornered tigress? Mother bear?

DELPHINE: I *so* know you are just fucking with me. Didn't you listen to the tapes? Look, she would've escaped without me!

CELESTE: So your choices don't count?

DELPHINE: They don't mean anything either way! Any of them!

CELESTE: (*Imitating* DELPHINE.) "I'm helping you—remember that, okay? Afterwards?"

(*Slight pause.*)

DELPHINE: So?
CELESTE: So it's afterwards. Remember?
DELPHINE: But is it good that I helped her or is it bad that I let her get away?
CELESTE: (*Sighs.*) What do *you* think?
DELPHINE: (*Sobbing.*) I don't know!

(*Slight pause.* CELESTE *exhales through her bared teeth, staring at her.*)

(*Sharp blackout. Lights up.*)

(DELPHINE *sits forward in the chair, her face streaked, hugging herself as if cold.* CELESTE *sits cross-legged on the table, her hands in poised mudra positions.*)

CELESTE: Tell me about the hotel.
DELPHINE: I have told you.
CELESTE: Tell me again. I'll be good.

(*Slight pause.*)

You look a little chilly. Want a smoke?
DELPHINE: I finished his pack.
CELESTE: There's a pack in your robe.
DELPHINE: No there isn't.
CELESTE: Yes there is, Delphine.

(DELPHINE *reaches into the pocket, finds a new pack. She looks at* CELESTE, *who smiles.* DELPHINE *takes out a cigarette, lights it.*)

DELPHINE: It isn't my robe.

CELESTE: The hotel, Delphine.

(*Slight pause. DELPHINE takes three quick puffs, then exhales slowly.*)

DELPHINE: Something's gone wrong, everyone fans out—someone for every floor, every exit, the kitchens . . . I'm new, so I get sent to one of the upper floors, where no one expects anything to happen. I'm in the elevator, the whole interior is polished steel—it's a mirror, but dark—like your reflection's coming up through the water, or the fog, or . . . or hell . . . and I actually laugh out loud, because I'm thinking "hell" when the door opens—it's the fourteenth floor, and everything—the carpet, the walls, the ceiling—is red, blood red. I just let go with this crazy laugh and somehow I'm out and the doors close behind me . . . and then . . . then it's really quiet.

(*Slight pause.*)

I have a cell phone in one hand and some pepper spray in the other, which is my idea. No one's given me a weapon, but that seems stupid—to me. Anyway, I'm in a maid's uniform, looking up the hall, totally unprepared, and thinking, "What am I doing here?"

(*Slight pause.*)

Halfway down the hall one of the doors is open—a big bright slab of light. In the doorway is a pair of black heels.
CELESTE: You didn't call in.
DELPHINE: I know. Nothing had happened.
CELESTE: But inside—
DELPHINE: I know.
CELESTE: You didn't call inside either.
DELPHINE: I thought I'd call any second, each second.

(*Slight pause.*)

The windows were open—red curtains, billowing across the room—the wind fourteen stories up . . . it was cold. I am cold. I'm so cold.

CELESTE: It's okay.

DELPHINE: It was a suite. It was bigger than my apartment. Something had happened in the bed—the mattress was slashed—and the bathroom, which was huge, there were puddles—footprints—and in the sink—

CELESTE: You told me this part.

DELPHINE: Okay.

(*Slight pause.*)

When I woke up?

CELESTE: Sure.

DELPHINE: When I woke up on the floor—the shower was still on, hot water, and because the windows were open it was making even more steam than normal. It was a cloud over my head. I tried to sit up. I was naked. My head hurt. My arms hurt—there were bruises. Handprints. Small hands—like my own hands, like they'd picked me up and thrown me into the wall.

(*Slight pause.*)

The maid's uniform was gone. Hanging on the shower curtain was this Chinese dress.

CELESTE: Did you put it on?

DELPHINE: Not at first.

CELESTE: Did you try to wake up?

DELPHINE: Not at first.

CELESTE: Did you realize you were being watched?

DELPHINE: Not at first. Nothing at first.

(*Slight pause.*)

I heard something, voices . . . in the other room, but it wasn't in the other room . . . it was on the balcony. I went out. I was naked. I wasn't thinking—it was so cold. It was dark. Silent—stars above my head, lights below my feet—I was alone . . . I don't know how long—I was numb—I had this sense that the entire earth was spinning, all around me. Then I was back in the room. There was no bed. Everything was painted white. In the middle of the room was a dressmaker's dummy, with the Chinese dress.

(*Slight pause.*)

I put it on. I looked up . . .

(*Slight pause.*)

Later: a window. A woman's hand against a leather strap. Wool blankets, mothballs, sexual hunger in the middle of meaningless nights. The world still spinning on my little bed.

(*Slight pause.* DELPHINE *dries her eyes on the robe, looks up.* CELESTE *smiles.*)

CELESTE: Is that everything?

(*Sharp blackout. Lights up.*)

(CELESTE *leans her back against the closed right-hand door. The left-hand door is open. The chair is stained with more blood.* PIERSON *is still on the floor.*)

(CELESTE *claps her hands together sharply.* PIERSON *erupts into a coughing fit. He lurches up on his elbows, sees* CELESTE *on the other side of the chair, across the room. He looks around for anyone else. He stands slowly. His gaze falls on the chair.*)

PIERSON: Yes . . . yes, well, best to continue. That's my godforsaken motto.

(*Sharp blackout. Lights up.*)

(PIERSON *stands against the far wall, away from both doors and the chair.* CELESTE *stands on the other side of the chair, hands behind her back, facing him intently.*)

PIERSON: The doctor-patient relationship is delicate enough in normal circumstances—but well, we were up against it—a lot of trust, a lot of reaching out—I can only speak for myself, but if Irene were here—despite her—understandably—her emotional perspective, I think she might admit to—to having—there being—a benefit.

(*Slight pause.*)

She'd no memory. I was helping to find it. Parts of it—still, better than none. She would agree.

(*Slight pause.*)

Heard from her? Just curious. Not only—our position—but, professionally—and personally.

(*Slight pause.*)

I think she broke my nose. Or thereabouts. And our discussions—like college again—all hours, wide-ranging—heartfelt experience freely shared. You can check the recordings.

CELESTE: Did she ask about a daughter?
PIERSON: Did she? Perhaps. There was so much.
CELESTE: Did she ask rather soon before she left?

(*Slight pause.*)

PIERSON: Now that I'm reminded, I think perhaps she did. What could I say? My task was to help her in her present situation, not in some other life, which may never have ever even been real.

(*Slight pause.*)

Ideologically.
CELESTE: Huh.

(*Sharp blackout. Lights up.*)

(CELESTE *behind the chair, idly tracing her finger over its stains, watching* PIERSON *at the right-hand door, trying to pull it open with all his strength as he speaks.*)

PIERSON: I'd be lying if I said I was different—it's a human condition, you want your work to matter, to register your existence—cave painting. In the young, the naive, the obscenely privileged, this desire is for a universal importance—Napoleon, the Pope, film stars—but most people of intelligence progress to desiring importance in their field—the wonder drug, the invention, the vitally thin volume—but most people who are intelligent and who have lived and who are not obscenely privileged resign themselves at some point to making their mark within their own immediate world—scar the children, cuckold the brute, sodomize the virgin—

(PIERSON *lets go of the doorknob with a snarl, which he turns into a clearing of his throat. He ambles to the left-hand door, which is also closed. He snatches at the knob, furiously working it as he speaks, again pulling with all his strength.*)

PIERSON: And then of course, beyond this, beyond the world, where one is doomed, one tries to make one's mark in one's own mind—a desperate battle—hopeless—but my point is that one never gives up, their ideals or their efforts. The arena shrinks, but the more it shrinks, the truer the struggle. Myself as an example—here—this woman—in some ways only here to test me—

(PIERSON *lets go of the doorknob. He stands not quite facing* CELESTE.)

An ancient struggle. I'm reminded of a poem:

> Wind-seduced blossoms
> Snowfall in springtime
> This cold stream choked with petals

Chinese.
CELESTE: Japanese.
PIERSON: Is it? I believe you.

(*Slight pause. PIERSON returns to the knob, pulling.*)

CELESTE: Wait a sec.
PIERSON: Hmm?
CELESTE: Stop it.

(*PIERSON is still. He abruptly darts away, back to the right-hand door. CELESTE stands still, sighs.*)

PIERSON: I'm not a child. Nor am I blind. I am not blind. Work with compassion and detachment—isn't that the goal?
CELESTE: Depends on the work, I think.
PIERSON: Well I know that.

(*Slight pause.*)

Of course it depends.
CELESTE: Uh huh.
PIERSON: Jesus Christ!

(*Sharp blackout. Lights up.*)

(*PIERSON sits in the chair, hunched, holding one hand over his left eye. CELESTE sits cross-legged on the table, one hand in a poised mudra position, the other tapping the scalpel on her thigh.*)

CELESTE: Tell me again.

PIERSON: Tell you what? I told you—I just fucking told you—I did what you asked, and you—

CELESTE: Tell me again. I'll be good.

(*Slight pause.*)

PIERSON: I woke up on the floor of my room, hands and knees. I looked up—my door was ajar. I had locked it. The walls had been painted bright red. I slapped myself across the face. I sat up on my bed. The light was on, the radio seething static. Night sweats. Filthy. I'd fallen asleep—as usual—in my clothes. I looked at my door, which was locked, and it popped open before my eyes, like a magic spell. I slapped myself across the face. I woke in the hallway, in darkness, barefoot, somewhere behind me the sound of sobbing . . . ahead of me . . . a light. I slapped myself across the face. I was still in the hallway.

(*Slight pause.*)

You've really hurt me, you know—

CELESTE: It's okay.

PIERSON: I too was a tender lad.

CELESTE: I know.

(*Slight pause.*)

PIERSON: Have they found her? Irene? Is it? Irene? Is it?

CELESTE: They haven't found her.

PIERSON: She was injured. Her passions are fierce. Anyone can kill. Your inquiry is pointless. This is no place for love—

CELESTE: Settle down, sheesh.

PIERSON: I can't—I really can't—

(*Slight pause.*)

CELESTE: The hall, the light . . .

PIERSON: I walked down the hall and ran into a wall of glass.

Behind it was the light. It was a two-way mirror.

CELESTE: You slapped yourself across the face.

PIERSON: Changing nothing. Through the glass are figures, head-phones, some kind of instruction. A woman enters, holding her shoe, limping, out of breath. A Chinese dress. She's given a syringe. The second woman points at me.

CELESTE: You slapped yourself across the face.

(*Slight pause.*)

PIERSON: I'm awake all night.

(*Slight pause.*)

Delphine kicks on my door.

(*Slight pause.*)

"*Dottore . . .*"

(*Slight pause.*)

Another chance to save my life.

CELESTE: As for me, I am filled with power, with the spirit of the Lord, and with justice.

(*CELESTE taps the scalpel on her cheek, smiles.*)

The other one?

(*Sharp blackout. Lights up.*)

(*The chair is gone. IRENE stands in the center of the room, in DELPHINE's dress. Her feet are bare and bloodstained—whether from injury or from walking in blood is unclear. In her right hand is a scalpel. Her left hand is held before her, palm out.*)

(Behind her stands CELESTE, *with a hand over each of* IRENE *'s eyes.* CELESTE *has put on her shoes.* IRENE *is still, and does not acknowledge* CELESTE's *presence.* CELESTE *whispers into* IRENE's *ear.)*

CELESTE: Breathe. I want you to remember a story you've heard before.

(Slight pause.)

An elegant Chinese dress is bunched around your waist. A man whose name you don't know is bringing you off with his mouth. You're in a hotel room. He's on his knees. You're leaning against a desk that no one's ever used. Except perhaps for this. One hand is holding up the dress, the other entangled in his hair. You're silent . . . deliciously suspended . . . grinding into his tongue.

(Slight pause.)

Your eyes are closed. You are unable in this moment to see yourself, to imagine yourself in this situation, though you know yourself to be in it. In the moment it is happening the last thing you are able to do is to reconcile this moment with the rest of your life. As a girl someone tells you: in twenty-two years you'll enact this very scene. It's impossible.

(Slight pause.)

Outside the room, they're looking for you. The elevator. The suite. The bathroom. Cries in the street. Cobblestones. A red room. A white room. A man behind a wall of mirrors. Slaughter. Everything follows.

(Slight pause.)

But for this moment, you've hidden yourself in the arms—in the mouth—of chance. Your own tenderness. Now, when your heart is hard. Remember.

(*Slight pause.*)

    You're a doctor. You can heal.

(CELESTE *lifts her hands from* IRENE's *eyes and steps back. She disappears through the open left-hand door.*)

(IRENE's *eyes are closed. She opens them. Her arms remain in position, as before.*)

IRENE: Is anyone there?

(*Slight pause.*)

    I've kept one step ahead of the wind. Zion *is* a field. Jerusalem *is* a ruin. It feels like I've been very busy. I feel quite alive. And I've remembered . . . all kinds of things.

(*Slight pause.*)

    Eyes changing color in the light. The tide in my own body. The smell of my own little girl. I wanted to tell someone how free I feel. If anyone can hear me.

(*Slight pause.*)

    She's the one face I can't remember, but I've got hold of her inside.

(*Pause.*)

    You are all forgiven.

BLACKOUT

Tilt Angel
A Deadpan Tennessee Fairy Tale
by Dan Dietz

No performance or reading of this work *Tilt Angel* in any medium may be given without express permission of the author. Inquiries regarding performance rights, publication, duplication of any kind should be addressed to: Dan Dietz, c/o Salvage Vanguard Theater, 1705 Guadalupe Street, Suite 301, Austin, TX 78701.

⇒ BIOGRAPHY ⇐

Dan Dietz is a playwright living in Austin, Texas. His plays include *Dirigible, Blind Horses, Tilt Angel,* and *tempOdyssey,* and have been seen in New York, Los Angeles, Seattle, Wilmington, Austin, and elsewhere. Dietz has been honored with a James A. Michener Fellowship, a Josephine Bay Paul Fellowship, and the Austin Critics Table Award for Best New Play. He is a two-time finalist for the Princess Grace Award and a nominee for the George Oppenheimer New Play Award. His short play *Trash Anthem* received the 2002 Heideman Award from the Actors Theatre of Louisville and was produced at the 2003 Humana Festival of New American Plays.

Dietz has developed his work at Annex Theatre (Seattle, WA), Horizon Theatre (Atlanta, GA), The Playwrights' Center (Minneapolis, MN), Salvage Vanguard Theater (Austin, TX), and the Millay Colony for the Arts. He received his Bachelor of Arts in Theater from Kennesaw State University in 1995 and his Master of Fine Arts in Playwriting from the University of Texas at Austin in 1999. Dietz is a Resident Company Member of Salvage Vanguard Theater and the Artistic Director of Austin Script Works.

⋙ PRODUCTION HISTORY ⋘

Tilt Angel by Dan Dietz
Produced by Salvage Vanguard Theater
October 18-November 3, 2001
Directed by Jason Neulander

Cast

OLLIE .... Jason Phelps
LOIS .... Cyndi Williams
RED .... Robert Pierson
ANGEL BONES .... Victor Steele

Designers & Technical Staff

Original Music .... Chris Black
Set Design .... Kimberlee Koym
Lighting Design .... Diana Duecker
Costume Design .... Meredith Moseley
Sound Design .... Jeremy Lee
Stage Manager .... Gwen Hilker

Salvage Vanguard Theater

Salvage Vanguard Theater is a nonprofit arts organization located in Austin, Texas, committed to fostering a dynamic exchange between visionary artists and audiences new to their work. To that end, Salvage Vanguard Theater seeks to combine explosive energy with expert technique, creating forms that defy theatrical traditions and define a new American avant-garde.

Salvage Vanguard Theater was founded in 1994 with the purpose of introducing Austin audiences to America's new generation of avant-garde playwrights. Since that time, the company has produced more than fifty world and regional premieres by some of the most exciting writers around, including Dan Dietz, Ruth E. Margraff, Lisa D'Amour, Suzan-Lori Parks, and Caridad Svich.

In an effort to create transcendent experiences, many of Salvage Vanguard Theater's productions combine music and theater in unique ways. Not only has the company produced three operas, but also almost all of its productions over the past three years have featured live music in one way or another, including music for solo violin, a complete orchestra, and even a custom-made instrument constructed from glass jugs and hubcaps. And, of course, the live soundtrack for *Tilt Angel*.

The creative team behind Salvage Vanguard Theater believes that their audience is smarter than they are. As such, they produce work that speaks up to, rather than down to, their audience. The results can be electrifying. The company has received numerous local and national awards for its theater work and its audience has grown every year since the company's inception.

In addition to producing new plays, Salvage Vanguard Theater runs an educational program for teens called ArtReach; publishes scripts and releases CDs through Salvage Vanguard Press; and is paving the way for living wages for Austin theater artists through its paid Resident Company.

—Jason Neulander
Artistic Director
Salvage Vanguard Theater
2003

≫ SETTING AND CHARACTERS≪

Characters

OLLIE: Early 20s, big lopsided body, small lopsided brain, a few clumps of colorless hair on an otherwise bald lopsided head

LOIS: 40s, in Act I a memory, in Act II self-transubstantiated into a body composed primarily of fresh vegetables

RED: 40s, right arm ends in a prosthetic pincer-type deal controlled by a harness he wears over his shoulders, brilliant red hair

ANGEL BONES: Impossibly tall and thin, skeletal wings, attached to heaven's umbilical, got a voice box born to sing the blues, from the corner of your eye resembles an airline pilot

Music

The landscape of this play is defined as much by music as by anything else. Angel Bones' songs are all a rough-edged kind of blues, hoarse and soulful and wry. His music weaves through the play, becoming Body Shop Music (connected to Red), Underworld Music (connected to Lois), Cleaning Music (connected to Ollie), and Phone Line Music (disconnected).

Setting

Tiny run down town in East Tennessee. Settings include Red's Body Shop, the House, the Vegetable Garden Out Back the House, the inside of the Phone Line, the Airplane Place, and the Underworld.

Note

An asterisk (*) next to two or more characters' names indicates text which is spoken simultaneously.

— ACT I —

INTRO

HOWL

(*LOIS tumbles through a hard blue sky. ANGEL BONES, perhaps unseen, begins to sing.*)

ANGEL BONES:
> sister sister tell me darling what i gonna do
> i was only born an hour ago and now i'm ninety-two
> sipping from a glass and slipping into bed
> trying to keep the gasoline from dripping out my head
>
> my razor's all rusted and my jeans are fulla holes
> my baby's gonna fly away the second it gets cold
> i got no hair and i got no skin
> my bones are poking out and my face is caving in
>
> sister sister please tell me where i gonna go
> there ain't no windows, someone's banging on the door
> sticking wrinkle fingers through the cracks in the wall
> got my mouth inside a mason jar cause i'm about to howl
>
> i know jesus loves me sister, take me by the hand
> wrap me in those wings of his and help me understand
> but here i'm hanging halfway tween the rising and the fall
> got my mouth inside a mason jar cause i'm about to howl

(*LOIS falls fast. The earth tilts its lips up to meet her.*)

ONE

TILTING BETWEEN POLES

(*OLLIE in the House—a tiny cruddy dwelling, too little to contain his big body. OLLIE is spinning from the pull of multiple gravities.*)

OLLIE: My stomach hangs willowlike from my bones. I'm like some weeping tree, barely hanging on to verticality.

Ma died. Up there. Silver ship, go boom. Commercial Flight Forgets It Has Wings, Abruptly Greets the Planet's Crust, Earthy Embrace Kills 72. Like I said, go boom. Black box, if found, may reveal secret pilot talk. Instrument chatter, coffee and peanuts. But for now, "go boom" will have to do. Ma died. Ma dead.

Dad won't come home from work. Been there since I gave him the news. He says he's got sandwiches enough. Is what he says. Backed up besides he says. This town's become Accident City, USA. Ma dead. Dad working.

Me. Me at home. As per usual. Home is my domain, though my shoulders strain the ceiling beams. Home is my occupation, raison d'etre. Even if I wanted to step out that door (which I don't, heck no, no way, huh-unh) and claim some gainful employment for myself, it would essentially be for naught. Even before they kicked me outta Jeff Davis Junior High I noticed the way people on the street behave in my presence which is to say they take one look at me and sort of tilt, you know, away. So I stay. Me. Me at home.

Home but not alone.

(*Phone rings.*)

OLLIE: Never alone home when you got the phone.

(*OLLIE picks up the phone. Strange breathing sound, like sucking through a straw.*)

OLLIE: Sky Representative, Mister Airline Man, keeps ringing on the line. Dad ain't here, and I ain't fluent in the airline language. Never flown. What some folks might refer to in this modern world as a handicap-type situation. If there's one thing I don't know, it's the sky. But Mister Airline Man don't give up easy. Got a message to deliver, and he's as all-fire serious about getting in your head as fumes off a Clorox bottle.

Mister Airline Man.

And Dad.

And Ma.

And me.

Some days you just wanna get nailed to your bed and stay there.

(*Sucking sound gets louder.* OLLIE *is getting sucked into the phone.*)

OLLIE: Dad? It's for you! DAD!!!!!

(OLLIE *manages to hang up the phone.* RED *appears, deep inside a sweet auto shell. Sure enough, he's got piles of sandwiches, all saran-wrapped, glorious sandwich pyramids, mystic shapes.*)

OLLIE: Dad works in bodies. They are his stock in trade. He bangs out dents with hammers of various sizes, smoothes wrinkled metal back to a perfect curve, reconnects wires torn to shreds and hiss-spitting electric all over the place. He's a surgeon. Cups new plastic over the gap of a broken taillight. Welds a new latch into the waiting mouth of an open hood. He works on bodies. Body Shop.

(*Body Shop Music begins.*)

OLLIE: Body Shop got a music all its own. Percussion ground zero, hollow hole like a bell inside a bell, like a church inside a church. Choir type stuff, I'm serious. Back when I was in the single digits age-wise I'd stand out the side and just tilt my head into the brick and listen. They talk about the sound of salvation when it comes time for Revelations on Sunday Morning Preacher TeeVee. The roar and the clanging, those wheels churning down from heaven to grip and rip the skin off this here earth. The angel horde descending, etc. And I know it's gonna sound like this.

And I take a breath.

And I wonder how I'm gonna stand the wait.

Dad works in bodies, on bodies. On top, on the sides, in the middle, like some great snake he winds round and thru the car. Head under the hood, feet sticking out the trunk. Knee poking outta the glove compartment. Neck rubbing up against ignition. Left hand out the right rear window. Right hand . . . oh. I almost forgot.

Right hand buried in the backyard by the garden. By what was tomatoes, but is now serranos on account of Uncle Emory coming home from Texas with seeds tween his fingers. Right hand buried fleshy side up, fingers flat and mangled, palm cracked, wrist like a chicken neck. Whole thing so like nothing like a hand. Buried. Burst. And reaching.

Right hand kissing the earth. New hand . . .

New hand not a hand. New hand whole like nothing like a hand.

Those serranos don't grow right. Tennessee soil makes em way too hot. Like jalapeno's ugly brother or something. Something bout the soil. Or maybe it's the hand.

Dad is the car. Dad is Detroit Southern-Fried, American-made and pride pride pride. Dad got spark plugs for teeth, electric saliva, burns when he kisses you good night, which he don't do no more on account of I'm a man now, but still when my memory goes loop-the-loop I feel him kissing, burns. Burns when he smiles, too. You can't look at Dad's face directly. Gotta find out who he is by reflection, a pinhole for an e-clipse, a police sketch taken second hand.

Dad got my heart in his hand now.

RED: Quit talking about me.

OLLIE: Heart like nothing like a heart.

RED: Every time you talk about me I get a twitch. Right here.

OLLIE: I wonder if he knows.

RED: I know.

OLLIE: You sure?

RED: I know everything I need to know. I know the third step down from the porch is cracked, makes a creak. I know the big sander over here is shaking, needs replacing. I know eggs fry up best if you don't poke the yolk. What more I gotta know.

OLLIE: You gotta know you gotta come on home.

RED: Nope.

OLLIE: Dad.

RED: Busy.

OLLIE: But . . .

RED: Up to my chest in a '78 Camaro.

OLLIE: But . . .

RED: From the appropriate angle and viewed from a distance you'd swear I was drowning in Chevrolet Steel.

OLLIE: But . . .

RED: But nothing. Okay?

OLLIE: Okay.

RED: Mm-hm.

(*Pause.*)

OLLIE: Dad.

RED: What.

OLLIE: We gotta talk.

RED: No.

OLLIE: It's important.

RED: Work is important. Talk is salad dressing. Okay?

OLLIE: Okay.

RED: Mm-hm.

(*Pause.*)

OLLIE: But Dad.

RED: What.

OLLIE: I'm hungry.

RED: Look in the mirror.

OLLIE: All right.

RED: See that horizontal line below your nose? The one flanked by pucker-pink petals?

OLLIE: Uh-huh.

RED: Stick your fingers into it. Notice the gaping space behind the line.

OLLIE: Uh-huh.

RED: With fingers firm, pry open the line.

OLLIE: Uh-huh.

RED: See the space? The one that gapes?

OLLIE: Uh-huh.

RED: Stuff it with something and shut it. End of lesson. Okay?

OLLIE: Okay.

RED: Mm-hm.

(*Pause.*)

OLLIE: Except but Dad.

RED: What.

OLLIE: There's no food. You took it all.

RED: Only what's mine.

OLLIE: Picked the whole garden clean.

RED: Yep.

OLLIE: Stuffed it between a buncha wonder bread.

RED: Zucchini on white, tomato on white, all my little babies.

OLLIE: Sandwiches enough.

RED: You bet your ass.

OLLIE: I'm starving.

RED: Again, I refer you to your own personal horizontal line.

OLLIE: My stomach . . .

RED: Should only be reached indirectly, like your father.

OLLIE: It's howling. Loud.

RED: Then go down to the piggle-wiggle store and get it some god-damn food. Okay?

(*Pause.*)

RED: OKAY?

OLLIE: I can't.

RED: Sure you can. See those chunks of flesh sticking off the bottom of your legs? The ones made up of flat parts and toe parts?

OLLIE: Uh-huh.

RED: They are forward motion machines. The toe parts grip the earth and then the flat parts launch you precisely one step ahead. Stick one machine in front of the other and get your butt out the door.

OLLIE: NO!

RED: You make me sick. What would you do in the event of a fire?

OLLIE: Uh.

RED: Of an earthquake?

OLLIE: Uh. Call 911?

RED: You know what they'd do?

OLLIE: What?

RED: Send over a buncha paramedics to propel your lousy ass outta the goddamn house straight into the pollen-stained air that's what.

OLLIE: NO!

RED: You're a grown man, Ollie. Twenty-one. Ain't you got grand plans or something? When I was your age I had grand plans.

OLLIE: I'm too busy to plan.

RED: Busy doing what?

OLLIE: Cleaning.

RED: Jesus. I ask God for a son, he gives me a maid.

OLLIE: I'm beautifying the home.

RED: Nine years. World's changed, Ollie. Evolved. Ain't you the least bit curious?

OLLIE: I got a window.

RED: Which you avoid like a dogdoo soufflé. Christ. Your skin's like wax paper.

OLLIE: I'm busy, I'm cleaning!

RED: You're see-thru! As in translucent. As in you'd get sunburn from a bright idea. Now do me a favor and silence yourself. I am currently earning the cash to keep us on this earth.

OLLIE: I can't silence my self.

RED: Again I mention those forward motion machines (hereafter referred to as FMMs) at the bottom of your legs.

OLLIE: What about them?

RED: Place one hand firmly around one of the FMMs.

OLLIE: All right.

RED: Using the fingers of the free hand, pry open the previously deliberated-upon horizontal line.

OLLIE: Uh-huh.

RED: Now. Lift the FMM way up and place it directly and entirely within the gaping hole behind your horizontal line. Two birds, one stone, end of lesson. Okay?

OLLIE: (*Muffled.*)

RED: OKAY?

OLLIE: (*MUFFLED!*)

RED: Mm-hm.

OLLIE: DAD MA DIED!

(*Pause.*)

RED: This information does not fall under the category of "breaking news," Ollie.

OLLIE: She died and I'm home alone and the guy called again.

RED: What guy?

OLLIE: Sky Guy.

RED: Tell him we ain't in the market.

OLLIE: He's real insistent.

RED: Oh yeah? Well, I am immovable. Where the hell's that ratchet wrench . . .

OLLIE: Then talk to him.

RED: No time.

OLLIE: Dad, we gotta get her back.

RED: Huh?

OLLIE: Whatever's left. The remains.

RED: Ain't no remains. She was incinerated, son.

OLLIE: Personal effects.

RED: Fried. The final blight upon a family unit already gone freakishly awry.

OLLIE: Well, something's hanging on, cause Sky Guy won't quit. Maybe he wants to pay for the funeral.

RED: Ain't no funeral.

OLLIE: Or cremation or whatever.

RED: Nope.

OLLIE: What do you mean?

RED: She made her bed, etc.

OLLIE: We gotta do something. To put her to rest.

RED: Says who?

OLLIE: She's our Ma. We're supposed to. Rest in Peace. It's like a natural law.

RED: Your Mother was not a natural woman. She did not obey laws. She ate breakfast at 11 P.M. Took walks at 3 in the morning. Had long distance phone conversations that cost an arm and a leg and two toes besides. She subscribed to *The New Yorker* for god's sake. Your Mother and Nature never got along.

OLLIE: Her body's in a mess, Dad. We gotta get it straight.

RED: . . . piece of shit body panel, come on! . . .

OLLIE: It's what's done. It's how the world stays clean.

RED: Goddamn, Ollie, peek out your window and digest the landscape a moment. You see anything that could be classified as clean around here? You're in modern-day Tennessee, son. Even the country music's contaminated.

OLLIE: It's what's done. What's dead is put to rest. It's how the world stays clean.

RED: Fucking moron . . .

OLLIE: It's how the world stays . . .

RED: CLEAN! OUT! YOUR! EARS! And get it thru your head. She abandoned us both.

(*Pause.*)

OLLIE: She's gonna be mad.

RED: Oh yeah? Well, let her. Let her!

(*RED bashes at the car body around him furiously.*)

RED: LET HER! LET HER! LET HER!

(*He stops, catches his breath.*)

RED: Let her do her worst.

(*The Chevy swallows RED whole.*)

OLLIE: (*To Audience.*) Ma was flying off. Silver ship. Left a note. Went something like this:

(*Sound of a jet plane racing overhead. LOIS appears.*)

LOIS: Dear Red,
  If you're reading this, I am far and long gone. I imagine at some point we'll have to figure out the legalities, etc., but for now just think of me as gone. This backwater red dirt Tennessee town has spit me out and I am flying headfirst for new horizons. I saved up some cash through coupons and other slow dripping means of accrual and am heading over to Memphis. I got accepted fair and square and I'm going university and you can't stop me. Anyhow, I'll call when the ground levels out.
  You never broke my bones. You never much complained. You never let us starve. You can sleep easy. You held up your end. But this house is full of wrinkling fingers and plastic place mats. I know where everything is, and no matter how I rearrange the pots and pans, I can still find them in a tick. Without thinking. All the spices are labeled, and they rattle in the rack every step I take. Oregano. Marjoram. Like teeth in wintertime. My ribcage burst when you weren't looking. And a pearl popped out. That's about all I can say. Tell Ollie I love him and I know one day his brain will catch up with the rest of his body.
  Goodbye,
  Lois
  P.S. Those serranos of yours are taking over the garden.

Someone oughta do something.

OLLIE: Ma?

LOIS: Yes, baby?

OLLIE: Maybe I can follow?

LOIS: (*Affectionate.*) You never did know how to place a question mark.

OLLIE: Ma, you can't go. There's too much to do. Washing the dishes and scrubbing the tub and polishing the chromy-type shower handles and folding the laundry so's the corners don't bunch up and the collars don't get crumply and I miss you and making the beds and rearranging the beer bottles inside the fridge and attempting to start up the nasty old vacuum that's a two-person job Ma that thing's pure evil you said so yourself—

LOIS: I'm sorry, Ollie.

OLLIE: Ma! Wait! Can we play it once? Before you go?

LOIS: Okay. Pick a category.

OLLIE: Uh . . . Southern Hemisphere for 100.

LOIS: Southern Hemisphere for 100. The answer is: This country shares its name with a song by Ary Barroso and S. K. Russel and a film directed by Terry Gilliam.

OLLIE: What is . . . um . . . shoot.

LOIS: Need some help?

OLLIE: Yes, please.

LOIS: (*Whispers.*) What is Brazil?

OLLIE: (*Triumphant.*) WHAT IS BRAZIL!

LOIS: DING! DING! DING! You got it!

OLLIE: Again! Again!

LOIS: Pick a category.

OLLIE: Um. Arachnids for 200.

LOIS: The answer is: This little family man is the most poisonous spider in the world. Lucky for us his teeth are too small to pierce a person's skin.

OLLIE: Um.

LOIS: Come on, baby. You can do it.

OLLIE: Um . . . it's . . . I . . . I think I knew it once, but . . . shoot.

LOIS: Help?

OLLIE: Yes, please.

LOIS: (*Whisper.*) What is a Daddy Longlegs?

OLLIE: WHAT IS A DADDY LONGLEGS!
LOIS: DING DING DING!!!
OLLIE: Again! Again!
LOIS: Can't. Gotta go.
OLLIE: No!
LOIS: You got a phone call.
OLLIE: Huh?

(*LOIS disappears. Phone rings. OLLIE answers. Sucking sound.*)

OLLIE: Dad! Dad, it's him again!

(*OLLIE struggles with the phone.*)

OLLIE: (*To RED.*) It ain't right, you know. Everybody deserves some kinda funeral.
RED: If the whole world thought like you there'd be bones popping up in my garden like weeds.
OLLIE: Come home. Answer the phone.
RED: Whole world thought like you, you couldn't take a step without stubbing your toe against a tombstone.
OLLIE: Come home and answer!
RED: Whole world . . .
OLLIE: DAD! PLEASE!
RED: AIN'T YOU GOT WHITES TO WHITEN OR SOMETHING?! GO AWAY! GET A JOB!
OLLIE: Answer. Home.

(*RED stops working, stares at OLLIE. Then he grabs a sandwich and—without removing the plastic wrap—takes a huge defiant bite.*)

TWO

OLLIE WORKS IN THE HOME

OLLIE: AND I GOT A JOB! It's marrow'd through my bones. Right

here. Dad don't understand it cause there's only one job good
enough for a son of his to have and that's . . .

(The earth begins to tilt on its axis.)

OLLIE: NO!!!!

(Earth tilts back. Everything is normal.)

OLLIE: Nine years. Nine years? Can't be that long.

(OLLIE ties a frilly filthy teeny-weeny apron on.)

OLLIE: Work? Dad don't comprehend the Webster's of the word. I'm
the one that knows from work. Knee-deep in dirt here, this
house don't clean itself. You would not believe the mold situation. You would not believe the bathroom, what's growing on
the grout. I scrub, rub deep, like a Chattanooga stripminer, peel
up paleolithic layers, and still it won't come clean. And the
dust? Thick, like mudpies hanging in the air. Dad says it's cause
the house is so old. Three generations. The dirt is entrenched.
Feels like we ain't living here so much as we're planted here. In
soil. Stinks. Work? Watch me. I bear Home on my back like
Atlas, carry it thru the day. I scrub.

*(OLLIE hits the floor and starts scrubbing. The earth rotates, sick-
orange sun rolls over the sky, rattles off the edge, yellow moon follows suit. OLLIE scrubs. His housework makes a kind of music:
Cleaning Music.)*

OLLIE: Grease. Car-grease. Tracked in by Dad. Scrimshawed into the
vinyl tile. I peel up a layer of dirt, read it like tea leaves.

(OLLIE reads the dirt. RED flickers into OLLIE's mind's eye.)

OLLIE: Dust. Book-dust. Sandstormed in from the library by Ma. I
suck up a bit, listen.

(*OLLIE listens to the dust. LOIS comes into view.*)

OLLIE: Our history is contained here. We walk upon it, an uneven gait. And new history falls from our feet to feed the old. We walk. We tilt. And all the Windex in the world won't take that away. Fresh starts are for commercials. This here's for real.

(*OLLIE peels a layer of soil from the linoleum floor. He reads it like a filmstrip from the underfunded school he was forcibly removed from.*)

OLLIE: They breathe. The air is full of almost raindrops. They can smell each other.
RED: You like it here?
LOIS: It smells like gasoline.
RED: Always. Grandpa Red said it smelled like that even before he laid the foundations. The very soil told him how to shape his life. What he was gonna be.
LOIS: It's a serious stink. I like it.
RED: You get used to it. Me too.
OLLIE: They breathe. The air is a cupful of questions. Surface tension.
RED: I can see you in my life.
LOIS: Huh?
RED: You fit perfectly over this gray area in my dreams. It's like a e-clipse. It's that bright.
LOIS: I like your hands.
RED: You got these lips just make me lose my mind.
LOIS: My lips?
RED: They talk to my mind and I lose it.
OLLIE: The air is a surface. They cup it with their bodies. And breathe. And ...

(*The layer of dirt crumbles to dust. RED and LOIS crumble and are gone. OLLIE just crumbles.*)

OLLIE: When the old dirt filmstrips get to be too much, I stop reading with my eyes. Start reading with my hands and feet. Find something far back. Or maybe future. Fresh. Fast fast forward.

And when I got it in my bones I go like this:

(*OLLIE begins his Home Beautification Dance. It is a patchwork of different styles, from tango to cha-cha to hip-hop. He dances around the house, which begins to gleam. It feels like some big musical number, larger than life, OLLIE is joyous and magnificent. Then the phone rings. Music quits. Gleam dies.*)

OLLIE: DAD? DAD!

(*Phone continues to ring. OLLIE circles it.*)

OLLIE: (*To phone.*) I can't. You hear? It's him you want. I'm just me.

(*Phone rings.*)

OLLIE: I'm busy. Home Beautification is an eternal struggle. One lapse and . . .

(*Phone rings.*)

OLLIE: Please. I can't go. I don't know how to breathe out there. I don't know the air. I . . .

(*Phone rings. OLLIE shuts his eyes.*)

OLLIE: Ma.

(*Phone rings. OLLIE opens his eyes.*)

OLLIE: Okay.

(*OLLIE picks up the phone. Sucking sound.*)

OLLIE: Yes. This is Ollie. I am ready to take your call.

(*OLLIE is sucked into the phone.*)

THREE

RED SPEAKS I

(Body Shop Music. RED works. Music fizzles and dies. RED stops, stares at audience. He starts again, music jerks back to life . . . then chokes and quits again. RED stops, stares at audience. He goes back to work. Music starts, instantly dies. RED throws a hammer at the wall. He strides down to the audience and stares at them. His prosthetic claw clicker-clacks impatiently.)

RED: Say it. Spit em out. Don't just sit there thinking, making brainwave patty cake like I can't hear you. Car body is a natural sounding board, amplified with live wires and wheels, I can hear every little thought you send my way. So speak it. You're just like her. She did the same thing. Got so's I couldn't keep my own thoughts in my head anymore, hers were always ringing to be let in. She had a problem, it was like fucking Tchaikovsky in the house, this brutal silent symphony, cannons and shit going off, Fourth of Fucking JUST SAY IT!!!

(Pause.)

RED: Sorry. I don't mean to. We're backed up body-wise. It's all I can do to keep upright and angled appropriately. I apologize. You wouldn't believe the number of wrecks in this town. We got at least one wreck per person, seems. Maybe more. This continuous buckling under, getting so the cars gonna crumple up on their own. Without impact or provocation.

And now a plane. Can't fix that. Something dis-integrates, body shop ain't gonna do much good.

(RED pulls out a piece of paper, unfolds it. LOIS appears.)

LOIS: Dear Red,

If you're reading this, I am far and long

(RED *stuffs the paper back in his pocket.* LOIS *vanishes.*)

RED: College. Shoulda seen it coming. All them initials started popping up in the house: PBS, NPR, fucking ACLU. Shoulda known. Come home from a hard day, no more Patsy Cline or even Clint Black cooing at me from the stereo, nothing but

(RED *hums the theme to* NPR's All Things Considered.)

RED: Drive a man to drinking habits, know what I mean?
  I mean, Christ, it was supposed to be Ollie! Ollie was supposed to be the one eating up the history books and the physics books and the, not Lois! He was the one born lopsided skull-wise, same as Einstein, doctor said, could be a genius, doctor said, oughta encourage that, said. And I did. Even after he got kicked outta sixth grade for good, I said Home School the little bugger (course he was six foot by that time, but still little on the inside, you know), I said, Lois: Teach! Start watching *Jeopardy* with the little guy, see if something sticks. And then one day I get home and . . .

(LOIS *appears.*)

LOIS: . . . and Alex Trebek was shooting through these categories, Songs, American Geography, Rhyme Time, and they start getting kinda weird, you know, insane categories, Former Clockmakers, Swedish Cuss-Words, just nuts, and Alex is getting faster and faster, his voice spilling outta his lips, and the contestants can't keep up, everything just speeding up crazy and then Alex Trebek turns his face to the camera and screams
  AAAAAAAAAIIIIIIIIIIIIIIEEEEEEEEEEEEEEEE!!!
  like a banshee caught on a barb wire fence
  AAAAAAAAAAIIIIIIIIIIIIIIIEEEEEEEEEEEEEEEEE!!!
  And then he sprouts golden wings his eyes turn to fire his voice ringing like bells inside bells inside bells. And he sticks his head through the teevee into my living room, his neck long like a snake, his face bobbing up and down and then Alex Trebek

says to me, "Lois, isn't it about time you found some questions to these answers?"

And then the teevee goes dead. Nothing but black glass.

RED: How does a man respond to that? His own home. Wife. What is the correct response?

LOIS: Books.

RED: Never read a book in her life that wasn't published by Better Homes and Gardens, now look at her.

LOIS: Walked over to the library and checked out a pile of books so high there was bird's nests in the top one by the time I got home. Plato's *Republic*. Robins.

RED: Said she was teaching the baby.

LOIS: I was teaching the baby.

RED: Teaching yourself.

LOIS: And the baby.

RED: Baby didn't learn.

LOIS: Baby can't learn. Info drips out his ears, stains his pillow blue.

RED: Baby can too learn.

LOIS: And he wasn't a baby, he was a pubescent, and a big one!

RED: He can too learn. Learns words. Big words. Belches em out like a antitank gun, you gotta do a duck and cover every time he finds a crossword.

LOIS: Red. Face it. He don't have any understanding. You look behind his eyes and it's just blue sky. On and on and on.

RED: You gave up on him.

LOIS: Well if that ain't the whole pot/kettle equation.

RED: Took the books for yourself and handed him a sponge. List of chores a mile long. Did permanent damage to his male-type ego. He coulda been a genius.

LOIS: Bullshit.

RED: Einstein's head, Lois. Like this.

LOIS: You know damn well why his head came out like that, Red.

(*Pause.*)

RED: You gave up on us. Whole little family. Shot to shit. High school wasn't good enough for you?

LOIS: I got hungry, Red. Ain't you ever got hungry?
RED: That's what a garden's for.
LOIS: Ain't my garden. Never been.

(*LOIS disappears as an airplane passes overhead.*)

RED: Form of a question, my ass.
　　　Don't look at me like that. I ain't trying to keep her from learning. Learning's good. I'm for it, hundred percent. But University? Memphis? Now? Shoulda thoughta that before we got married, had a kid, settled into gear. I can't go nowhere. Shop's been in the family three generations now. Horseless Carriage Repair for my Granddad, Automobile Fixer-Upper for my Daddy, and for me, Body Shop. Three lives bound up in here, bouncing off the brick, sticking to the corners. Can see my Granddad sticking a bit over there, in a place the broom don't reach and the hose don't wanna go. Like a cobweb, thick and stringy, only red. We all been Red. Until Ollie.

(*RED looks down at his prosthetic claw.*)

RED: I guess some things ain't supposed to be passed down. Some things supposed to go extinct. Better that way.

FOUR

BLACK ICE FIBER OPTIC BOBSLED

(*OLLIE is sliding/soaring/sucking through the phone line. It's like a vertical bobsled, all forward motion, slick as black ice. The sucking sound is very present, along with Phone Line Music—the voice of disconnect.*)

OLLIE:
　　　shhh shhh shhh shhh
　　　shhh shhh shhh shhh

Hello?
shhhhhhhhhhhhhhhhh
Hello?
Hello?
shhhhhhhhhhhhhhhhhh
Hello?
receiver like a pinprick
shhhh shhhh shhhh
licking at my chin
shhhh shhhh shhhh
lips first face first
shh shh shh shh
eyes I'm diving in
Hello?
Hello?
voice like a razor blade
stony bony mouth
breathing like a compass spinning
norther wester south
shhhhhhhhhhhhh
receiver like a pinprick
licking at my chin
shhhh
lips first face first eyes I'm diving oh
Hello?
Hello?
Hello?
ohhhhhhhhhhhhhhhhOHHHHHHHHHHHHHHHHHHHHHHH
Wrong number
Wrong number
There's no one
here by that—

(*The phone spits* OLLIE *out at the other end of the line. It's dark. A shadow behind him speaks.*)

ANGEL BONES: Hello.

FIVE

RED SPEAKS II

(*RED is moving his prosthetic pincer open and shut, open and shut.*)

RED: It's an old model. Made it myself, right here in my shop. Ain't pretty, but that's life when you got no HMO. I use my shoulders. See? Shift them in and out, up and down. Open. Shut. Open. Shut. Reach. Grab. Hang on. Let go. I use my shoulder muscles. Feels like I got wings back there. Sometimes.

(*RED slowly removes his prosthesis, hangs it over the car door. He flexes and stretches his real hand beneath it.*)

RED: Funny. I can still see it. After damn near a decade. Feel the fibers pulling when I go like this. Like it never left. But it ain't here. This is what some folks would call a mirage. Trick of the mind, cornea practical joke, lonely nervous system calling long distance for an old friend. Calling collect. How many fingers am I holding up? None. Do not believe what you see.

Sometimes, when I go like this . . . I feel earth between my fingers. Soil. Little rocks. Bugs and worms and what have you. Sometimes, I go like this . . . and I can feel it moving. Creeping underground. Crawling toward the carrots, cabbages, brussel-type sprouts. I been practicing. The goal I have set for myself is to touch the subterranean tip of my finger against the root of one of my vegetables. That's it. I'm miles away right now. But I got time.

She just about killed me when she found out I buried it in the backyard. "Red!" she says.

(*LOIS appears.*)

LOIS: Red!
RED: "Red," she says.

LOIS: Red!

RED: "You're like

LOIS: You're like some goddamn dog. Bad enough you're always digging stuff up out there, letting that snarl of a garden take over what was once a perfectly good backyard sitting-type area. Now you go and bury your ripped up smashed in burst out HAND back there?

RED: What am I supposed to do with it? Hang it from the ceiling fan?

LOIS: You give it to a specialist. A medical waste operative at the hospital. They got baggies, sealed baggies for situations like this.

RED: Sealed baggies. Bullshit.

LOIS: You have created a biohazard in our backyard.

RED: Biohazard?

LOIS: What is a risk or danger to life or health, especially that resulting from biological experimentation?

RED: (*To audience.*) See what I gotta live with?

LOIS: That does it. From this moment forward, I will not eat a single piece of produce from that garden. Do you hear me? Not a single nibble on a single leaf.

RED: Just what do you think fertilizer is, Lois?

LOIS: It ain't thumbs and digits and metacarpal—

RED: Meta-what?

LOIS: WHAT ARE ANY OF THE BONES OF THE PART OF THE HAND CONSISTING OF THE FIVE BONES BETWEEN THE WRIST AND THE FINGERS!

RED: (*To audience.*) You think this is bad, you should hear her rattle off the reasons why I oughta be a Democrat.

LOIS: Well they can't, cause I'm dead.

(*Pause.*)

RED: I know. I got ears.

LOIS: Can't seem to hear the phone.

RED: Hey. Like so much of this America, I am currently overworked.

LOIS: Bury his hand, won't bury his wife.

RED: Your body ain't my fault. You shoulda took the bus.

LOIS: Wings, not wheels. Understand?

RED: No. I don't. Weren't you happy? Weren't we happy?

LOIS: Are you serious?

RED: Guess that's a "no"?

LOIS: Red. None of us were.

RED: Don't speak for me.

LOIS: Right. Don't speak. Your answer to it all. And me stuck in that silence, tween a father and son who decide one day out of the blue to up and start a cold war on each other. No rhyme or reason. And no talking. Just circling each other, day in, day out, year after year, like a pair of fucked-up homing pigeons.

RED: You don't know nothing about it.

LOIS: So educate me! Tell me what happened.

RED: That's between him and me.

LOIS: Come home from the grocer, twelve-year-old boy curled up in the tub, bellowing enough to rattle water from the faucet. Water from his eyes. And then you. Four in the morning. Stumble in drunk with . . . without.

RED: I remember.

LOIS: Neighbors saying they don't want Ollie around their kids no more . . .

RED: I remember plenty.

LOIS: Then kicked outta school.

RED: I remember from that night on you wouldn't take a touch from me without shrinking into the wallpaper.

LOIS: That ain't fair.

RED: I come home needing some support, little reassurance, you turn me into a monster.

LOIS: You didn't need my help with that.

RED: Turn yourself invisible. Regular Houdini, you are.

LOIS: I was thrown for the proverbial loop, Red.

RED: The Amazing Lois and her Vanishing Act! Watch as she disappears before your very eyes! Oh her body's still there folks, but her heart and soul have flown the fucking coop!

LOIS: Me? You're the one went dead cold. I swear some nights in that bed you'd think it was more than your hand got chopped off.

RED: Cause I could tell your heart wasn't in it. Married to a cripple. I don't need that kinda charity, Lois.

LOIS: I wasn't offering charity, I was offering me.

RED: Can you blame me for not believing you? You turned our bed into a fucking library.

LOIS: That was after you shut down!

RED: No it was why I shut—

LOIS: Yes! Yes, Red! It's true! If I couldn't make it with you, I was damn sure gonna make it with Nietzsche! With Proust! With Kant!

RED: YOU TRYING TO TELL ME YOU'RE A LESBIAN?!

(*Pause.*)

LOIS: That is the dumbest thing ever fell outta your face.

(*Pause.*)

LOIS: Look. Maybe I was nervous at first, but . . .

RED: Nervous? If I stroked your cheek we had to call the paramedics to peel you from the ceiling.

LOIS: You never stroked my cheek, that ain't your style.

RED: Here it comes.

LOIS: Here. Here. And here.

RED: Here we go.

LOIS: That was your favorite pattern, wasn't it, hon? And I memorized it. Got so I could flinch in the right rhythm, minimize the pain. Don't worry. I don't blame you.

RED: You can't blame me.

LOIS: I had eyes. I knew what I was getting into when I took the heat of your ring around my finger. And I didn't care. Raging man with good hands. Even when they were bad.

RED: You're talking fog again Lois.

LOIS: But one time you went just a little too far.

RED: Misting up my windshield.

LOIS: Here. Here. And here.

RED: Hot air and condensation.

LOIS: (*Points to her abdomen.*) But in here . . .

RED: You know, half of these incidents you refer to I got no recollection of . . .

LOIS: In here was more than lung power this time.

RED: . . . and the other half I got alibis out the wazoo.

LOIS: More than hot air and condensation.

RED: You make this shit up and sew it all over me like skin. I must look like fucking Frankenstein to you. A crazy quilt of open hand and back hand and full on fist.

LOIS: If the glove fits.

RED: In my entire life, I hit you once.

LOIS: Once upon a time.

RED: Beg pardon?

LOIS: Sorry. Thought you were starting another one of your fairy tales. If you're so damn innocent, reach out for your son. See if he comes running to take your hand.

(RED *looks like he just got socked in the gut. Beat.*)

RED: (*Slow and vicious.*) I hope it hurt. I hope that fuselage ripped you into a hundred ugly pieces. Like you're doing to me right now.

LOIS: I'm just talking true.

RED: Don't talk about my son. I know my son.

LOIS: Bull. I'm the one spent year after year walking through the empty rooms in his head, trying to put up curtains and shit. Make something stick.

RED: He and me got things in common. Somewhere in our bodies. I bet we got identical kidneys.

LOIS: He's about as far from you as summer to frost.

RED: I bet we got identical teeth.

LOIS: Oh no. Your smile. Like an e-clipse. That hazardous. No body on this planet got such teeth.

(*Pause.*)

RED: All these years you were hating my guts.

LOIS: No.

RED: You hated my guts so you left.

LOIS: I left because the questions changed. Because my signature started unraveling and I liked the new shapes it made. Because I knew you wouldn't go with me.

RED: Well. You won't be going anywhere anytime soon.

LOIS: Red.

RED: Nope. You made your choice.

LOIS: Bury his hand, won't bury his wife.

RED: No wife of mine. Or did you forget the whole "Goodbye Forever" letter you left.

LOIS: You're the one who said you'd never move.

RED: Body Shop, Lois.

LOIS: Don't you ever get sick of this trailer town?

RED: Three Generations.

LOIS: Three generations of trash.

RED: You wanna repeat that to my face?

LOIS: I said I married a piece a trash come from a long line of garbage.

RED: Yeah? Well, this piece of trash from that long long line is still stepping around on top of the ground. More'n you can say.

LOIS: I married the dumbest man on earth.

RED: Yep. And "I do" was the dumbest thing I ever did.

LOIS: Bastard.

RED: Bitch.

LOIS: Loser.

RED: Bitch.

LOIS: No-good, brainless, spineless pile of—

RED: BITCH!!!! Get outta my head! Stay in pieces at the airplane place where you belong. Stay in flight. Forever. Scattered. And gone.

(*LOIS vanishes. RED puts his prosthetic hand back on.*)

RED: (*To audience.*) What?
    Mm-hm.
    That's what I thought you said.

(*RED goes back to work.*)

SIX

CLAIMING REMAINS

OLLIE: Huh?
ANGEL BONES: Said hello. Extended you a greeting.

(*ANGEL BONES extends impossibly.*)

OLLIE: Shadow extends, drips over, says howdo. Shadow with wings,
all flying the friendly. My head's still buzzing from phone line
static, I tip sideways and clear the conversations from my ears.

(*He beats his ears, and bits of phone conversations tumble out.*)

OLLIE: Sorry.
ANGEL BONES: Not at all, friend.

(*ANGEL BONES picks up the conversations, holds them above his
open mouth. They writhe like insects. He drops them in and swallows. Burps—sounds like redial.*)

OLLIE: Are you Sky Guy? Mister Airplane Man?
    You been dialing our house, looking for identification?
ANGEL BONES: You must be Oliver.
OLLIE: I prefer Ollie.
ANGEL BONES: (*Making a notation.*) "Ollie."
OLLIE: How'd you know my name?

(*ANGEL BONES holds out a file. OLLIE touches the file. LOIS
and RED appear.*)

RED: We can't name him Oliver, it sounds like a vegetable.
LOIS: Oliver Cromwell.
RED: Vegetable.
LOIS: Oliver Wendell Holmes.
RED: Please pass the olivers.

LOIS: Shut up.

RED: Why, which olivers do you mean: the black or the pimento-
stuffed?

LOIS: We aren't naming him Red.

RED: What's wrong with Red?

LOIS: It's creepy. Like having a clone around the house.

RED: Tradition.

LOIS: What if he's a blond?

RED: He ain't gonna be blond. My family has one gene that will
steamroller over anything that gets in its way, and that's hair
color for males. You're a male, you're a Red. Period.

LOIS: Okay. I'll make you a deal. If his hair is red, we'll call him Red.
But if it is any color other than a brilliant, dominant strain of
red, we shall name him—

(*LOIS and RED vanish.*)

ANGEL BONES: "Ollie."

OLLIE: I come to identify remains.

ANGEL BONES: You're late.

OLLIE: Nope. Just slow. Wingless.

ANGEL BONES: Give me your hand.

OLLIE: Sky Guy got a grip makes me question my masculinity.

ANGEL BONES: so nice

OLLIE: Makes me question compass points and road signs.

ANGEL BONES: to make

OLLIE: Makes me question opinion polls and teevee game show
hosts.

ANGEL BONES: your

OLLIE: Makes me question the very punctuation of my life.

ANGEL BONES: acquaintance

OLLIE: (*Sings.*)
    unravel me fingers
    ghost man is here
    beneath nails slip me
    lodge and remain
    within wingspan

his fingers
his hand

(*Pause.*)

OLLIE: Scuse me. Don't usually sing like that. Strange outbursts are not my stock in trade.
ANGEL BONES: What is your stock in trade?
OLLIE: I work in the home.
ANGEL BONES: Telecommuter?
OLLIE: Do what now?
ANGEL BONES: Area of expertise?
OLLIE: Cleanliness.
ANGEL BONES: Could you be more specific?

(*OLLIE jumps into his Home Beautification Dance for few seconds, then stops, exhausted.*)

OLLIE: Sorry. Ain't really up for that kinda revelation.
ANGEL BONES: You're right. My bad.
    Age?
OLLIE: Indeterminate.
ANGEL BONES: Come again?
OLLIE: Dad insists it's twenty-one. But I feel I'm on a different kinda time line.
ANGEL BONES: Height.
OLLIE: Gargantuan.
ANGEL BONES: Weight?
OLLIE: More'n enough to tie me to the ground.
ANGEL BONES: Hair color?
OLLIE: Disappointing.
ANGEL BONES: Fingerprint.

(*ANGEL BONES reaches for OLLIE. OLLIE shies away.*)

OLLIE: You got enough of me already.
ANGEL BONES: Fair enough.

OLLIE: You got something for me to sign?
ANGEL BONES: After.

(*ANGEL BONES uncurls an eighteen-foot finger and points toward a box.*)

OLLIE: Oh.

(*Pause.*)

ANGEL BONES: Cigarette?
OLLIE: Ain't flights supposed to be nonsmoking?
ANGEL BONES: Yep. Non-crashing, too. Want one?
OLLIE: Never tried it.
ANGEL BONES: Really? Not a single drag?
OLLIE: I got innocent lungs.
ANGEL BONES: Cleanliness.
OLLIE: Huh?
ANGEL BONES: Just had a vision of you slipping quick and sideways through the eye of a needle. Leaving no filmy residue behind.
OLLIE: Funny. I just had a vision of you. Stuck screaming on the head of a pin.
ANGEL BONES: You ain't far off, Ollie.

(*OLLIE reaches for the box. He opens it a crack. LOIS suddenly appears, along with the roar of jet engines.*)

LOIS: ladies and gentlemen at this time

(*OLLIE shuts it, LOIS vanishes.*)

ANGEL BONES: Ask me, it's a job for the husband.
OLLIE: He's got sandwiches enough.
ANGEL BONES: I like you, Ollie.
OLLIE: Well you creep me out a bit.
ANGEL BONES: You'll change your tune.
OLLIE: Think so?

ANGEL BONES: Know so. I got a way of growing all over you.

(*ANGEL BONES exits. OLLIE opens the box.*)

OLLIE: Hello?

(*LOIS and jet engine sound come back.*)

LOIS: ladies and gentlemen at this time ladies and gentlemen at this time this time ladies and I'm going to have to ask you to ladies and gentle to ask you to remain calm and assume the ladies and gentlemen crash position assume the calm crash at this time position ask ladies and gentlemen I'm going crash and ask ladies and remain gentletime maybes and tentlight position and babies and candlemen crash time this time this time have to ask i'm going to have to ask maybes and brittlemen at this time i'm going i'm going i'm gentle i'm going i'm gentle and time is this brittle maybe
> time is this brittle maybe
> time is this brittle maybe
> time is this

(*OLLIE shuts the box.*)

OLLIE: It's her.

(*Pause.*)

OLLIE: I SAID IT'S HER!

(*RED appears in the Body Shop, asleep in a pile of sandwiches. He jolts awake.*)

RED: Who's there?

(*ANGEL BONES goes to OLLIE.*)

ANGEL BONES: Ollie?
RED: Ollie?
OLLIE: That's me.
ANGEL BONES: Sign here.

(*OLLIE signs. His name appears on RED's body. RED scratches if off like a rash. Won't go away. Finally, RED takes a brushful of red touch-up paint and smears the word "RED" over OLLIE's name.*)

ANGEL BONES: On behalf of Cloud Umbilical Airlines, let me say how sorry we are for your loss.
OLLIE: I gotta go now. Gimme my mother.

(*OLLIE takes the remains.*)

OLLIE: You got a phone I can hitch a ride on?
ANGEL BONES: She won't fit.
OLLIE: On foot then. Less you can carry me.
ANGEL BONES: Gotta work late today.
OLLIE: You and my Daddy oughta split a ball game sometime.
ANGEL BONES: Split something anyway.
　　Bye Ollie.
OLLIE: Bye Sky Guy.

SEVEN

MOTHER WEIGHT

(*OLLIE heaves the box onto his shoulders like some kind of Atlas, bears it home. ANGEL BONES sings.*)

ANGEL BONES:
　　dirt black
　　clay red
　　chewing on my shoes

heavy heavy bones
make me sink

big flat
rain drops
plastic wrap my eyes

heavy heavy bones
make me sink

family
pine tree
sing to me
vertically
prick the sky
needle-wise
thread the eye
stitch up my
mouth
stitch up my
howl
ing
mouth

heavy heavy bones
and i think i'm gonna sink

EIGHT

BURIAL

(*OLLIE gets home. He sets the box down. The earth shudders. He
picks up the phone, dials. ANGEL BONES answers.*)

ANGEL BONES: Heaven's Anchor Funeral Home.
OLLIE: I got a Mother to bury.
ANGEL BONES: Can you hold please?

OLLIE: Busy day?
ANGEL BONES: Accident City, USA.
OLLIE: I'll wait.

(*Hold Music, a Phone Line Music negative.* OLLIE *waits.* RED *comes up behind him.*)

RED: House looks nice.
OLLIE: Dad!
RED: No one can polish up the dust like you, kid. Each grain got its own particular shine.
OLLIE: You scared me.
RED: That's unfortunate. Son scared of his father. Ain't right.

(RED *smiles.* OLLIE *looks away.*)

RED: Doing something on the phone?
OLLIE: Dad.
RED: Got some kinda objective there?
OLLIE: Shouldn't you be at work?
RED: Came home.
OLLIE: Why?
RED: Ain't that what you wanted?
OLLIE: I got what I wanted. On my own.
RED: So what's in the container?
OLLIE: She deserves it, Dad.
RED: That your lunch? Some kinda box lunch?
OLLIE: Go away.
RED: Mind if I chew on a bit?
OLLIE: Thought you were all sandwiched.
RED: Man craves variety.
OLLIE: She deserves it, Dad. Everyone deserves some kinda peace.
RED: She was abandoning us, Ollie. Leaving us to our own devices. Taking off blue yonder-wise, greener skies, pastures, what have you.
OLLIE: She'd have come back.
RED: You don't know her.

OLLIE: She'd have come back for me.

RED: You really don't know her.

OLLIE: (*To phone.*) Hello? I been on hold for years here!

(*RED snatches the phone out of his hand with his claw. Hold Music cuts off.*)

OLLIE: OW!

RED: I've told you before, son. Keep clear of this thing. Mind of its own. Bleeding? Lemme see.

OLLIE: You got some kinda bitter in you, Dad.

RED: I eat what grows.
Lemme see. Come here. Come on.
Father's arms. Open wide. Waiting.

(*OLLIE doesn't move.*)

RED: See, there's another natural law floating around this ball of muck, Ollie. It pertains to the living. Man gets treated like Monster, Man becomes Monster. Reverse Physiology. Or something. Now I am trying to take care of you. Come here.

(*OLLIE doesn't move.*)

RED: I can see we've come to an impasse.

OLLIE: Go away.

RED: Give me the box.

(*Pause.*)

RED: Wait a minute. How'd you get ahold of that? You leave the house? I'll be damned. Look at you. You got sun. Give me the box.

(*Pause.*)

RED: I am her husband. Her body, upon giving up the ghost, is my territory.

(*Pause.*)

RED: Hey, Ollie. I was thinking. You and me oughta spend more time together.

OLLIE: We got teevee.

RED: I mean worktime.

OLLIE: I work at home.

RED: Look.

(RED *shows* OLLIE *the place where the name appeared on his body.*)

RED: I have had what our more religious neighbors would refer to as a visitation. Change of heart-type stuff. A physical manifestation of an idea which occurred to me today as I was beating the shine back into an old Impala. You and me need to overlap more, son. We got things in common, somewhere, we got to have. Genes and whatnot.

OLLIE: I am not quite following your gist, Dad.

RED: Then let me arrive at my point. I want you to come back to work. At the shop.

(*Sudden sound of a machine, harsh and grating. The earth tilts on its axis.*)

RED: My hand!

OLLIE: Dad!

RED: (*In pain.*) JESUS CHRIST, TURN IT OFF!!!

OLLIE: I'M SORRY I'M SORRY I'M

(*Earth tilts back. Everything is normal.*)

OLLIE: The shop.

RED: That's what I said.

OLLIE: But I.
I am currently cleaning the house. It is a shockingly full-time position.

RED: Uh-huh. And how's that position working out for you?

OLLIE: Just fine.

RED: Floor's filthy.

OLLIE: Your boots brought it in.

(*RED removes his boots, slow, eyes on* OLLIE. *He sets them outside the house. Wiggles his bare toes.*)

RED: There. Clean feet. Pink as newborns.

(*RED places his feet upon the floor of the house.*)

RED: I do believe the dirt on this floor is tickling me. Deliberately. Hee hee.

OLLIE: Please go.

RED: Just gonna throw it back in my face, huh?

OLLIE: I got laundry.

RED: No, Ollie, what you got is a losing battle. A cold war what's going nowhere. You need a Job. Man Needs Job. We have a place where Job is waiting. Unfilled. Family position, a claiming of heritage, a pile of old bricks with your name on it.

OLLIE: Red bricks.

RED: Your name.

OLLIE: My name is—

RED: LISTEN, YOU—

Listen. I ain't very good with words, so just listen.

(*RED begins to bang out a rhythm. Body Shop Music envelops the space, wraps around* OLLIE. OLLIE *begins to move to it, hypnotized. He dances over to the Body Shop, dances around the cars. Meanwhile,* RED *drags the container out to the Vegetable Garden Out Back the House.*)

RED: You want it, Lois? You want mud and clay and all that's ground-bound?

(*RED reaches up into the air with his prosthetic hand, straining. A rumbling sound begins.*)

RED: You want a lit-up landing strip to slap you back to earth?

(*RED strains harder, the rumbling gets loud.*)

RED: Well Today's your lucky day.

(*RED yells. A huge mangled hand breaks through the surface of the earth.*)

OLLIE: (*Snapping out of it.*) Huh? What's that?
RED: Here, Lois. Take my hand.

(*The giant hand takes hold of the box.*)

OLLIE: Oh no.
RED: You will slowly fuel this garden. You will never leave this house.
OLLIE: No!

(*The hand drags the container under the earth. OLLIE dives after it. The hand comes back up and grabs OLLIE.*)

RED: OLLIE!

(*The hand squeezes OLLIE. OLLIE screams in pain. RED tries to stop the hand, but it drags OLLIE beneath the earth. The earth seals up like a ziploc. RED stares in horror at the ground. Silence.*)

RED: (*To Audience, quiet and scared.*) What? You got something to
say, then say it.
Talk to me.
Please.

END OF ACT I

— ACT II —

INTRO II

WHISPER SONG

(*Underworld music begins. Lights up revealing* OLLIE *in the Underworld. The Underworld looks like the underside of a vegetable garden. Roots and tubers sticking off the ceiling. Layers of soil in strips. Fossils grinning out at us.* OLLIE *is trapped in the vicious grip of the giant hand. He struggles fiercely, slowly prying each finger loose. He can barely breathe.* ANGEL BONES *sings.*)

ANGEL BONES:
　　funny (ha ha ha)
　　how my nerves got
　　all on the outside
　　(ha ha ha)

　　stomach (ho ho ho)
　　and intestines
　　swinging from the skyline
　　(ho ho ho)

　　fingertips (hee hee)
　　waving change the weather
　　up above the mason dixon line

　　funny enough
　　to choke me down
　　to a whisper

(RED *appears, above ground. Every time* OLLIE *yanks at a finger of the giant hand,* RED's *limbs twitch and jerk.*)

ANGEL BONES:
>   tugging (ah ah ah.)
>   on a infrastructure
>   born before my lifetime
>   (ah ah ah.)
>
>   tickling (oh oh oh)
>   at the spinal cords
>   of everyone I know
>   (oh oh oh.)
>
>   fingertips (oh no.)
>   ripping through the history in the
>   SOIL
>   on the
>   FLOOR
>   and the
>   DIRT
>   on the
>   WALLS
>   and the
>   DUST
>   in the
>   HOUSE
>   where my
>   LIFE
>   UN
>   RAV
>   ELS
>
>   funny enough
>   to choke me down
>   to a whisper
>
>   funny enough
>   to choke me down
>   to a
>   shhhhhhhhhhhhhh

(OLLIE *frees himself from the hand, gives a fierce battle-yell and begins to beat the hand to bits.* RED's *body is flung around above ground like a puppet.* OLLIE's *rage subsides. He starts to cry.*)

ANGEL BONES: Shhhhhhhhhhhhhhh now. Shhhhhhhhhhhhhhh.

NINE

EVERY LAST ONCE UPON A TIME

(ANGEL BONES *speaks to the audience, the human face he once wore shining through from behind his skull.*)

ANGEL BONES: It's an easy flight, Chattanooga to Memphis. Like walking cross the room. I done it a hundred times. I could do it blind. I got it in my bones. Flying bones, I got. Like birds do. My wife's words. Bones that got to go, she said, nonstop, she said. She about lost her religion over my restlessness. No matter how tight she tuck me into bed, she'd find me every morning in a different place. Sitting on the couch. Leaning against the door-frame. Facedown, kitchen table. Snoring away in some crazy position on the floor. Sleepwalker. Motion. Me.

But truth is, and this is something I never told her: I don't sleepwalk. I sleep fly. Second I shut my eyes the instruments are all there in front of me.

(*Cockpit sounds fill the air, pilot voices, faint like tuned in on an old radio.*)

ANGEL BONES: Compass. Altimeter. Blade rotation. Gas temp. Fuel flow. Airspeed indicators. Artificial horizon. Everything but a copilot. In dreams I fly solo.

And in all those night flights, those sleeping voyages counterclockwise round the world, I never once had nothing but scotch-smooth sailing.

Like walking cross the room. That simple. Think about it:

You're home. Phone rings. You get up to answer. Automatic. You don't even think. You take step, step, step and

(*Sound of a THUMP on the old radio. Shuddering. Cockpit sounds and voices start to get a little panicked.*)

ANGEL BONES: Floor ain't there no more. Gone. Yanked out from under you. Whole house yanked out from under you. You feel gravity. You feel for the first time that it is a thing with teeth. And you feel them first, those teeth, right here. Your stomach.

(*Shuddering gets loud. Sound of air traffic control asking questions, sound of pilots trying to keep it together.*)

ANGEL BONES: And in that moment, that moment when you hang there, floor gone, house gone, nothing but cold blue air under your feet . . . in that moment, everything comes true. Every story they poured into your baby ears to rock you off to sleep. Every fairy tale about ladies turning into spiders and little green people with tiny-ass wings. Every Last Once Upon a Time. Comes True. Laws of physics unravel. Whole world cracks open. And you find yourself staring straight into every myth you ever heard.
Then you fall.
I tried everything. Believe me. Every maneuver and combination, every sequence we got taught. And my final thoughts, even as I looked straight ahead out the window to see the earth tilt its lips up to meet mine, my thoughts were of . . .

(*Radio cuts off. Quiet.*)

ANGEL BONES: . . . you. All of you. I felt you behind me. The whole way down.

(*A shadow spills into the underground. It whispers frantically, indecipherably, growing louder and louder.*)

SHADOW (LOIS)*: time is this brittle maybe time is this brittle
maybe time is this brittle maybe time is this brittle maybe . . .

ANGEL BONES*: Last one. Number 72. Time to get you where you
need to be. Then we can all get some rest.

(*ANGEL BONES vanishes. The shadow's whispering is loud
enough to hear clearly now.*)

SHADOW (LOIS): time is this brittle maybe time is this brittle
maybe time is this brittle maybe time is this
NO!

(*Pause.*)

SHADOW (LOIS): No? Go. Hello?

(*The shadow shifts and jerks and spreads and rises.*)

SHADOW (LOIS): Oh.
Uuuuuppppp. Up? WHOA. Up.
Climb. DNA chain rebuild grindmotion linkchild slippery-
thick UP. Climb.
Reach. Limbstretch clusterself layerlight reach and stretch
and CLIMB.
Song. Bloodsong selfsong bluesong chewsong SING. Self.
Me.
Mind. Mine. Mind got a mind of it's own. Old. Grow.
Reactions, equal and opposite and otherwise. Chain reactions,
unequal, tilted, tension the only way to hold it together, keep
the cup from spilling baby, CLIMB.
This is not the drink I ordered.
This is not the meal I made.
But feed. Grow. Climb.
And SING

(*The shadow sings a gorgeous note.*)

SHADOW (LOIS): My name is Lois.
My mind says it knows this.
My body is of a different opinion.
The word "choice." The words "free" and "will". I sheds them and chews them and swallows them piece by piece. I grows them back as skin.
Damn if I ain't evolving. Darwinizing. Right before my very eyes. Survival. Walk away from disaster. Fittest. Fit the pieces back together, what once was swallowed now is mine, eat what others leave behind, make a whole outta hunks of grime, find your way back to bright daytime and CLIMB!

(*The shadow sighs.*)

SHADOW (LOIS): Soil like sugar. Candy apple earth.
I never felt better in my life.

TEN

THE NEED OF YOU

(RED, *above ground, battered.*)

RED: Family. Family tree. Uprooted, ripped and roaring. Upside down growth patterns making hungry pine needles reach for the sky in reverse. The world is all atumble. My son is all atumble. My hand is all atumble. My wife is in my hand. My son is in my fist. The world is all gone under. My heart is all atumble.
I have no hand no more. My son took it and shook it from my bones. As sons are wont to do. Instinctively. I have no heart no more. My hand has took my heart—my son—and shook him bones and all. The teaching of the shaving. The teaching of the changing of the tire. The teaching of the cooking of the bar-beque'd meats. The teaching of the watching of the television sports season free-for-alls. The teaching of the glazing of the eyes upon witnessing cheerleader tumbles. The teaching is

atumble. It has gone all under.
Prosthetic me.

(RED *heaves a grief-moan so deep the Underworld shakes.* OLLIE *appears under the earth.*)

OLLIE: What was that?
LOIS: (*Voice in the dark.*) A phone call from this guy I used to know.
OLLIE: Hello? Somebody talking?
LOIS: Some body.

(LOIS *steps up behind* OLLIE *and we finally see her clearly. She has stitched herself a new body made up almost entirely of fresh vegetables. She is grotesque and somehow beautiful.*)

OLLIE: Shadow slips up behind me, says howdo. Serves me up a great big helping of the steaming heebie-jeebies.
Who is it?
LOIS: Don't turn around.
OLLIE: Who is it?
LOIS: Don't look yet.
OLLIE: I got to.
LOIS: That's what Lot's wife said.
OLLIE: Yeah well her day ain't nothing next to mine. Now tell me your name or—
LOIS: Famous Survivors for 100.
OLLIE: What?
LOIS: This Scottish sailor spent five years on a desert island at the turn of the eighteenth century and served as the real life inspiration for Daniel Defoe's famous fictional castaway, Robinson Crusoe.
OLLIE: Uh . . .
LOIS: Who is "Alexander Selkirk"?
Famous Survivors for 200. This Russian gentleman wasn't a feline, but the fact that his assassination was rumored to have required beating, shooting, drowning, and massive amounts of cyanide suggests he had nearly as many lives.

OLLIE: Uh . . .

LOIS: Who is "Rasputin"?

Famous Survivors for 500.

OLLIE: The answer is the DAILY DOUBLE!

LOIS: DING DING DING! How much would you like to wager?

OLLIE: I'll bet it all.

LOIS: You've grown some courage.

OLLIE: I'm betting it all.

LOIS: Okay. For the whole shebang: This woman died in a plane crash just when her new life was about to burst into being. This woman's body and memory were subsequently defiled by being buried in her husband's ratty-ass vegetable garden like some family fucking pet. This woman has since transubstantiated herself, stitched herself a new body new corpus new DON'T TURN AROUND!

OLLIE: sorry

LOIS: please

OLLIE: i won't

LOIS: please stitched herself a new body new corpus new self new me made primarily out of primarily out of out of out of out of out of

AAAAAAAAAAAAAAAAAIIIIIIIIIIIIIIIIIII-IEEEEEEEEEEEEEEEEEEEEEE!!!!

Do you know the answer?

OLLIE: My Ma?

LOIS: Contestants must phrase their answers in the form of a question.

OLLIE: My life is in the form of a question. Crook-backed and wingless.

LOIS: Rules are rules. Do you know the answer, baby?

OLLIE: Who is "My Ma"?

LOIS: DING DING DING DING DING!

(*She turns* OLLIE *around to face her. He hugs her fiercely.*)

LOIS: Whoa! Watch the zucchinis.

OLLIE: Who is My Ma! Who is My Ma!

LOIS: My sweet sweet boy.
OLLIE: I came after you. I got dragged down here and—

(*OLLIE jumps back, looks at LOIS.*)

LOIS: Baby?
OLLIE: What . . . what . . . your body . . .
LOIS: There wasn't much left. I had to improvise.
OLLIE: I can't see the you in there.
LOIS: I'm in here. I promise.
OLLIE: Is your blood green?
LOIS: You use what you got.
OLLIE: You eat what grows.
LOIS: Now you sound like him.
  You're looking at me funny.
  Am I . . . ugly?

(*OLLIE shakes his head.*)

LOIS: Am I pretty?

(*OLLIE shakes his head.*)

LOIS: What am I then?

(*OLLIE slowly moves toward her and reaches out his hand.*)

LOIS: What are you doing?
OLLIE: My stomach . . .

(*OLLIE touches a tomato hanging from LOIS's body.*)

LOIS: Don't.
OLLIE: Please. I ain't had nothing. My insides gone all outside. Bare
  to the sky.
LOIS: What are you saying?
OLLIE: I'm hungry. Please, Ma.

(*Pause. LOIS nods. OLLIE plucks the tomato from her body. LOIS shivers. OLLIE eats.*)

LOIS: Just like when you was new. I held you to my breast. A big swaddled semicolon in my arms. You punctuated my body. You taught me pause.

OLLIE: I missed you.

LOIS: I missed you too. So hard. I'm sorry I had to leave.

OLLIE: You're here now.

LOIS: Yes.

OLLIE: Don't go like that no more.

LOIS: I won't. I promise.

(*RED is gazing through grief-rimmed eyes at the sky.*)

RED: The sky. I've never seen such an angry blue. Like some robin's egg come out all wrong.

(*The sky splits. ANGEL BONES appears in full celestial glory, hanging effortlessly in the air.*)

RED: Huh. I seem to be seeing things.

ANGEL BONES: Red.

RED: Huh. I appear to be hearing things.

ANGEL BONES: Your name is Red.

RED: Huh. In my grief-stricken state, I am hallucinating an angel man with bony wings and white fire shooting outta his eyes.

LOIS: But I need you, Oliver.

ANGEL BONES: I need you, Red.

OLLIE*: Huh?

RED*: Huh.

OLLIE: Need me? What for?

LOIS: A two-person job. Famous Survivors.
      I ain't leaving. It ain't fair. I just found out what life was.

RED: What are you?

ANGEL BONES: The need of you.

LOIS & ANGEL BONES: Will you help me?

OLLIE: You know I will. Whatever you want.
RED: I don't know what you want. But sure.

(RED *takes ANGEL BONES' hand with his prosthetic claw.*)

RED: (*Sings.*)
    unravel me fingers
    ghost man is here
    beneath nails slip me
    lodge and remain
    within wingspan
    his fingers
    his hand
OLLIE: Did you hear something?
RED: Scuse me. Don't usually sing like that.
LOIS: I got ears made outta radishes. You wouldn't believe the things
    I hear.
RED: Strange outbursts are not my stock in trade.
ANGEL BONES: I know. You work in bodies.
RED: Body Shop.
LOIS: Come with me.

(*LOIS leads OLLIE through a tunnel.*)

RED: But what can I do for you?
ANGEL BONES: Listen to this:

(*ANGEL BONES opens his mouth. Music pours out: an overwhelming overlapping of all the musical themes in the play. RED
shudders in rapture.*)

ANGEL BONES: You read me?
RED: Loud and clear.
ANGEL BONES: Over and out.

(*ANGEL BONES stretches out his wings. They eclipse the sun.*)

ELEVEN

WHY THE WORLD TURNS

(*LOIS and OLLIE underground. RED at the Body Shop door.*)

LOIS: Here we are. Smack dab center underneath.

OLLIE: Under what?

LOIS: Center of the world. Home.

OLLIE: What do we do now?

RED: Work.

LOIS: Work.

OLLIE: I know from work.

RED: Work is it.

LOIS: Work is what's next, Ollie.

OLLIE: I know the Webster's of the word.

LOIS: Work is the answer.

OLLIE: What is a physical or mental effort exerted to do or make something?

RED: As our forefathers thought.

OLLIE: What is employment at a job or in a position?

RED: And taught.

OLLIE: What is an occupation raison d'etre profession business trade craft etc. etc. and etc.?

RED: They were right about so many things and they were not wrong about this.

OLLIE: The answer to the question is Work.

LOIS: That's right, baby. Work makes the world go round (take it from someone who lives at the pivot-point), makes the world spin and is therefore revolutionary, a season shifting activity. The axis turns because Atlas got his work cut out for him.

RED: Work.

OLLIE: What kinda work?

RED: Construction.

LOIS: Excavation.

RED: Building up.

LOIS: Moving up.

OLLIE: I don't get it.

LOIS: Digging. That's what I need you for, Ollie.

RED: Screw this repair business.

LOIS: Your big arms and big big hands.

RED: Fenders and windshields, sealing and bending and undenting.

OLLIE: Hands?

RED: Screw that noise.

LOIS: Straight back up to the goddamn land of the living.

RED: Screw that music.

LOIS: Whether he likes it or not.

OLLIE: Who likes it?

LOIS: Ghost man with eighteen-foot fingers. I can feel him. Reaching right for me.

OLLIE: Sky guy.

LOIS: Wants to rip me off the earth and hurl me into the blue.

OLLIE: NO!

LOIS: Exactly.

OLLIE: No way.

LOIS: Exactly. I got the right. More than him.

OLLIE: Who?

RED: Well, as of now it's over.

LOIS: Way more than him.

OLLIE: Who? Sky Guy?

RED: Three Generations.

LOIS: Oh no. Much fleshier than that.

RED: Father to Son to Son to . . .

OLLIE: Who?

LOIS: Time to erase what's past.

RED: Gone.

OLLIE: Ma, what's his name?

LOIS: His name?

RED: I hereby declare this Body Shop

LOIS: His name is

RED: Closed For Business.

LOIS: Fingerprints on the Fridge.
        His name is

RED: Closed For Repairs.

LOIS: Rust Between the Sheets.
　　　His name is
RED: Closed For Personal Reasons Too Larger Than Life To Carve On This Skinny-Ass Sign.
LOIS: A Baby a Son That's Born With a . . .
RED: Closed!
LOIS: Spent his whole life unraveling this family like a sweater.
RED: CLOSED!
LOIS: Tearing at the seams till we spilled out all over the floor.
RED: CLOSED!!!
LOIS: A mess.
　　　Well guess what, Ollie?
OLLIE: What, Ma?
LOIS: You and me are gonna clean it up.
OLLIE: Clean?
LOIS: Clean it up for good. No more past.
OLLIE: Scrubbed up and gone.
LOIS: Just us. You and me.
OLLIE: You and me. For good.
LOIS: Forever.
OLLIE: Future.
LOIS: Fresh.
OLLIE: Fast fast forward.

(*Cleaning Music begins. It has a strange distorted edge to it this time. OLLIE and LOIS do the Home Beautification Dance together. The gleam is sharp. The earth quakes.*)

RED: Earth howling out what you done all wrong. Sky screaming down what you better do right. Now I know how Noah felt. Got a vision in my head that ain't mine. Blueprint superimposed on my eyeballs, and all I can do is
LOIS: Let's get to work.
RED: work.
OLLIE: Work!

TWELVE

WORKSONG

(RED *welds together big pieces of car bodies behind a big drop cloth.* OLLIE *digs his way up through the earth.* ANGEL BONES *sings.*)

ANGEL BONES:
    lift it up
    pull it up
    rattle it, shake it, bend it, break it
    make it up

    gotta little job to do boys
    gotta little mission in my bones
    i can change the world with my itty bitty song
    and this is how the itty bitty goes

    lift it up
    pull it up
    rattle it, shake it, bend it, break it
    make it up

    ain't a house got built without chopping down a tree
    no omelet cept for cracking up some eggs
    you can't change the thinking in this great big world
    if you won't go knocking on some heads

    lift it up
    pull it up
    rattle it, shake it, bend it, break it
    make it up

    gonna get my ass promoted
    gonna get to know the people at the top
    but first i gotta build a tall tall ladder
    outta sweat and blood and fingernails
    and body parts and moans and wails

and never ever ever gonna stop

lift it up
pull it up
rattle it, shake it, bend it, break it,
scrub it, rub it, polish it, powersand it, double-hand it, detail it,
    weld it all together till it hangs tite, outta site, just rite,
    gotta have it posthaste, yesterday, doubletime, on the line
    overtime climb baby climb baby climb baby climb baby
CLIMB!

(shit. you think the big guy even knows i exist?)

THIRTEEN

CLOSED MANIFESTO

(RED *is laboring like crazy behind the cloth. Sparks fly and steel* *screams.* RED's *heart is a big fat American radio needle. He tunes* *it viciously, snatching up stations.*)

RED:
    Bang bang clanging on the door
    WE'RE CLOSED!
    Bang bang bang-a-lang
    YOU HEAR?
    Closed!
    Not open!
    Sorry we're!
    Come back later!
    Gone to Lunch!
    Gone Fishin!
    Gone Huntin!
    Gone Joggin!
    Gone West!
    Gone to War!

These are the times that try men's!
A day that will live in!
Four score and seven!
There comes a time in every!
Boogie woogie bugle!
Ask not what your country can!
The summer soldier and the sunshine!
Are we not men we are!
One small step for!
One if by land, two if by!
We will we will rock!
Can we stand by idle while our!
Highway to the danger!
Gonna party like it's!
Walk softly and carry a big!
Nothing to fear but nothing to fear but
FIX IT YOUR GODDAMN SELF!

(RED *collapses into a pile of sandwiches.*)

FOURTEEN

STUFF IS WEIRD

(*The House. All is quiet. Then a loud rumbling and a big yell and* OLLIE's *hand busts straight through the floor into the House. His other hand busts through. Then* OLLIE *busts through. He climbs up out of the earth, reaches back down into the hole, and pulls* LOIS *up like a giant carrot. She remains buried from the shins down. She looks like a tree that's been planted in the middle of the floor.*)

OLLIE: Dang! Filthy again! Whole house. I just cleaned, Ma, I swear!
    Let me get my sponge . . .
LOIS: No! Leave it be. It's perfect
OLLIE: Huh?

LOIS: Just like I remember.

OLLIE: But Ma, it's covered in dirt.

LOIS: Dirt is good.

OLLIE: Dirt is huh?

LOIS: Dirt is good.

OLLIE: Dirt is . . . good?

LOIS: Yes.

OLLIE: Uh. That goes against just about every philosophy I use to guide my life.

LOIS: It's true. Dirt is good.

OLLIE: You never said anything like that when you was . . . when you wasn't . . .

LOIS: In case you haven't noticed, stuff has changed.

OLLIE: Some stuff don't change.

LOIS: Stuff has rearranged.

OLLIE: Some stuff stays the same.

LOIS: Stuff has gone thru winter and come up spring, sprouted up rosy and glowy and homey and hungry and STUFF EATS DIRT!

OLLIE: Stuff eats dirt?

LOIS: Stuff eats dirt plus sun plus rain.

OLLIE: Stuff is weird.

LOIS: Stuff is your mother now get me DIRT!

OLLIE: Plus sun?

LOIS: Plus rain! Sky! Get me sky!

OLLIE: I can open a window. How's that?

LOIS: More!

OLLIE: All the windows. How about that?

LOIS: MORE!

OLLIE: More than windows? More than doors?

LOIS: I want weather. Sun and rain. Life is out there, beating to get let in. Let it in!

OLLIE: Well, ceiling beams. Guess time come to shrug you off my shoulders for good.

(*OLLIE smashes a fist through the roof. Shaft of light smacks him in the eyes.*)

OLLIE: Sunlight got a fist that sends me reeling. But Ma needs sky.
So . . .
GOODBYE CEILING!

(*RED appears in the Shop, eating a sandwich.*)

RED: Sounds like thunder.
OLLIE: GOODBYE ROOF!
RED: Nope. Not a cloud.

(*OLLIE tears the roof off the house. A huge hunk of light pours in.*)

OLLIE: HELLO WEATHER!

(*LOIS basks in the light.*)

LOIS: YES! YES! GOT SUN AGAIN! LOVE MY SUN!

(*OLLIE smiles.*)

OLLIE: Love you too, Ma.

FIFTEEN

WHAT RED'S BEEN BUILDING

(*RED in the Body Shop. He is finishing up a sandwich.*)

RED: Last one. Onion on white. Bitter.

(*He swallows.*)

RED: Good. Gone. No more sandwiches enough.

(*ANGEL BONES appears in full radiant glory. RED winces, turns
away.*)

RED: You again. Mind turning that lightshow down a bit? You convinced me last time.

(*ANGEL BONES turns down his glory.*)

ANGEL BONES: How's it coming, Red?
RED: How should I know? I'm just a power tool. You're the boss.
ANGEL BONES: More like the link above you. And I got a link above me. Connected to a link above that. Etc.
RED: I'm tired.
ANGEL BONES: Let's see.

(*ANGEL BONES removes the cloth, revealing a huge pair of wings built from car body panels.*)

RED: About what you had in mind?
ANGEL BONES: Picture perfect.
RED: Ask a question?
ANGEL BONES: Shoot.
RED: How the hell am I supposed to get off the ground in that?
ANGEL BONES: You flap.
RED: I can't flap. What the hell you think I am, a red-breasted yellow-bellied—
ANGEL BONES: You flap every day. Here.

(*ANGEL BONES touches RED's shoulder blades. RED moves them, opening and shutting his prosthetic claw. He and OLLIE shiver simultaneously.*)

RED: Sometimes I can still feel it.
OLLIE: Hand like nothing like a hand.
RED: Do not believe what you see.
LOIS: (*To OLLIE.*) What'd you say, baby?
OLLIE: Nothing. Just got a bad feeling.
ANGEL BONES: Built up some serious muscle tissue back here.
RED: Careful, you're gonna make me blush.
LOIS: What kind of feeling?

ANGEL BONES: You're perfect.
RED: I'M TIRED.
OLLIE: Like something's coming.
RED: And flapping my ass up to heaven ain't exactly my idea of R&R.
OLLIE: Or going.
RED: Know what I mean?
OLLIE: Or gone.
ANGEL BONES: "Heaven" ain't exactly the right word.
RED: What is the right word?

(*ANGEL BONES opens his mouth. No sound comes out, but RED seizes up like a dog to a silent whistle. ANGEL BONES closes his mouth, RED collapses.*)

RED: Uh-huh. And how do you spell that?
ANGEL BONES: You can say no, Red. It's a volunteer mission.

(*Pause.*)

ANGEL BONES: You loved her.
RED: Shut up.

(*Pause.*)

RED: It's complicated.

(*Pause.*)

RED: Yes.
ANGEL BONES: You can prove that. By doing this.
RED: And . . . Ollie?
ANGEL BONES: He stays.
RED: He's alive then? He's still around?
ANGEL BONES: Affirmative. And closer than you think.

SIXTEEN

ONE THING FALLS

(*OLLIE and LOIS. OLLIE is watering her, LOIS is gulping it down.*)

LOIS: Paradise. More.
OLLIE: Home sweet house.
　　　You had enough?
LOIS: Enough? The word fails. Roots green and reaching. Light in my blood. Bursting with abundance. And sunk in soil. I got toes dipping straight into mysteries I never dreamed of in all my library books. Proust was a doofus. Kant a backwards half-wit. University? Universe. I am my own philosophy now.
OLLIE: I mean enough water.
LOIS: Think so. Thank you.

(*OLLIE sets down the watering can, lies down in the shade of his mother.*)

LOIS: Soaking up sky. Boy by my side. This is niiiiiiiice.
OLLIE: Yep.

(*Pause.*)

OLLIE: I'm feeling something.
LOIS: That's called "happy."
OLLIE: Wow.

(*Pause.*)

OLLIE: Now I'm feeling something else. It's called "hungry."

(*LOIS drops a carrot down onto OLLIE's head.*)

OLLIE: Like Newton and his apple.

LOIS: One thing falls, and a whole new physics gets born.
OLLIE: Natural laws.
LOIS: Mmm-hmmm.

(*OLLIE devours the carrot.*)

RED: I still don't get why me. Why not you?
ANGEL BONES: You buried her, Red. You took responsibility.
RED: Me?
ANGEL BONES: No tears. Not a single gesture of respect for what
   had passed. She wasn't buried. She was planted. Ain't no way
   the earth can swallow something like that.
RED: Well. Hate to break it to you, but she ain't exactly gonna be
   happy to see me.
ANGEL BONES: I never said it'd be easy.
RED: Shit. If I'da known when I got up today I'd be helping some
   angel man deliver salvation I'da stayed behind my eyelids where
   I belong.
ANGEL BONES: "Salvation" ain't exactly the right word.
RED: Do me a favor. Don't tell me what the right word is.

(*ANGEL BONES laughs.*)

ANGEL BONES: I like you Red.
RED: Yeah, well you creep me out a bit.

(*They laugh together.*)

LOIS: (*Startled.*) Sun's setting.
OLLIE: Pretty.
LOIS: Jumping over the walls like a convict.
OLLIE: Going, going, gone.
LOIS: Make it stop.
OLLIE: Huh?
LOIS: Hold it back with your big big hands. Please. Quick.
OLLIE: But Ma. There'll be more tomorrow.
LOIS: MAKE IT STOP! BRING IT BACK!

(*OLLIE looks around frantically, then bashes down a wall. Sun shines back in. LOIS sighs.*)

LOIS: That's right you ball of fire. I ain't through with you yet.

(*She basks.*)

RED: What was that shaking?
ANGEL BONES: Whole world's in a snarl. You ready?
RED: In a second. Knees all wobbly. Earth feels funny.
ANGEL BONES: I always thought that. Never felt at home on solid ground.

(*Pause.*)

RED: You know. I ain't never been what you'd call a sweet person. Giving. I ain't used to sweating without collecting something green in return. Don't understand family that don't love you no matter how much you put on the table. Bodies that crack apart in your hands when all you wanna do is make them whole. Sky that falls down no matter how much you try to prop it up. I guess what I'm asking is: is there a logic? A reckoning?
ANGEL BONES: There are failures. Moments of disconnect. We forget our wings and plummet hard. But an actual crash is statistically unlikely. Most of the time, we stay in the air. We fly pretty okay, I guess.
RED: But when we crash, is there an answer?
ANGEL BONES: There is a black box. But I don't know how to open it.

(*Pause.*)

RED: I should have buried her right. I should have wept.
ANGEL BONES: Go ahead.
RED: Can't. Disconnect. Tears fail me.

(*OLLIE bashes down another wall.*)

RED: I miss my family.
ANGEL BONES: Me too.
RED: I wanna see them.
ANGEL BONES: They're waiting.
RED: Okay then.

(RED *straps himself into the wings.* OLLIE *bashes down another wall.*)

RED: So, uh, when I get up there, wherever, with her in my arms, who do I ask for? I mean, surely I don't knock on the big guy's door. Ask for an interview. Right?
ANGEL BONES: There are no doors.

(OLLIE *bashes down the final wall.*)

ANGEL BONES: No one knocks.
OLLIE: Walls down. Air rubbing its elbows all over me. Sun running fingers thru what some might call my hair.
LOIS: Mmmmmmm.
OLLIE: Walls gone. Family history picked up by the wind. Blown off into the lungs of others.
    I got no house no more.
    Uncontained me.

(OLLIE *removes his apron. He holds it. He looks around for a place to put it. He holds it. He looks around. He holds it. He holds it.*)

OLLIE: I'm feeling something. I think it's called "being twenty-one."

(*Wind picks up, sends everything spinning.* RED *is flapping like crazy, grunting and heaving his shoulders.*)

RED: I don't believe it. I'm airborne. I'm eating clouds. I'm about to break my back.

(*OLLIE looks up.*)

OLLIE: Eyes wide crazy. See my daddy coming.
      MA!

(*LOIS looks up.*)

LOIS: Eyes wide wild. See my husband coming.
      Red?

RED: See my family tree a long way off.

(*RED flies toward his wife and son.*)

SEVENTEEN

NO MORE

(*OLLIE and LOIS watch as RED steps slow through the air to
where they stand. As ANGEL BONES sings, each family member
moans along with a different stanza: RED with the first, LOIS
with the second, OLLIE with the third.*)

ANGEL BONES:
    woman don't want me no more
    woman don't want me no more
    she seen where my feet
    done walked while she was gone
    now my woman don't want me no more

    baby don't love me no more
    baby don't love me no more
    heard all bout my hands
    and the ways they done gone
    now my baby don't love me no more

weather don't want me no more
weather don't want me no more
the clouds they got mouths
saying get out of town
no the weather don't want me no more

(*RED, LOIS, and OLLIE moan together for one last wordless stanza. It is rich and devastating. It is the voice of this family.*)

EIGHTEEN

RECKONING

(*RED lands.*)

LOIS: Well, well, well.

RED: Did that tree just talk?

LOIS: Well fucking well well well.

RED: Is that tree my wife?

LOIS: Well looky here. A useless puddle of flesh done fall down from the sky.

RED: Lois? That you?

LOIS: A useless puddle of flesh with wings. Look, Ollie. It's your Daddy.

OLLIE: I am seeing, but I am not entirely believing.

RED: Ollie. Thought maybe you was gone for good.

LOIS: Cut the bleeding heart act, Red. We all know you got nothing but 10W40 in your veins.

RED: I been thru some stuff, Lois.

LOIS: You been thru some stuff?

RED: I have had certain eyes of mine opened.

LOIS: Ollie, listen to this. Red has been thru some stuff.

OLLIE: I am hearing, but I am not quite comprehending.

RED: Ollie. Son.

(*RED opens his arms to embrace OLLIE. OLLIE hits RED, knocking him to the ground. RED slowly rises.*)

RED: Okay. I deserved that.

LOIS: Red, if you got what deserved you'd be flattened down to a bloody pulpy throw rug.

RED: I know, and believe me I . . .
     What the hell happened to the house?

OLLIE: I done some remodeling.

LOIS: Ollie has made it a little more livable in here.

RED: There is no more "in here." It's all out there.

OLLIE: It was cramped.

LOIS: It was dark.

OLLIE: Now we got room.

LOIS: Now we got light.

RED: Now we got jack. Now we got no more address.

LOIS: That vanished a long time ago, Red. Swallowed by a fold in the map.

OLLIE: Not anymore. I pulled us out. Dusted us off. Made us new. All with these hands. These are my hands, Dad.

RED: Son, I—

OLLIE: LISTEN TO ME.
     These are my hands, Dad. These are my arms. My legs. My feet. And this is my head. My parts are connected and working together. I am standing here before you. Do you see me?

RED: Ollie.

OLLIE: I am shaping sounds with my tongue and teeth. Do you hear me?

RED: My son.

OLLIE: I am placing my palm upon your chest. Do you feel me?

RED: I am so so sorry.

OLLIE: DO YOU FEEL ME?

(*RED grabs OLLIE's hand. The earth tilts on its axis.*)

OLLIE: Let go of me!

RED: Not until you learn.

OLLIE: Please. I'm sorry. Please let go.

RED: How many times do we have to go over this? This is a car body. And these are its parts. When I ask for a taillight, you give me a taillight. When I ask for a radiator, you do not give me a rearview mirror.

OLLIE: Dad!

RED: You give me what I want! You learn the difference. When I teach you, you learn.

OLLIE: Stop, please!

RED: It's in your blood. Three Generations. Learn!

OLLIE: STOP!

RED: LEARN! LEARN! WHY CAN'T YOU—

OLLIE: I SAID STOP!

(*OLLIE makes a loud grunting sound, as if shoving against a huge weight. Sudden sound of a machine, harsh and grating.*)

RED: My hand!

OLLIE: Dad!

RED: (*In pain.*) JESUS CHRIST, TURN IT OFF!!!

OLLIE: I'M SORRY I'M SORRY I'M

(*Earth tilts back. Quiet.*)

RED: I feel you. I hear you. I see you.

OLLIE: End of lesson.

LOIS: Good. Now hear this: Get lost, Red. You are on private property.

RED: Lois. I'm sorry.

LOIS: You oughta be.

RED: I done you wrong.

LOIS: Fiercely and repeatedly.

RED: And I beg your forgiveness.

LOIS: No.

RED: I love you.

LOIS: Again, the only appropriate response is the word, "No."

RED: And I wanna do what's right.

LOIS: Too late. Things have shifted, Red. New life. I am on my own.

OLLIE: We're on our own.

LOIS: We are on our own, Red. You got no place in this family.

RED: Lois. You're dead.

(*LOIS screams.*)

OLLIE: SHUT UP, DAD!

RED: It's true. And my heart is split over it. And I don't want it. But there it is. Lois. You're dead.

(*LOIS screams.*)

OLLIE: SHUT UP, DAD!

LOIS: Oh, Red. I've only just begun to live.

RED: What, you're gonna live like this? This what you think life is? What pop-up book did you crawl out of?

LOIS: You never could recognize a good thing when you saw it.

RED: What I see is an earth all out of whack. A sky tilted fit to spill.

LOIS: Let it spill! Let it rain hairy angels down on all of us. I'm staying.

RED: Ollie. Look at her.

LOIS: Red. Get your sorry ass the hell out of here.

RED: Look at her, son.

LOIS: Get your lousy wrinkled butt back to the Body Shop where it belongs.

RED: She's gone.

OLLIE: no

LOIS: Crawl back into your hunks of rust and vinyl and gears and NOISE

RED: She's over.

OLLIE: She's here. Right here. And I'm taking care of her.

LOIS: AND STAY THE HELL AWAY FROM ME AND MY SON.

RED: I can't. Been given a mission.

LOIS: That ain't a mission. That's an ugly-ass sculpture that by all rights never shoulda got you off the ground.

RED: More things in heaven and earth I guess.

LOIS: Why Red. You almost made an allusion.

RED: I ain't leaving without you.

(*RED reaches for LOIS.*)

LOIS: Don't!

(*A big rumbling. The whole earth shakes.*)

LOIS: Don't you dare. I got my roots around this whole town. I got them stretched all through the foundations of your goddamn multigenerational Body Shop, Red. You take hold of me, and everything comes crashing down.

(*Pause.*)

RED: You take what you need, Lois. You do what you gotta do.

(*RED reaches for her.*)

LOIS: Can't you leave me be? All thru my life, you . . . can't you leave me be?
RED: Ollie, help me.
OLLIE: Why? What you got I want, Dad?
RED: Nothing.
LOIS: (*To RED.*) That's right. You starve him with what you call love.
OLLIE: Tell me, Dad. What you got I want?
RED: Nothing. Oughta be me. Dead and gone. But it ain't.
       I can't fix this, Ollie. I don't know nothing no more.
       But you do. Show me. Please. Show me how the world stays clean.

(*OLLIE shuts his eyes.*)

LOIS: You've done enough, Red. Go.

(*RED looks at OLLIE. Long pause. Then RED nods, gets ready to go.*)

OLLIE: Dad.
LOIS: Son? What are you doing?

(*OLLIE opens his eyes.*)

OLLIE: Ma?

LOIS: Yes, baby?

OLLIE: I love you.

LOIS: I love you.

OLLIE: But you're stuck.

LOIS: No I'm not.

OLLIE: Rooted all wrong.

LOIS: I'm happy.

OLLIE: It ain't right.

LOIS: Who says?

OLLIE: I know.

LOIS: You don't know! You're just letting your father shove you against a wall.

OLLIE: Wrong, Ma. I know.

Dad. I'm pretty mad at you.

RED: You got a right.

LOIS: Ollie.

OLLIE: Dad. There's lots in this family that's a mess because of you.

RED: I accept that.

LOIS: Please.

OLLIE: Dad?

RED: Yes?

OLLIE: My Ma . . . My Ma . . .

RED: Yeah?

OLLIE: I'm feeling something.

RED: What is it?

(*OLLIE begins to cry, to mourn. RED joins him.*)

LOIS: Stop. Stop. There's nothing to cry about.

Ollie. Ollie, look at me. Your Ma ain't dead. I'm alive. Look at me.

Red, don't do this. If you ever loved me, let me have this now. Please.

I can't. It ain't fair. I won't.

I got so many questions left. So many days. Suns strung together like pearls.

The people I could have been in those pearls.

String breaks. All spill out onto the floor.

Rattle of bones. Teeth. Peeling of skin. Heart blown apart. Impact.

Why is the world so hungry? Why can't it just stay full? Why can't it just stay full?

(LOIS begins to moan. Her moan turns into a wordless grief-song. ANGEL BONES joins her. RED and OLLIE join in. LOIS slips from her vegetable skin like a dress. She is whole and lovely. She and RED face each other, look into each other's eyes. LOIS reaches out to him. RED takes her hand. Song stops. Full electric quiet for a moment.)

LOIS: Let me drive.

(RED leaves the wings, and LOIS steps slowly toward them. As each foot lands, we hear the sound of a shovel digging through soil, the sound of burial. She reaches the wings and straps herself into them. She looks up to the sky.)

LOIS: Over.
ANGEL BONES: Out.

(Lights out.)

EPILOGUE

(OLLIE stands in the ruins of the House.)

OLLIE: My stomach sits square at my center. It tells me what it needs. I feed it best I can. I eat what grows.

Ma died. Up there.

Ma dead. Buried and wept over.

Ma gone.
World back on its axis.
Dad . . .

(*RED appears, standing outside the Body Shop. He stares at the "CLOSED" sign he nailed to the door.*)

OLLIE: I ain't waiting around for him. This backwater red dirt Tennessee town has politely offered me an open door. And I am graciously accepting.

I will walk out into the sun. I will step step step and stop. I will build a home. A first-generation home. One that fits. And in my home I will build some windows. And around my windows I will build some walls. And in my walls I will plug a phone. And with my phone I may reach out and touch my father's hand. Hand like nothing like a hand. Someday.

But first, before I drive a single nail into waiting wood, I'll lay a foundation.

(*OLLIE takes some dusty dirt from the ruins of the house, holds it in his hands.*)

OLLIE: Trace out a space and scatter some family dirt like seeds.
Whisper my questions into the black box of the earth.
Listen for how it answers back.
I'll go like this:

(*OLLIE gently blows on the dust. It billows from his hands. A plane passes overhead. RED looks up, watches it cross the sky. OLLIE doesn't look up, but he knows it's there. Simultaneously, the two men smile.*)

END

17 reasons (why)
by Naomi Iizuka

No performance or reading of this work *17 reasons (why)* in any medium may be given without express permission of the author. Inquiries regarding performance rights, publication, duplication of any kind should be addressed to: Morgan Jenness at Helen Merrill, Ltd., 295 Lafayette Street, Suite 915, New York, NY 10012; (212) 226-5015.

⇛ BIOGRAPHY ⇚

Naomi Iizuka has previously collaborated with Campo Santo + Intersection on *Language of Angels, Polaroid Stories,* and *Scheherezade* part of *Pieces of the Quilt.* Other plays include *36 Views; War of the Worlds* (written in collaboration with Anne Bogart and SITI Company); *Aloha, Say the Pretty Girls; Tattoo Girl;* and *Skin.* Her plays have been produced by Berkeley Repertory Theatre, Actors' Theatre of Louisville, the Dallas Theatre Center and Undermain Theatre in Dallas, Frontera@Hyde Park in Austin, Printer's Devil and Annex in Seattle, the New York Shakespeare Festival, the Brooklyn Academy of Music, Soho Rep, Tectonic Theatre in New York, San Diego's Sledgehammer Theatre, and the Edinburgh Festival. Her plays have been workshopped at the Kennedy Center, San Jose Repertory Theatre, Geva Theatre, Breadloaf, Sundance Theatre Lab, A.S.K. Theatre Projects, the McCarter Theatre, A Contemporary Theatre, the Bay Area Playwrights' Festival, Brava, Midwest PlayLabs, New York Shakespeare Festival's New Works Now, En Garde Arts/P.S. 122, and New York Theatre Workshop. *36 Views* is published in *American Theatre. Language of Angels* is published in *Theatre Forum; War of the Worlds* and *Aloha, Say the Pretty Girls* are published by Smith and Kraus; *Polaroid Stories* is published by Dramatic Publishing; *Tattoo Girl* is included in *From The Other Side of the Century,* published by Sun and Moon; and *Skin* is included in *Out of the Fringe* published by TCG. Iizuka is a member of New Dramatists and the recipient of a Whiting Award, a Rockefeller Foundation grant, an NEA/TCG Artist-in-Residence grant, a McKnight Fellowship, a PEN Center USA West Award for Drama, Princeton University's Hodder Fellowship, and a Jerome Playwriting Fellowship. She has taught playwriting at the University of Iowa, the University of Texas, Austin and Cornish College in Seattle, and is currently teaching at the University of California, Santa Barbara. She is working with Campo Santo + Intersection on a play based on *Hamlet-Blood in the Brain,* based in Oakland, California, in the 1980s.

➤ PRODUCTION HISTORY ◆

17 reasons (why) by Naomi Iizuka
Produced by Campo Santo + Intersection
October 24-November 24, 2002
Directed by Delia Macdougall

Cast

Luis Saguar:
THE SUNSET SCAVENGER, JERRUSHA FITZGERALD,
RINALDO D'AMATO, ANTONIO SANDOVAL
Catherine Castellanos:
MARY HOLLAND SPARKS, HAZEL SCHUMER,
GLORIA KANTOR
Beth Wilmurt:
TRICIA SULLIVAN, MAY FITZGERALD, FLORA O'SHEA,
Roxana Ortega:
MILDRED NUÑEZ, IRENE D'AMATO, LEYLA COSMOS
Joe Lopez:
THE DJ, TOMAS SANTIAGO, MALCOLM XAVIER KEENE,
HERNAN SANDOVAL
Hank Di Giovanni:
BLACK BART, DR. JOHN GRAVES, FRANK WILDER,
COLIN DIXON
Sean San José:
RAOUL NUÑEZ, JAVI NUÑEZ, GABRIEL MOLINA,
DETECTIVE VICTOR OLVIDADO
Margo Hall:
EVANGELINE MADRUGA, HETTIE MCCUE,
MAEVE DIXON
Michael Cheng:
JOSIAH WOODS, TOBIN SCHUMER, IGNATIUS LIU

Video Cast

Brandon Callender . . . . Young Malcolm Xavier Keene
Darren Hochstedler . . . . Dream Hillsborough
Liam Vincent . . . . Dream Taylor

Designers & Technical Staff

Michael G. Cano . . . . Stage Manager
Suzanne Castillo . . . . Costumes
Kevin Cunz . . . . Set
Christopher Studley . . . . Lighting/Videography
Drew Yerys . . . . Soundscape
L. Peter Callender . . . . Fight Choreography
Cory Johnson . . . . Motion Graphics
Andy Kaden . . . . Set Assistant
Elizabeth Rodriguez . . . . Costumes Assistant
Niloufar Talebi . . . . Choreography
Tanya Vlach . . . . Research Director
Charmin King . . . . Assistant Stage Manager
Steve Mitchell . . . . Photography
Dan Hamaguchi . . . . Graphic Design
Melyssa Jo Kelly, Lena Monje,
Elizabeth Scott, LeAnna Sharp . . . . Production Team

17 reasons (why) was a recipient of a grant from the Wallace Alexander Gerbode New Production Fund. The play was written for Campo Santo + Intersection as part of their trajectory of plays written specifically for the company and space. During the development process, the project received two public workshop presentations at Intersection. Campo Santo + Intersection continued project development with the director, designers, historians, researchers, and neighborhood residents through workshops and readings at Intersection, including public readings in November 2001 and April 2002 in the Campo Santo Open Reading Series and Intersection's Literary Residency Program. World Premiere by Campo Santo

(Margo Hall, Sean San José, Luis Saguar, Michael Torres) + Intersection (Executive Director - Deborah Cullinan).

With thanks for the stories of: Malcolm E. Barker, Jeannie Barroga, Dorothy Bryant, Deborah Cullinan, Kevin Cunz, Benton Greene, Jeffrey Hamilton, Susan Harloe, Marcie Henderson, Bill Issel, Nancy Landolinda, Leyla Ovando, Adam Palafox, Rassan Queen, Javier Reyes, Rand Richards, Luis Saguar, Sean San José, Marilyn Shaw, Michael Torres, Nancy Traynor, Tanya Vlach.

And the research help of: Bill and Marina Jones, Victor Miller, New Mission News, Tim Wilson, Tom Carey, Alan and all the staff at the San Francisco Main Library Historical Room, Mission Branch Library, Alejandro Murguia, Bill and Norita Vlach, Stephen Parr, Sgt. Robert Fitzer of the Police Museum, Judy West, Carlos Cordova, Yolanda Lopez, Rene Yanez, Brava Theater Center, Lalo Cervantes, Lelenita's, All the Ghosts in the Machine, all the people of the Mission who let Tanya take pictures, California Historical Society, Bancroft Library, Mark Hofstatter and Peter Straus of MUNI, 33 Ashbury Muni Bus Driver, Noelia of Galeria de La Raza, Point Blank, Walter Swan of the Mission High Alumni Museum, Rose, Ramon and Lavann of St. Francis, Carole Deutch, Bud Gundy, Peter Booth Wiley, Mission Police Station, Spain Rodriguez, SFSU Labor Archives, Mormon Family History Center Genealogical Center, Audrey Revell of Dore Studio, Tracy Lin of the China Books & Periodicals Inc, Wells Fargo History Museum, Mission Dolores, Cyclops, Cliff from Sacred Rose Tattoo, Pancho and Mauro at the San Francisco Public Library, John from Whiz Burger, Notre Dame Senior Citizens Housing.

Gracías a: Selana Allen, Gabriela Barragan, Dorothy Bryant, Beth Donohue, Benton Greene, Bill Issel, Ian McConnell, Alexander V. Nichols, Rand Richards, Paul Santiago, Mark Swetz, and all who attended and worked on the readings.

Campo Santo

Like the roots of the name, Campo Santo, we are a mix of cemetery, sacred ground, and santos: The cemetery, taking new plays and bringing them to life, taking the sacred form of storytelling and using it as a tool to bond community through socially relevant plays; forming a family and passing the flame. To bring the theatre to the people: simple, direct and accessible. To let the power of the words carry and create the productions, Campo Santo cultivates writers—not just playwrights, but also fiction writers and poets—to work in a small, community-based space with actors, designers, directors and audiences to create new theatrical experiences that reflect and reinvent our society as it is today, its sins and saints, to live and learn from it. Intimate enough so the words and life spill onto the audience. We want to show the audience the world we live in and see in the audience the world we come from. We need to make a new generation of theatre audiences part of the community.

Founded in 1996, Campo Santo's core members are Margo Hall, Luis Saguar, Sean San José, and Michael Torres. We came together in an effort to create theater that is socially relevant and is accessible to a diverse inner-city population that is often marginalized or excluded from mainstream culture. While performing Octavio Solis' *Santos and Santos* at the California Youth Authority, a water pipe broke in the auditorium and we continued the reading in the living space which was only 5 x 20 feet. Though we had only the words, no set and no lights, the youth were at the edge of their seats. This experience reminded us of the power of storytelling and the essential role audiences play in bringing theatre to life.

Since our founding in 1996, we have produced over twenty highly successful productions of new works by contemporary writers including Premieres by Jorge Ignacio Cortinas, Migdalia Cruz, Philip Kan Gotanda, Naomi Iizuka, Denis Johnson, Jose Rivera, Luis Saguar, Greg Sarris, John Steppling, Erin Cressida Wilson, and others. Future works being written for the company include world premieres by Jimmy Santiago Baca, Dave Eggers, Philip Kan Gotanda Naomi Iizuka, Denis Johnson, and others.

We have achieved an enormous amount of artistic and organizational growth evidenced by an increasing number of grants including support from the San Francisco Art Commission, The Flintridge Foundation, the NEA, Theater Communications Group, The Rockefeller Foundation and others: and numerous awards including the Will Glickman Award for Best New Play for Erin Cressida Wilson's *Trail of Her Inner Thigh* and the Bay Area Theater Critics Circle Award for Best New Play for *Hellhound on My Trail* by Denis Johnson.

One of the most important elements of our growth has been our ability to cultivate long-term relationships with internationally known writers and some of the Bay Area's best theater artists—all artists who, despite their success, choose to work in our intimate, collaborative, community-based space where experimentation and risk are welcome. All of these elements have made it possible for Campo Santo to thrive artistically, to build a solid constituency, and to develop strong management, internship, and outreach structures. We have also found a home at Intersection for the Arts and, together, we are committed to taking risks, to working with writers and artists on projects that might fail and to allow our audience to experience work that is edgy and alive.

Currently all of the plays we present are written specifically for Campo Santo and are developed collaboratively over long periods of time. We feel that our greatest opportunity lies in sharing this with our community and in creating opportunities for people to engage not only in the product but in the process of making plays.

—Sean San José
Campo Santo Core Member
2003

⇒ CHARACTERS ⇐

the SUNSET SCAVENGER, collector of unrecognized treasures
JERRUSHA FITZGERALD, a miner killed for his gold
RINALDO D'AMATO, a pawn shop owner who was an ohlone chieftain in a past life
ANTONIO SANDOVAL, a tattooed resident of the sunrise hotel and thief
MARY HOLLAND SPARKS, the oldest living mormon
HAZEL SCHUMER, a laundress at the new method laundry
GLORIA KANTOR, the mambo champion of 1957
TRICIA SULLIVAN, a punk rock girl who ran away
MAY FITZGERALD, a dancing girl and the ex-wife of a gravedigger
FLORA O'SHEA, a ghost
MILDRED NUÑEZ, a nurse at a retirement home
IRENE D'AMATO, a laundress at the new method laundry
LEYLA COSMOS, a painter of murals and beautiful dyke
THE DJ, maker of music and static and echoes and noise
TOMAS SANTIAGO, a guy who was there the night of the whiz burger murder
MALCOLM XAVIER KEENE, a tattoo artist
HERNAN SANDOVAL, the mambo champion of 1957
BLACK BART, a stagecoach robber who lived in the mission
DR. JOHN GRAVES, a police surgeon
FRANK WILDER, an ancient irishman with one glass eye
COLIN DIXON, a gravedigger
RAOUL NUÑEZ, a resident of the sunrise hotel
JAVI NUÑEZ, an auto mechanic and ghost
GABRIEL MOLINA, a movie projector operator at the old roosevelt
DETECTIVE VICTOR OLVIDADO, a cop
EVANGELINE MADRUGA, a resident of the sunrise hotel
HETTIE MCCUE, the operator of a "fancy house" and opium smoker
MAEVE DIXON, a laundress at the new method laundry
JOSIAH WOODS, a young reporter from massachusetts
TOBIN SCHUMER, a runaway from kenosha, wisconsin
IGNATIUS LIU, a levitating immortal who worked in a laundry and later as a baker

1.

(*darkness. pieces of junk and debris in a vast space, an ancient building in the mission. the* SUNSET SCAVENGER *enters with a welding torch. he starts to weld a giant #1. the flame lights up the darkness. sparks. more sparks. a DJ in the shadows. he spins. the sound of static. through the static, the sound of a dial moving across different radio stations. a sea of channels. fragments of songs, hip hop, mambo, doo-wop. the* SUNSET SCAVENGER *turns off his torch. an old song starts to play. faint big band. benny goodman, guy lombardo. something like stardust.*)

SUNSET SCAVENGER: seventeen reasons why. stories from the mission. one. the beginning. or maybe it's somewhere in the middle. maybe it's just the part where you came in on, because the thing, it started already, started before you even got here. time the present, time the past, time the future. place: a senior housing facility in what used to be the old mission dolores.

(*light up on* MARY HOLLAND SPARKS, *the oldest living mormon. she's lived in the mission most all of her life. she sits in a plain old chair. behind her is a window.*)

SUNSET SCAVENGER: there's a window, looks out onto the parking lot out back. back in the day, they used to fight bears and bulls out there. big old grizzlies they brought down from up around the foothills, truckee and redding, put them in a ring with a bull, watched them fight till the death, the bulls charging and the bears clawing their way through, men shouting from the stands, clouds of dust and blood, so much blood. a contest to the death, life or death. the place is all paved over now. the blood's all washed away. the people who used to watch, they're all bones and ash now. ghosts. if you believe in ghosts.

(from the shadows, the GHOSTS IN THE MACHINE *say the names out loud, like an incantation, like a shout out, like a whispered secret, like a double dutch rhyme. they echo and overlap.)*

GHOSTS IN THE MACHINE:
    valencia
    dolores park
    mccarthy's
    cha cha cha
    lucca
    guerrero
    san carlos
    st. francis
    st. peter's
    duggan's
    south van ness
    el capitain
    el oso
    woolworths
    the york
    la victoria
    red tiger
    the new mission
    lelenita's
    whiz burger
    iglesia de dios
    falstaff
    hamm's
    payless
    cancun
    farolitos
    wang fat's
    siegel's
    the graywood
    the norma
    the sunrise
    the thor

the arlington hotel
the roosevelt tamale parlor
guadalupania
discolandia
joyeria la joya
el tico nica
king's bakery
st. mary's
new method
las palmas
duc loi's
seals stadium
marinellos
queen shoes
hunt's donuts
hamburger johnnys
valencia gardens
cesar's latin palace
roccapulco
levi strauss
folsom
shotwell
army
cesar chavez
the dovre club
doc's clock
the sunshine creamery
the roozie
the mish
miguel guadalupe hidalgo
b'nai david
ohlone
ohlone
ohlone
17 reasons why
liberty
balmy

lucky
lucky
lucky
lucky
a place called lucky street

(*the* SUNSET SCAVENGER *lights up.*)

MARY HOLLAND SPARKS: i smell marijuana. o yes. i'd know that
smell a mile away. i was at a party in the hollywood hills, this
was 1953, my starlet days. robert mitchum was there. we shared
some reefer—that's what we used to call it back then, reefer. he
was very tall and he had a very large face, his face was just huge.
we were very high, and he leaned in close and he said, "mary
sparks, you're alright." that's all. no big moral of the story.
Sometimes memories are like that. sometimes that's all there is.
i've lived in the mission most of my life, since i was a girl. i'm
mormon. i came here from new york way back when. i came by
ship, down one side of the americas, and up the other. 24,000
miles of storms and sharks and howling winds. six months at
sea. i'm the last mormon in these parts. maybe there's some
others, but i'm the oldest. that's what counts. i've lived through
earthquakes and world wars. i've lived through men on the
moon and fibre optic cable. i've lived through thirty some odd
presidents, god help me. i've seen this place go from irish, italian, german, jewish, norwegian, poor white okie to mexican,
nicaraguan, el salvadoran, guatemalan, vietnamese, arab, filipino, laotian, you name it. i seen it go from poor to rich to
poor to rich to mixed up-and-i-don't-know-what. i seen it all.
i'm old. you have no idea. the nurses here, they think i'm about
ninety-five, ninety-six. nice girls. belen and marta, mildred and
inez. i like them, but they don't know shit. i'm one hundred and
sixty-seven, give or take a day. they don't ask and i don't tell.

(*the image gradually comes into focus. it's the face of a young girl
seen close up. her eyelids are shut tight and flickering. she's
dreaming.*)

MARY HOLLAND SPARKS: because i knew, i knew the answer, and i wanted to tell you, too, right then and there, i wanted to say it out loud, but i didn't. you get to be a certain age, i don't care what anybody says, you forget. it's like you go looking for a thing, but it ain't right in front of you anymore. it's in some box in the attic, and you gotta hunt through all the old photographs, the knickknacks and the souvenirs, the vinyl records and the eight track tapes, the dried flowers and the mass cards, the blue dress, blue like the color of sky, that kind of blue, you know, robin's egg blue, folded in tissue paper, silk, the scent of lavender coming up from the creases like a memory. all the things you know by heart—the smell of your mother's skin, the sound of your father's shoes on the cement, that part in the movie that used to make you cry, that song you used to listened to on the am radio.

(*the sound of a girl singing an old english folk song, eerie and beautiful, strange and familiar. the sleeping girl opens her eyes. the image of the girl fills the whole space. her face is the universe. her eyes are huge. they blink. they blink. TRICIA emerges from out of the girl's retina, out of the dark, black pupil of her eye. she comes closer and closer. we see she's the singer of the song. she's a punk girl circa 1989 with a mohawk and piercings and steel toe boots, a tattooed tear drop at the corner of her eye. she starts to sing. she sings and MARY begins to speak. TRICIA singing grows fainter.*)

MARY HOLLAND SPARKS: yes o yes. i can still see her face, old-fashioned face. you could see her mother and her mother's mother in the bones of her face, in the blue grey blue of her eyes. i thought, you look like so many girls i used to know. all the girls i used to know. big dreams. hard lives. tricia, flora. mary, may. yes, i know the answer. i know it in my bones. she knows and i know, but she's not here to say, only i am. i'm the last one standing.

(*TRICIA fades away. city sounds. people you can't see outside MARY SPARKS' window. voices. laughter. the sound of a boom box. salsa music. hip hop music. the sound of the music outside the window grows louder. MARY HOLLAND SPARKS fades away. smoke rings in the air. the SUNSET SCAVENGER takes a long drag from his cigarette. he writes the #2 with a finger of smoke. the sound of traffic. the sound of evangelicos talking about hell and salvation on the microphone and the men against the wall going pssssss pssssss, chiva, coca, pssssss pssssss pssssssssss.*)

2.

(*am radio. seventies soul and then some sweet dopey love song you secretly know all the words to. i'm thinking like "didn't i blow your mind this time" by the delfonics. mission street. june 1977. TOMAS SANTIAGO and MILDRED NUÑEZ are waiting for the #14 bus. they're fifteen years old. they're kissing on each other, while the whole world spins around them.*)

MILDRED: hold up, tomas, hold up hold up.
TOMAS: what? what is it?
MILDRED: i smell something funny. you smell that? smell.
TOMAS: whiz burger.
MILDRED: no.
TOMAS: gasoline diesel oil.
MILDRED: no uh uh something else. it's like, it's like it's blood and shit and piss and death—
TOMAS: mildred—
MILDRED: seriously, i smell all this dead shit in the air. it's going to rain. i'm telling you, you can smell butchertown all the way over from hunter's point, and that means rain.
TOMAS: i smell something, i don't know what it is.
MILDRED: that be dead cow. it stinks. dang. where's the bus? come on, bus. come on, bus. i'm willing you to come on and get here already, stupid bus.

(*the sound of a car bass thumping.* MILDRED *and* TOMAS *stare at a passing car. it rumbles by. it shakes the world with its bigass bass.*)

MILDRED: '64 impala.

TOMAS: i see it.

MILDRED: all chopped and riding down low, all red red candy apple red.

TOMAS: i said i see it.

MILDRED: who are those guys?

TOMAS: i don't know.

MILDRED: tomas.

TOMAS: don't look at me like that.
(*pause.*) what? what?
what does it matter? it don't matter, so don't even worry about it, cause you don't know them.

MILDRED: tough guy.

TOMAS: that's me.

MILDRED: you think that.

TOMAS: i don't think it. i know it.

MILDRED: tss.

TOMAS: listen up, mildred, the world's a hazardous place. full of liars and hucksters and natural born killers, demons, and angels, too, mysteries and natural wonders, freaks of nature and miraculous goings on, things we can't even get our brains around. you don't even know.

MILDRED: what are you talking about, noodlehead?

TOMAS: what i'm talking about? what i'm talking about, "miss-straight-a-know—it-all-cause-i-read-it-in-some-book"? goddamn, you don't know nothing. okay, let me give you an example. let me illuminate you.

MILDRED: yeah you do that, illuminate me.

TOMAS: i'm trying see i'm trying. it's like, you know that old chinese guy, the one who works at the panaderia?

MILDRED: yeah. so? what about him?

TOMAS: like i saw him, like i saw him last night. through his window.

MILDRED: what were you doing all peeping around on the old chinese guy, looking in his window?

TOMAS: i wasn't peeping around. he had his blinds up and the lights on inside. i was just walking home, minding my own business, and i look up and i see he was all doing these kung fu moves in slow motion. like wah. wah. wah. wah. and then he started to like levitate, like some kind of ancient wizard man, just rising up, higher and higher, till he was just like floating there in the middle of the room, just floating. i could see his little chinky slippers floating there, like he was walking on air.

MILDRED: it's not nice to say chinky.

TOMAS: you're missing the point, mildred—

MILDRED: that's like calling somebody beaner or wetback. or (*whispers.*) nigger.

TOMAS: say again.

MILDRED: you heard me.

TOMAS: did you say "nigger"?

MILDRED: you heard me, tomas.

TOMAS: see that big black girl over there. you say that word one more time, she's going to hear you and she's going to come over and kick your ass but good.

MILDRED: oh yeah? well i'll kick her ass right back.

TOMAS: oh you will?

MILDRED: yeah i will.

TOMAS: she's big. she's a big girl.

MILDRED: i don't care. i'm fast.

TOMAS: you ain't that fast.

MILDRED: shut up. you don't know. you don't know anything.

TOMAS: i'll take care of you, mildred.

MILDRED: i don't need taking care of. i don't. where's that bus? goddamn bus. it's like it never comes. and then when it comes, it's like you get on, and everybody's all giving you the once over, and it's loud and funky smelling and drab-like, and somebody's always fighting over some stupid thing, and then you got some idiot spilled his drink all over the place and it's all sticky and wet and shit, and there's no place to sit except all the way in back where everybody's all spread out, taking up way too much room, and they ain't gonna move one inch, and so you gotta squish up next to somebody all thigh to thigh, and the seat's all warm, and some creepy guy's looking at you with these weird old fish eyes.

TOMAS: it's just the bus.

MILDRED: what i'm saying, what i'm saying is it's too many people. in general. there's no room. it's just way too many people. i mean what the hell, i mean who are all these people?

TOMAS: "these people," what do you mean "these people"? girl, you know practically every damn person on this street. there's that guy antonio who hangs out with your brother raoul, and there's that guy malcolm who does the tattoos, and there's old man molina who used to work at the york, and old lady dixon with the cane and mrs. d'amato, and that's some faggots i don't know—

MILDRED: shut up don't say that—

TOMAS: —and there's victor and mando and daniel and luis, and joachim and manolo and frankie and martine, and elena's tia gloria with vanessa's baby and the older brother i forget his name, and there over there, there's that that old irish guy with the glass eye like columbo—

MILDRED: i know i know. i know all them people.

TOMAS: i know you know. that's what i'm saying, mildred. you know every single one of them, almost, so don't be talking about all "these people." you're a homegirl. face it. hometown, homegrown, homegirl.

MILDRED: i know what i am, tomas. i don't need you telling me what i am, alright. like you even know anything. telling me something i don't know—yeah right. fool. (*pause.*) what? what?

TOMAS: i like you, mildred. you got moxie.

MILDRED: say again?

TOMAS: moxie. the old irish guy taught me that word.

MILDRED: what old irish guy?

TOMAS: you know—columbo. the one with the glass eye. he lives in the old church up by 15th and dolores. i think his name is like frank, frank something.

MILDRED: why were you talking to him?

TOMAS: i don't know. i was just talking to him.

MILDRED: what's it mean?

TOMAS: moxie? it means like sass. you know. attitude.

MILDRED: i don't like that guy.

TOMAS: he's okay. he don't hurt no one.

MILDRED: he's nasty. and he drinks.

TOMAS: i drink.

MILDRED: i know you drink. you don't have to tell me you drink. i smell it when you drink. and it's nasty, too. all stinky beer breath. you didn't never used to drink. you never used to drink.

TOMAS: mildred—

MILDRED: i swear, tomas, you got no sense sometimes, kicking it with all those low class, hoodlum types, drinking and being all boisterous and ignorant and shit. you ain't even like that. you ain't nothing like that. stupid, it's so stupid.

TOMAS: you love me, mildred. admit it. just confess your love for me. just go on and get it over with.

MILDRED: get away from me, cause i ain't going to even kiss you now. now i'm pissed off.

TOMAS: i'll wait.

MILDRED: you'll wait a long time.

TOMAS: okay. then i'll wait a long time. i can wait. (*pause.*) you still pissed off?

MILDRED: yeah. (*pause.*) did you—? i mean did you really—? did you see that chinese guy, you know—?

TOMAS: yeah.

MILDRED: for real?

TOMAS: uh huh.

MILDRED: that's crazy.

TOMAS: yeah it is.

MILDRED: i didn't tell you my dream. i was going to tell you, but then i forgot.

TOMAS: what dream?

MILDRED: nah it's stupid.

TOMAS: (*tickling MILDRED.*) come on come on, tell me tell me tell me.

MILDRED: quit it, don't don't—okay. alright. last night, last night i dreamt that you and me, i dreamt we was dancing. but it was this kind of dance i don't even know how to do. not in real life anyways. like kinda like a samba or a mambo, foxtrot, i don't know. and we was in this old ballroom, and there was like shiny wood floors, and a mirror ball, you know, all spinning and spinning, and then the music started going, and it was us, but it wasn't us. it was like us if we had lived a long time ago, like if we were people from before we were like even born. and we looked different, but inside, you know, it was us. and you were all done up in a suit and tie, and you looked sharp, too, and i was wearing this blue dress, i remember that, silk, and it was beautiful. it was like the most beautiful dress in the world. (*pause.*) wait. wait. you feel that?

TOMAS: (*pause.*) rain.

MILDRED: rain.

TOMAS: it's starting. come on, come on. run.

(*MILDRED and TOMAS run for cover. the rain begins to fall. it falls and falls. sheets of rain. the bus comes. and then another and then another. they speed by. a blur of metal in the rain. the sound of radio stations switching one to the next. static. the #3 in an oil stained puddle, slick and opalescent like mother of pearl.*)

3.

(*DETECTIVE VICTOR OLVIDADO appears in the shadows.*)

VICTOR OLVIDADO: what i remember, what i remember—see cause it was like a place, it was like a place we all went to, corner of 18th and south van ness. there was a big neon sign, whiz burger, nice, you know, kinda retro style—this was when everything was all fifties retro, happy days and shit—and everybody went there, older kids, but families, too, everybody. i mean i knew, i knew that guy cordova, he was like friends with my uncle tomas, i remember him hanging around, just kicking it. he was somebody, i mean he was somebody i knew, and i think about that, i think about that i knew him, and then afterwards everything that happened, but how would you know that, how would you know how fucked up somebody is just to look at them. i wasn't there that night. this was 1977, i was just a little kid. it was summer, right after school got out. robert hillsborough, that was his name, the guy who got killed. he was a gardener. i don't know why i remember that. i used to have these dreams. i'd see him and his boyfriend in like this garden, you know, all trees and green. it was a sunny day and they were happy, you could tell just by looking at them. and then they kissed, and i remember thinking in my dream that it was kinda fucked up, but then i didn't think that anymore. i just thought they seemed happy, you know, they seemed happy like people at the end of a movie who live happily ever after, like that. then i'd wake up, and i knew that guy, that he was dead, and what i dreamt, it wasn't real. afterwards, this was a long time afterwards, my uncle tomas, he told me he was there that night. he had gone out dancing with this girl mildred nuñez he used to know, and then he went and met up with those guys after. it wasn't planned or anything. things just got, they got out of hand. he said it was like cordova, it was like he went crazy. he told me he watched the whole thing go down, he just watched, and then he ran away. he never told nobody but me. and i never told nobody either, but i never looked at him the same after that, i never did.

(*MILDRED and TOMAS appear again. the moment right after they stop kissing. not a movie. but real. VICTOR and TOMAS look at each other across time.*)

MILDRED: tomas?

(*TOMAS walks away. MILDRED watches him disappear into the night. the sounds of the city. the sound of a car bass rumbling, drowning out all the other noises.*)

MILDRED: tomas. tomas!

(shouts and screams. the sound of mayhem. a siren. a #4 in cursive writes itself like etch-a-sketch magic in the darkness.)

4.

(picture of a little boy standing in the void. his name's MALCOLM XAVIER KEENE. *he's maybe eight years old. his skin's the color of coffee. he's a beautiful little boy, dressed up in his sunday finest. the focus narrows to his face.)*

MALCOLM XAVIER KEENE: "To be, or not to be, that is the question:
Whether 'tis nobler in the mind to suffer
The slings and arrows of outrageous fortune,
Or to take arms against a sea of troubles,
And by opposing, end them. To die, to sleep—
No more, and by a sleep to say we end
The heart-ache and the thousand natural shocks
That flesh is heir to; 'tis a consummation
Devoutly to be wished. To die, to sleep—
To sleep, perchance to dream."

(the sound of static. the sound of an old vinyl record playing on the victrola. a crackling voice from long ago.)

BLACK BART: poetry. hell, you want some poetry. well alright then,
i'll give you some goddamn poetry. here's a verse i penned just
now. special. for you:
"i've labored long and hard for bread,
for honor and for riches,
but on my corns too long you've tread,
you fine-haired sons of bitches."

(a low, hoarse laugh. cold and bone dry, like if a skull could laugh. it reverberates in the echo chamber of time. the sound of ragtime, tinny and cheerful and faraway. in the far off distance, the image of a man in a long, white duster with a white flour sac over his

head, the eyes cut out. he holds a double barreled shot gun aimed straight ahead. he fires. an explosion of bright light. and then a cloud of dust particles swirling in the air. an old recording of nina simone's "my baby just cares for me." a neon #5 flickers on.)

5.

(the sunrise hotel. 1983. the music fades out. ANTONIO SANDOVAL is ironing a shirt. he has tattoos all on his back and arms and chest. scars, too. RAOUL and EVANGELINE are drinking tallboys.)

ANTONIO:
    the sun don't shine at the sunrise hotel,
    and the folks at the norma ain't normal,
    the folks at the thor are on thorazine,
    and the arlington is—what the hell is the arlington?
    hormal.
    formal.
    dormal.

RAOUL: dormal ain't no word. i think you're thinking dorsal.

EVANGELINE: yeah.

RAOUL: now, dorsal, see, dorsal is a word

EVANGELINE: uh huh, that's right.

RAOUL: like fin. like on a dolphin.

EVANGELINE: uh huh.

RAOUL: like dorsal fin.

ANTONIO: really?

RAOUL: yeah, like you know, like a fin. it's a kind of fin.

ANTONIO: i never knew that. man, you got vocabulary knowledge like nobody i know.

EVANGELINE: i knew that word. dorsal. i knew that word.

RAOUL: you knew that word?

EVANGELINE: what i say? yeah, i knew that word. i knew it before he said it even.

RAOUL: really?

EVANGELINE: yeah "really." what you chuckling at, chucklehead?

RAOUL: nothing.

EVANGELINE: you want to say something to me. spit it out, ugly.

RAOUL: that just surprises me, evangeline, that's all.

EVANGELINE: oh yeah, uh huh, and why does that surprise you?

RAOUL: no reason, i guess. i just didn't know you knew so much about marine life.

EVANGELINE: yeah? well, i got news for you, raoul, i know all about marine life, i know all about that shit. i got an uncle, his family, that side of the family, they're all like tuna fisherman down in san diego. they live right by the ocean, chula vista, point loma. and they have these boats. nice boats, you know, fifty feet, sixty feet, more even. nice wood inside and everything all neat as a pin. and they go out. and they fish with these big nets. and they make a shitload of money. they're fucking rich motherfuckers. tuna, i'm telling you, tuna is good business.

ANTONIO: i did not know that. i'm learning all kinds of new shit everyday.

RAOUL: he give you money ever, your uncle?

EVANGELINE: no.

RAOUL: you ever go down there and ask?

EVANGELINE: hell no. like i'm going to take a bus all the way down to san diego, show up on my uncle's doorstep all fresh out of nowhere, asking him for money. that's some tacky shit, raoul, hitting up your own family for scratch. you got no shame.

RAOUL: i got shame.

EVANGELINE: no you don't, you got no shame. you one shameless individual, raoul nuñez. besides, i don't even need their money. i got my own damn money.

RAOUL: oh yeah?

EVANGELINE: yeah. i got a check coming. injury settlement.

RAOUL: you don't look injured.

EVANGELINE: what are you, a doctor now? you got some degree in medicine i don't know about? they's internal injuries, my vital organs, my liver and my kidneys and shit. my neck, too. hell, you don't need to know all the details. it's personal. that's why they call it personal injury. it's personal. check's coming any day now.

RAOUL: is that right?

EVANGELINE: what i say? i swear to god, you plug-eared and ugly.

ANTONIO: how much?

EVANGELINE: a lot.

ANTONIO: how much is a lot?

EVANGELINE: honey, you don't even want to know. just imagine. imagine evangeline in a big old stretch limo cruising down easy street, wearing gold and diamonds and a big fur coat, big wad a hundreds in her pocket.

RAOUL: girl, that's so ghetto.

EVANGELINE: shut up, ugly.

RAOUL: listen up, if you really got some money coming, i got some investment opportunities i might maybe let you in on. get you in on the groundfloor. properties, you know, venture capital and shit. i'm telling you, new technology, evangeline, bio-pharmeceuticals, that's where it's at. play your cards, right, you gonna double your initial investment in the first six months. low risk, high yield, no shit. let your money grow instead of blowing it all up front.

EVANGELINE: what do you think, antonio?

ANTONIO: man's gotta plan, sounds like.

EVANGELINE: sounds more like a scam to me.

RAOUL: girl, you gonna be missing out, and then you gonna be sorry.

EVANGELINE: we'll see, we'll see. investments, tsss. what does that even mean? lots of talk, some paper, sounds like one step up from some kind of check kiting nonsense. hell with that. tell you what, with me, i like to hold a thing, you know, in my hands. cash, gold, car keys, jewelry, nice 45, what have you.

ANTONIO: i hear that, i hear that.

EVANGELINE: now you see now, antonio here, antonio, he gotta real business going on. he got it going on. he buys and sells. he moves shit from here to there and back again. he provides a valuable service. and it's hands on, you hear what i'm saying. ain't about venture capital investment bipharmaceutical bull-sheet. it's business. antonio here he understands business.

RAOUL: yeah? then what's he doing coming off a five-year stretch?

ANTONIO: cost of doing business.

EVANGELINE: mmhm, that's right.

ANTONIO: raoul, man, i can't even believe you bring that up. you know damn well that whole thing, that was crap. that was just some stupid shit. it wasn't even supposed to go down like that. just a little misunderstanding, that's all.

RAOUL: don't even talk to me about any that.

ANTONIO: you brought that shit up. you the one be dredging it all up.

RAOUL: you lucky, antonio. that's all i'll say. you a lucky man. you better hope that luck don't run out.

ANTONIO: see, raoul, let me tell you about luck. it works like this. i got nine lives, raoul. you forget that fact. i'm like a cat. i got spring in my step. i got a flick in my tail. i got a lucky charm. i got a lucky number. i got all my bases covered.

RAOUL: i'm serious.

ANTONIO: i'm serious, too. i'm a serious cat.

RAOUL: fuck you.

ANTONIO: raoul—

RAOUL: cause see this is some messed up shit, this is some kinda crazy shit is what i think. i think you're crazy is what i think.

ANTONIO: i don't give a damn what you think.

RAOUL: yeah you don't give a damn. you don't give a damn about shit.

ANTONIO: ain't for you to be worrying about.

RAOUL: stupid is what it is, fuckin stupid.

ANTONIO: just leave it be alright.

RAOUL: of all the dumb, lameass shit—

ANTONIO: i said leave it be. leave it.

RAOUL: fuck you, antonio. fuckin dumb motherfucker.(*pause.*) luck. yeah you tell me about luck. damn.

ANTONIO: man's gotta earn a living. man's gotta have a plan. you got your plan, raoul. i got mine.

RAOUL: whatever you say.

ANTONIO: that's right. whatever i say. you got that right, whatever i say.

(*silence. the sound of the steam hiss from the iron. steam, hiss. steam, hiss. steam, hiss.*)

EVANGELINE: how did that go again, that poem you was writing?

ANTONIO:
> the sun don't shine at the sunrise hotel,
> and the folks at the norma ain't normal,
> the folks at the thor are on thorazine,
> and the arlington is, the arlington is – damn. i can't make nothing rhyme with normal. i gotta maybe switch things around, you know switch the lines around. cause with thorazine, you got some more options, right. you got benzene.

EVANGELINE: visine.

ANTONIO: denteen.

EVANGELINE: blue jean.

ANTONIO: whip cream.

EVANGELINE: kerosene.

RAOUL: valvoline.

EVANGELINE: ketamine. tricycline. morphine.

RAOUL: evangeline.

ANTONIO: yeah, that's good, that's good. evangeline, i like that.

(*ANTONIO puts his shirt on, the one he just ironed.*)

EVANGELINE: slick. you look so slick, antonio. you do better than my own mother with them creases and the collar, the collar looks good. who taught you to iron?

ANTONIO: my uncle hernan. hernan sandoval. old school pachuco. lover and a dancer. mambo champion of 1957. that man had pleats in his pants so sharp they could slice meat.

EVANGELINE: yeah? well uncle hernan taught you good. i don't see one wrinkle, not a one. look and the sleeves, you did the sleeves nice. where'd you get that iron anyway?

ANTONIO: it was a gift.

EVANGELINE: that's a nice iron. with the steam action. sunbeam. yeah, sunbeam that's a good brand. i been thinking i need an iron. i got me some dresses they get so wrinkly, rayon you know. it's not supposed to wrinkle, that's what they say, but that's a damn lie, cause those dresses wrinkle like you can't even believe, i can't even wear em like that, all wrinkly and messy and shit. maybe i can have your iron. can i have your iron?

ANTONIO: no.

EVANGELINE: just to borrow sometime, when i need it.

ANTONIO: i tell you what, evangeline, anything ever happens to me, you can have my iron, how about that?

EVANGELINE: what if i want it now?

ANTONIO: then you gonna be sorely disappointed.

EVANGELINE: wouldn't be the first time. oh man, i like this iron. sunbeam. this is a quality iron. i want this iron. someday.

ANTONIO: someday.

RAOUL: where's my cigarettes?

EVANGELINE: honey, i smoke newports. i don't smoke no goddamn pall malls, so don't even look at me like that.

ANTONIO: (*retrieving a pack of cigarettes.*) here.

RAOUL: i just need one for the road.

ANTONIO: nah. keep em, just keep em.

RAOUL: you sure?

ANTONIO: yeah, keep em. it's only half a pack anyway.

RAOUL: i'll get you next time.

ANTONIO: yeah, get me next time.

RAOUL: i ain't just saying that.

ANTONIO: i know you ain't. i know that, raoul. ain't no big deal, ain't nothing. man, you take everything so serious. don't he take everything so serious.

EVANGELINE: yeah he does.

ANTONIO: yeah he does.

EVANGELINE: baby, you look so slick. where you going looking so slick?

ANTONIO: i got me an appointment.

EVANGELINE: oh yeah? is that right? what, you got a date or something?

ANTONIO: yeah something, something like that.

EVANGELINE: who you got a date with?

ANTONIO: honey, i got a date with destiny.

EVANGELINE: that her name?

ANTONIO: yeah, yeah that's her name.

EVANGELINE: that's a nice name. i like that name. what's she like, miss destiny?

ANTONIO: i can't get her out of my head, she's like that.

EVANGELINE: pretty? i bet she's pretty, i bet she's real pretty.

ANTONIO: yeah she is. kinda hard, kinda cold, but pretty, yeah she's pretty. more than pretty even. she's the kinda woman makes you want her just by how she looks at you. like a promise, like a dare. she don't even have to say a word. and if you want what she got, you gotta come to her, you gotta meet her where she stands. ain't no other way. and when you get close to her, when you get right up close, you never know, you never know what's going to happen. that's the thing. she could fuck you up. or she could make your dreams come true all at once, and for real. she's like that. that's what she's like.

EVANGELINE: antonio?

ANTONIO: i'll be back.

EVANGELINE: yeah?

ANTONIO: yeah.

EVANGELINE: antonio?

ANTONIO: i'll be right back. i'm just going around the corner. i gotta get something at the liquor store. i won't be long.

(*EVANGELINE and RAOUL recede from view into the darkness. ANTONIO remains. the light closes in around ANTONIO. the sound of radio switching stations. voices and static, through a sea of static, pieces of that old curtis mayfield song "back in the world," and through it all the sound of traffic, the sound of breathing, the sound of footsteps, somebody running, running for his life. ANTONIO is in a circle of light. he lifts a gun from his waistband. he aims. he hesitates. and in his hesitation, it opens a hole in time where everything stops and all the other sounds fade away. and all you hear is the sound of gorecki's third symphony. dawn upshaw singing, her voice so beautiful and lucid, so full of wanting that it breaks your heart. ANTONIO drops his gun and begins running towards the audience. the sound of a shotgun blast from behind him. a flash of bright white light. ANTONIO freezes in mid-motion, his legs in mid-stride, his arms in the middle of pushing through the glass door of the liquor store. he is filled with light. so much light. you can see his veins, you can see the muscle and the*

bone, you can see the heart beating through his skin. and then all
is darkness.)

6.

(in the darkness, a woman whispers the word: six. the buzzing of
the tattoo needle begins. light on the back of a girl. a tattoo artist
works on the field of her back. projected onto the back wall are
photographs of san francisco and the mission circa 1890s. sepia
tinted street scenes. cable cars and old buildings. portraits of people who lived a hundred years ago, women in long dresses, steel-
workers and shipyard workers, the faces of immigrants, children
playing stickball in the street. photos of old crime scenes, men shot
dead in stairwells and abandoned alleys. as the images are projected, a young reporter from massachusetts named JOSIAH
WOODS is in the midst of composing a letter home.)

JOSIAH WOODS: there is what one can only describe as a kind of
wild west mentality to the portion of the city which the locals
call the mission. the place teems with all manner of criminal
element—pickpockets, charlatans, fancy ladies and petty
thieves. i have in my brief sojourn here been witness to no less
than eight stabbings, two shootings, a host of public brawls,
and more instances of public intoxication than i care now to
enumerate. there are a disproportionate number of saloons,
dim, rather cave-like establishments frequented, it seems,
exclusively by men. of keen interest to me is the fate of one
black bart, known also as the gentleman bandit. the man wore
a mask over his face and fancied himself a poet, penning vers-
es and leaving them at the scenes of his various crimes. he was
captured in 1883 after a botched robbery. shot by one of his
would-be victims, he managed to escape, but in his haste, made
what would prove a fateful error, leaving in his wake a bloodied
handkerchief, in the corner of which was printed a distinctive
laundry mark. the wells fargo men traced the piece of linen
back to a chinese laundry in the heart of the mission, and from

there tracked down black bart, whose address, as it so happens, was a rooming house not far from that selfsame laundry. he was sentenced to six years in prison, after which time he was released, and disappeared without a trace. i have since undertaken a search for him, and if my luck and finances permit, to find out what became of him, and in so doing uncover the story of his life. why choose one man's story over another's? what quirk of fate? what strange compulsion? a kind of avarice, i imagine, a kind of greed to know another's secrets. and also, too, a sense, perhaps, that in the story of another, one might find for a brief instant the key that might unlocks one's own.

(JOSIAH WOODS vanishes. the buzzing of the tattoo needle stops. the tattoo artist pulls back. we see on the girl's back a tattooed #7 in a thick, ornate, old english script.)

7.

(the here and now. faraway you can hear some miles davis. bitches brew. a tattoo parlor in the mission. MALCOLM XAVIER KEENE, all grown up, takes a pause in his tattooing, and then resumes now and again throughout the scene. LEYLA COSMOS is the girl getting tattooed.)

LEYLA COSMOS: say again his name.

MALCOLM XAVIER KEENE: antonio sandoval. that man had beautiful tattoos. old school tats, color like stained glass on a sunny day. liquor store robbery. shotgun blast through the heart, shot right through the heart. all that work, all that artistry, all that hands of man would render—worm food in the end.

LEYLA: that sounds like the line to some poem or something.

MALCOLM: that ain't no poem. that's my natural everyday speech. you want a poem? girl, i'll give you a poem.

LEYLA: the red man wrote me a poem just before i got here.

MALCOLM: the red man? my poem's better than some red man poem. the red man ain't no poet. fuck the red man.

LEYLA: the red man's poem was pretty good.

MALCOLM: i don't want to hear about the red man no more. the poem's forming in my mind, i need some quiet whilst it takes shape:

in the black and blue, in the sacred rose, in cyclops and jerry's and frisco tattoo,

there is the history of a particle of human flesh,

which refused the consumation of death,

as if the inner eye in its thirst, its thirst you see, for a greater and greater reality

had converted those selfsame pores of flesh into hungry seeing mouths—

LEYLA: whoa whoa whoa who said that?

MALCOLM: i did. just now.

LEYLA: you're quoting, malcolm. who're you quoting—walt whitman?

MALCOLM: no—

LEYLA: william shakespeare—

MALCOLM: "to be or not to be, that is the question." i know my shakespeare, i know all that shit by heart, i learned that shit when i was a kid, and this ain't shakespeare.

LEYLA: allen ginsberg jack kerouac.

MALCOLM: hell no. allen ginsburgh jack kerouac my ass. i'm quoting myself—malcolm xavier keene.

LEYLA: somebody else said that, i know they did.

MALCOLM: somebody else said every damn thing there is to say. what makes it special is how i finesse it, how i massage the gist, the syntactical twists and turns, how i lay hands on a thing, the sense my fingers make, the secret patterns in my fingertips.

LEYLA: is that what makes you special, malcolm? (*admiring her new tattoo.*) that's nice. you made it look nice. i'm painting a mural right now—did i tell you that? down near 17th and mission. it's going to be like this history of the mission. like the place, you know, the neighborhood, but also all the people, it's going to be like all the people, from the ohlone indian goddess of light to just plain everyday people, people you don't even know their names, but they're all part of it, see, they're all gonna be in my mural.

MALCOLM: that's a big mural.

LEYLA: it's kicking my ass.

MALCOLM: i want to be in that mural. me and the goddess of light.

LEYLA: we'll see, we'll see.

MALCOLM: you got a nice back, leyla. it's all nice. nice back, nice elbows, nice knees.

LEYLA: knees? you never even seen my knees.

MALCOLM: i can tell. i got a sense about these things. you should wear more skirts. show off your knee caps.

LEYLA: you should wear a skirt, too, malcolm. i bet you got nice knee caps.

MALCOLM: girl, i ain't wearing no skirt.

LEYLA: a sarong. it's polynesian.

MALCOLM: i ain't polynesian.

LEYLA: you could be. i got some polynesian in me, as a matter of fact. no it's true. like one sixteenth. my mom's part polynesian, part guatemalan, part Filipino, part german, part equadoran, part el salvadoran, and part irish. and my dad's like part italian, part moroccan, part samoan, part swedish, part mexican, part indian, part chinese, and part greek.

MALCOLM: damn, girl. that's a lot of countries. i'm dizzy just thinking about it. it's fuckin dizzying.

LEYLA: it's the future.

MALCOLM: is that right?

LEYLA: in the future, everybody's gonna be like me. you're looking at the future right here, malcolm.

MALCOLM: i like the future. the future's real pretty. so leyla?

LEYLA: yeah?

MALCOLM: so you still like girls or what?

LEYLA: malcolm man, you ask me that every time i see you.

MALCOLM: i'm checking in just checking in. you never know. weather changes. you got your arctic cold fronts, you got your gulf stream moving in.

LEYLA: it ain't like the weather.

MALCOLM: i'm speaking metaphorically.

LEYLA: i still like girls.

MALCOLM: another incarnation maybe. a little further down river.

LEYLA: what river?

MALCOLM: what river? o now, o now. listen up and learn, miss leyla cosmos. right this second, we're sitting atop a river. no that's for real. it's all underneath us, a big old river running underground. put your ear to the sidewalk 16th and mission—

LEYLA: i ain't putting my ear to no sidewalk at 16th and mission—

MALCOLM: i'm serious, you do that and you can hear the woosh woosh of the water, down below the pavement and the cement and the asphalt. it's deep down deep, green black water, glistening and opalescent, looks still almost, but you get closer and closer and you see it's moving, it's moving so fast, the currents take you away.

(*the sound of water. old style music, a player piano. JERRUSHA FITZGERALD appears. HETTIE MCCUE takes shape. they pose for a photograph in period dress. HETTIE MCCUE is wearing a corset. circa 1870. sepia tinted. they stare out into the eye of the camera, into an unknown future.*)

MALCOLM: this is my great great grandfather, jerrusha fitzgerald. this is my great great grandmother hettie mccue. i'm not born yet. i'm not even close to born. i'm just a glint in the eye, an embryonic possibility. jerrusha struck gold, they say, made a tiny fortune when a fortune could be made. sewed the gold nuggets in the lining of his special coat. died in a brawl in a bar down by shotwell, lost the coat along the way. they say his ghost wanders the streets of the mission looking for that coat, touching the backs of strangers as they pass, pulling at the lining, tugging at seams.

LEYLA: what happened to hettie mccue?

MALCOLM: i don't know. no one knows. fell off the boat of history, and then she just, she just kinda floated away.

(*the sound of the river gets louder. MALCOLM XAVIER KEENE and LEYLA COSMOS recede from view. JERRUSHA FITZGERALD and HETTIE MCCUE remain. they are figures in a photograph. the photograph floats down the river. HETTIE*

MCCUE's *corset transforms into an hourglass #8. and then the people are carried away by the currents, and all that's left is #8. on the surface of the water you can see a #8, warped and shimmering.)*

8.

(*a river. the whole world becomes rushing water, green black and glistening. you get closer, and the water sounds like fire, rushing and roaring, the suck of oxygen, the suck of the current rushing out to sea. the photograph of* JERRUSHA FITZGERALD *and* HETTIE MCCUE *spins and swirls on the surface of the water, slowly crumbles and disintegrates.* HETTIE MCCUE *disappears. the light gets brighter and brighter. the blinding flash of the old-fashioned camera.* JERRUSHA FITZGERALD *begins to transform into* RINALDO D'AMATO. *as he transforms, the sound of a girls' singsong chant "my name is cece/come out and play with me. . . ." bleeding into "ninety-six tears" bleeding into the sound of an old-fashioned piano. an old theatre in the mission. 1899.* MAY FITZGERALD, *a dancing girl, appears. she's getting dressed for a show. ruffles in her skirt and feathers in her hair. she looks at herself in a mirror. she hikes up her skirt and adjusts a garter.* IGNATIUS LIU *appears. he wears a queue and a coolie jacket. he carries a stack of clean laundry.*)

MAY: pretty as lotta crabtree, prettier even, don't you think? wait, don't, don't go. i'm may, may fitzgerald. my mother married a chinaman. her second husband that was. her first was a miner, irish like her, beat her with a switch and locked her in her room. got himself killed one night, cheated at cards, got a knife in the gut, served him right, hettie said. that was her name. my mother, i mean. hettie, hettie mccue. her second husband, his name was wah. charlie wah. he had a laundry in the mission. he died, too. found him in the morning, till emptied out, neck slit ear to ear. my mother had no luck with men, cursed she was. charlie had a bunch of wives here and back in china, too. who knows, we might be brother and sister. is your name wah?

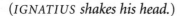
(*IGNATIUS shakes his head.*)

MAY: what's your name then, chinaman?
IGNATIUS: i can't tell. it's a secret.
MAY: why would a name be secret? names aren't secret. why should they be?
IGNATIUS: powerful. secret. like a magic spell.
MAY: a magic spell? do you know magic?

(*IGNATIUS nods.*)

MAY: like what?

(*IGNATIUS pulls a flower from MAY's ear. or something equally delightful.*)

MAY: ah. wondrous man. you're a treat you are. can you tell fortunes?
IGNATIUS: tea leaves, cards, palm of your hand.
MAY: can you tell me my fortune?

(*MAY extends her hand. IGNATIUS takes it in his own.*)

MAY: what do you see? what is it, chinaman? what do you see?

(*IGNATIUS won't say her fortune. he won't say it aloud. but you can see it in his eyes. he exits.*)

MAY: wait, chinaman, wait. wait for me.

(*RINALDO D'AMATO lights up a marijuana cigarette. a nimbus of smoke. MAY fades away. the sound of a projector. the numbers 1, 2, 3, 4, 5, 6, 7, 8, 9. then scratchy white, then black. the sound of film sputtering to the end of the reel.*)

9.

(*the roosevelt. 1958. the projection booth of an empty movie the-atre. GABRIEL MOLINA unloads a reel, loads another into the projector. RINALDO D'AMATO smokes a marijuana cigarette.*)

RINALDO D'AMATO: gabriel man, i'm so high right now. i think i'm seeing visions like a great ohlone chieftain, shaman, medicine man.

GABRIEL MOLINA: what are you talking about, medicine man?

RINALDO D'AMATO: ohlone ohlone, i am an ohlone.

GABRIEL MOLINA: what's an ohlone?

RINALDO D'AMATO: it's an indian. ohlone indian. the first people in the mission. peaceful people. wise people. i am an ohlone.

GABRIEL MOLINA: rinaldo, you're from sicily.

RINALDO D'AMATO: that's this life. i'm talking about my past life.

GABRIEL MOLINA: rinaldo, man, you smoke too much. look at all this smoke. you gonna get me in trouble with management.

RINALDO D'AMATO: you work too hard.

GABRIEL MOLINA: i'm saving up for a '55 ford crown victoria. canary yellow. javi fixed it up. he says he'll sell it maybe.

RINALDO D'AMATO: hahahahavi. nuhnuhnuh–ez.

GABRIEL MOLINA: man, you shouldn't make fun of his speech defect.

RINALDO D'AMATO: wwwwwwwhat sppppech dddefect? that boy makes me laugh.

GABRIEL MOLINA: yeah you laugh. javi's a good mechanic man. makes good money, too.

RINALDO D'AMATO: money money money. work work work.

GABRIEL MOLINA: seeing movies ain't work. westerns, man, that's the ticket. robert mitchum, john wayne.

RINALDO D'AMATO: i hate westerns. stupid cowboys. stupid cow-boy hats. stupid boots. jokers. i root for the indians.

GABRIEL MOLINA: you full of opinions for somebody who don't do nothing.

RINALDO D'AMATO: i do things.

GABRIEL MOLINA: you smoke weed.

RINALDO D'AMATO: i collect antiques, memorabilia.

GABRIEL MOLINA: junk nobody ever buys.

RINALDO D'AMATO: one man's junk is another man's treasure. don't be such a stiff.

(*RINALDO offers* GABRIEL *the joint. he takes it, inhales deeply.*)

GABRIEL MOLINA: is this from your garden?

RINALDO D'AMATO: it's good, huh. don't tell irene. she asked me the other day, "rinaldo, what's those plants?" i told her they was carrots.

GABRIEL MOLINA: carrots!

RINALDO D'AMATO: i said it was this special kind of carrot from mexico. i got em planted all along the side of the fence next to the tomatos and the zucchini, gets good sun. i take out the scraps and the coffee grounds, throw it all down there in the dirt, mix it up, water it. they grow like you wouldn't believe. i swear to god i shoulda been a farmer.

GABRIEL MOLINA: maybe you were in a past life. old mcdonald, that's you, rinaldo. "old mcdonald had a farm eee yai eee yai oh—"

RINALDO D'AMATO: no man no, i told you. i was a shaman. that's what i was. an ohlone shaman. i raised the dead. i communed with the spirits and the demons. don't tell irene.

GABRIEL MOLINA: your sister is kinda cute.

RINALDO D'AMATO: irene? you don't even know. "rinaldo do this, rinaldo do that, you're spoiled rotten, rinaldo." she's a pain in the neck that woman.

GABRIEL MOLINA: why didn't she ever get married do you think?

RINALDO D'AMATO: who'd marry her? bossy, everything's gotta be just so. besides she's too old.

GABRIEL MOLINA: she's kinda old now, but she's pretty good-looking for an older lady.

RINALDO D'AMATO: so you marry her.

GABRIEL MOLINA: maybe i will. you think i'm kidding. i ain't kidding. i marry her and that'd make you and me brothers—brother.

RINALDO D'AMATO: (*taking the joint.*) give that to me, brother. crazy, you're crazy.

(*RINALDO inhales. exhales.*)

GABRIEL MOLINA: irene still work at that laundry?

RINALDO D'AMATO: nah, she's working at adelines now.

GABRIEL MOLINA: what was that laundry called again?

RINALDO D'AMATO: new method.

GABRIEL MOLINA: that's right. new method.

RINALDO D'AMATO: man, i hated that place. all those big vats of boiling water with the bleach. all that steam, so hot you could hardly breathe. she took me there when i was a kid. the metal press made this hissing sound and the sheets hanging there all in a row, they'd flap, and you'd see something move, and i knew it was a ghost.

GABRIEL MOLINA: for real? when was that?

RINALDO D'AMATO: 1922. almost forty years ago.

GABRIEL MOLINA: what's a ghost look like?

RINALDO D'AMATO: some of them, they look like you and me. you'd never even know, but some of them, they're invisible. you don't see them, you just feel them, like fingertips on the back on your neck, like a palm against the side of your face.

(*GABRIEL MOLINA and RINALDO D'AMATO fade away. a clip from "night of the hunter." robert mitchum shows his hands. tattooed on one is "love"; tattooed on the other is "hate." the sound of a heartbeat. the sound of cards shuffling. hands shuffle and deal, flicking a card into the void. the card lands. ten of spades.*)

10.

(*the sound of a heartbeat continues. the faint sound of tinny ragtime. a saloon circa 1900. JOSIAH WOODS appears. BLACK BART emerges from the shadows.*)

BLACK BART: track me down, disturb my peace, the hell do you think you are? ask me all these questions, why i did what i did, if i feel guilty, if my conscience weighs heavy on my soul? do i sleep at night? do i dream? do i dream? the truth? hell i'll tell you the truth. they caught me on account of my handkerchief, dropped it at the scene of the crime. the tiniest thing. they traced that damn hanky back to a chinese laundry i used to go. when i got out, i went back to that chinese laundry, snuck in through the window in the middle of the night, slit the throat of the chinaman who gave me away. what do you think that chinaman dreams? what do you think a dead man dreams? does he dream his lifetime over like some picture show in his head? or is it just the smell of dirt, the darkness of the grave?

(*the ragtime transforms into mogwai. a loud wall of guitar. BLACK BART and JOSIAH WOODS fight. as they fight, JOSIAH WOODS transforms into TOBIN SCHUMER, BLACK BART transforms into FRANK WILDER. TOBIN SCHUMER smashes a bottle in FRANK WILDER's face. glass shatters. FRANK WILDER reaches up to touch his eye. blood flows. FRANK WILDER disappears into the night.*)

TOBIN SCHUMER: bad dream. bad dream. all gone. (*tunelessly, spoken almost.*) row, row, row your boat. (*beat.*) gently. down. gently down. gently down the stream. merrily, merrily, merrily, merrily. (*beat.*) merrily, merrily, merrily, merrily. life. is. but. a dream. row, row, row your boat. gently down. gently down. life is. life is.

(*the sound of a girl singing an old english folk song, the same song that TRICIA SULLIVAN sang from before. the song is an echo. mist seeps through the space. the sound of wind through a crack in the door, through a broken window.*)

TOBIN SCHUMER: tricia? tricia?

(*FLORA O'SHEA appears, obscured, ghost-like. she wears a dress from the turn of the century. TOBIN SCHUMER sees her, backs away, scrambles away. enter IRENE D'AMATO dressed in a new method uniform. she holds two votives. night. an empty church. the sound of wind grows. the sound of a tarp or curtain flapping.*)

IRENE D'AMATO: flora? flora, is that you?

(*darkness. two candles glow in the darkness. the wind whistles and howls. the song is stuck in a groove. the keening of the wind, the keening of human voice. FLORA O'SHEA approaches IRENE D'AMATO. the wind grows stronger. the flames go out. pitch black. silence.*)

INTERMISSION

11.

(*in the darkness, we hear the sound of wind. we hear the old english folk song. in the shadows, we see IRENE D'AMATO as she was before the act break. a woman's voice whispers "eleven." an intake of breath. the candles go out. IRENE opens her eyes. lights up. FLORA O'SHEA has vanished. the mist has turned into steam. the new method laundry. 1920. IRENE stands amid billowing sheets. white sheets. the smell of clean. hot water, lye, soap flakes. billowing steam. enter HAZEL SCHUMER and MAEVE DIXON in a flurry. they're dressed like IRENE.*)

HAZEL: daydreaming, irene?
MAEVE: daydreaming of her one true love, isn't that so, irene?
HAZEL: maeve.
MAEVE: love is in the air. hazel has a true love.
HAZEL: maeve.
MAEVE: hazel loves the butcher.
HAZEL: i do not.
MAEVE: butcher's wife, butcher's wife, hazel schumer the butcher's wife.
HAZEL: o pipe down won't you.
MAEVE: hands like hams and big fat belly.
HAZEL: that's enough from you.
MAEVE: you're sweet on him, confess.

HAZEL: he's sweet on me.

MAEVE: o but he's fat, he's so fat! and his mother she's just a tiny thing, how could such a tiny woman have such a big fat son?

HAZEL: you're a minx, maeve, and andreas is not fat anyways.

MAEVE: "andreas" is it. that's cozy.

HAZEL: he's big boned.

MAEVE: he's fat, hazel, he's a big fat man, no getting around that. but he's rich, i'll give him that. marry him and you'd be rich, too.

HAZEL: not rich.

MAEVE: rich enough.

HAZEL: what's rich enough?

MAEVE: what do you think, irene, what's rich enough?

IRENE: i don't know.

HAZEL: frank wilder has a maiden aunt won the irish sweepstakes. i'd say she's rich enough. clever, too. started up a sewing shop. bought some land outside modesto. made a bundle is what i hear.

MAEVE: if i won, i'd start my own business, too.

HAZEL: doing what?

MAEVE: i'd open up a restaurant. linen napkins, china, candelabras.

HAZEL: candelabras.

MAEVE: tea cups with little flowers painted on, a hundred different kinds of forks and knives.

IRENE: what would you serve then, maeve? what kind of food?

MAEVE: french cuisine i would say.

HAZEL: o french cuisine is it.

MAEVE: that's right. soufflés, sorbets, cognac, escargots.

HAZEL: escargots. oo lah. aren't we fine.

MAEVE: snails to you, butcher's wife.

HAZEL: you wouldn't know french cuisine if it came up and bit you on the tit.

MAEVE: is that right? well you know all about food, don't you. you eat enough of it, that much anyone with eyes can see.

HAZEL: shut your pie hole, maeve.

MAEVE: say that again, i'll yank your hair out by the roots.

HAZEL: i'd like to see you try, little irish pipsqueak.

MAEVE: what'd you call me? i'll knock you on your big fat german ass i will.

IRENE: that's enough. ladies don't talk like that.

HAZEL: yes but some of us aren't ladies. clearly.

MAEVE: talking about me.

HAZEL: if the shoe fits.

MAEVE: think you're a lady then is that what you think.

HAZEL: more of a lady than you.

MAEVE: o you'd like to think that you would.

HAZEL: ask anyone ask them.

MAEVE: i'll ask andreas what kinda lady you are.

HAZEL: call me a tart? o that's rich, coming from the likes of you.

MAEVE: i don't hike up my skirt for some big fat butcher, no i don't—

IRENE: that's enough. like cats in a bag you are, the both of you.

(pause. they fold the sheets. so many sheets from hotel rooms across the city, stripped from beds where strangers slept the night before, their bodies in sleep, splayed and curled, twitching and still. they dream. bodiless, they dream.)

HAZEL: hot.

MAEVE: don't i know it.

HAZEL: need some help?

MAEVE: i could do.

HAZEL: here.

(the tension dissipates. like a temperature shift. like ice cubes in an empty glass. HAZEL and MAEVE fold in unison. the thwap of sheets being folded. thwap. thwap.)

HAZEL: what if you won, irene? what if you won the irish sweep-stakes? what would you do?

IRENE: i don't know. buy the house outright, for my parents, you know. send my brother, rinaldo, to university when he gets old enough. stanford.

MAEVE: stanford?! listen to this one.

IRENE: rinaldo's very clever, he's a very clever little boy.

MAEVE: if clever means naughty, then clever he is. you think he's a handful now, you just wait ten years. you and your mother, you dote on him, spoil him rotten. if it were me, i'd smack him good when he smarted off.

HAZEL: maeve.

MAEVE: i'd wake him before sunrise, make him do some chores, grow some calluses on those baby soft hands, or else he'll grow up to be a no good layabout, you watch and see.

IRENE: he's going to be too busy with school. he'll need to study.

MAEVE: o for heaven's sakes.

IRENE: i'm thinking he might go into business someday. i think he has a head for numbers. what do you think, hazel?

HAZEL: i think he's a very sweet little boy.

MAEVE: god hates a liar, hazel.

IRENE: you're an awful girl, maeve. how'd you get to be so awful?

MAEVE: five younger brothers at home is how.

HAZEL: hush.

MAEVE: don't you hush me. i'm sick of her brother, sick of my own. boys have it easy, you ask me, they have it so easy it makes me want to scream.

IRENE: oh maeve.

MAEVE: don't "oh maeve" me.

HAZEL: no one has it easy, and if they do, it don't last long. the world sees to that. you know it's true. anyway, what's the point in whinging and whining, no point at all. besides it's my turn. ask me, go on ask me, ask. what, cat got your tongue, maeve? that'd be a first.

MAEVE: alright then fine. what would you do if you won the sweepstakes?

HAZEL: you really want to know?

MAEVE: yes, yes i really want to know. good lord.

HAZEL: first—

MAEVE: first yes first go on then—

HAZEL: first, i'd buy a mink coat.

IRENE: mm. mink. i like mink.

HAZEL: then i'd buy one in sable and silver fox.

(*music begins. a waltz. faint and faraway.*)

HAZEL: chinchilla.

IRENE: ah chinchilla. i like chinchilla.

HAZEL: and a closet full of dresses and lingerie.

IRENE: silk.

HAZEL: silk.

MAEVE: silk and satin.

HAZEL: satin, too, and that's just for starters. (*as HAZEL speaks, FLORA O'SHEA appears.*) i'd quit this job, move into a room at the fairmont hotel, top floor, penthouse suite, and every day i'd get my hair done, and my nails, have a girl bring up my meals on a tray, champagne and caviar, filet mignon, and i'd go to sleep at night in sheets like these, nicer even, soft and clean, that clean smell, soap flakes and lavender water, and somebody else to make my bed, somebody else to cook and to clean, somebody else to wash and iron and fold, some other girl, some other girl like the girl i used to be.

MAEVE: and every night, i'd go out dancing. i'd go out in my finest dress and dance in the middle of the dance floor in black shiny shoes with little straps around my ankles, i'd spin and i'd spin, and all eyes would be on me, thinking who is she, who is that girl, and i would be the lucky one, the luckiest one, the luckiest one of all.

(*the LAUNDRESSES begin to dance. FLORA joins them. the music transforms from a waltz into a big band number. the dance grows faster and faster, more frenetic. the swirl of skirts and sheets. laughter and sweat and the pounding of feet and the rooms spins, it spins. sweat on your back and neck, your hair gets in your eyes and your heart is pounding so hard you can feel it in your ears. the whole world blurs and warps into the chaos of a handheld camera. the flash of an old-fashioned camera. music cuts out. the end of the last song on the record. the sound of a needle on vinyl, the record spins in an endless rotation. slides of police photographs projected into the void. the bodies of nameless men and women, killed decades ago in apartments and city streets in and around the mission. they lie in stairwells and hallways and alleys and empty lots, their bodies rendered strange and alien in death, arms* askew, legs bent in impossible angles. the images turn to black. white cursive scratches itself into the void: "august 8th, 1912. flora o'shea." light up on DR. JOHN GRAVES.)

DR. JOHN GRAVES: august 8th. 1912. flora o'shea.

(all the other lettering disintegrates except for the "12." the blackness turns to flesh. a field of flesh like the expanse of a back, the tendons of the neck, the clavicle.)

12.

(the basement of the old mission police station. 1912. light on DR. JOHN GRAVES.)

DR. JOHN GRAVES: female. caucasian. sixteen years old. red hair, eyes—blue grey blue. five foot seven inches, one hundred and twenty pounds. distinguishing marks: small scar at the base of her spine. birthmark beneath her left breast. found in the early morning hours on camp and albion. stabbed repeatedly in the heart, the vital organs. no witnesses. no known motive. assailant unknown. the secrets of her body still secret. the last face she saw, the last sound she heard. the thoughts that ran through her brain, the hidden tunnels and passageways, the dark red room at the end of the hall. and beyond that room, another room and another one after that. dark and cool. potter's field. a wooden cross. a blanket of grass. all that sky. what if the dead could talk? what would they say?

(as he speaks, images of TRICIA SULLIVAN, FLORA O'SHEA and MAY FITZGERALD flicker in the darkness, like holographic souls. night. a church. the sound of wind grows. the sound of a tarp or curtain flapping. the wind whistles and howls. video close-up on TRICIA SULLIVAN. her image is projected into the void. as she speaks to us in the foreground, in the background we see her image pixilated and fragmented. her mouth. her mascara eyes. the

curve of her neck. her fingers pushing back a strand of hair.
pierced ear lobe. tattoo. her voice is an echo. the words overlap. a
susurration of names.)

TRICIA SULLIVAN'S VOICE:
my name is tricia sullivan
my name is may fitzgerald
my name is flora o'shea
my name is tricia sullivan
my name is may fitzgerald
my name is flora o'shea
my name is may fitzgerald
my name is tricia sullivan
my name is flora o'shea
my name is tricia sullivan
my name is may fitzgerald
and i was here. i was here.

(the sound of breathing. DR. JOHN GRAVES *lights a cigarette.*
the burning embers. close-up on the burning embers, black and
red, burning, moving. the sound of wind transforms into the
sound of fire. the images of TRICIA, FLORA, *and* MAY *overlap*
and bleed together. another image seen in choppy fragments, black
and white and technicolor. flesh on flesh. the sound of breathing.
struggle. DR. JOHN GRAVES *vanishes. the sound of fire. the*
sound of sex. COLIN DIXON *and* MAY FITZGERALD. *1906.*
their bodies seen in bits and pieces. an expanse of back. a belly
arching up. faster and faster and faster and faster. a trembling. the
room begins to tremble. the clattering of a window. the breathing
grows louder. teetering on the edge. COLIN *and* MAY *cry out. then*
their bodies are still. two bodies twisted in sheets. their skin is slick
with sweat. they are so still, you can barely see them breathing.
light up on MAEVE DIXON. *she stands with a cane. older, but not*
so different. you can see the young woman in the old woman's
face. she has the same eyes she had when she was young, sharp
eyes. they don't miss a beat.)

MAEVE DIXON: huh. huh. hm. hm. you know how they say, how they say lucky, unlucky. step on a crack, break your mother's back. step on a line, break your father's spine. hexes and curses, black cats and wishbones. the number thirteen.

(*MAY gets out of bed, begins to get dressed. COLIN watches her. far back in the background, TOBIN SCHUMER spraypaints the number 13 onto the wall. he's a tiny figure in the night, on the other side of the parking lot, barely visible, a sea of asphalt between him and you. the tickatickaticka of the spray paint can, then the sssssssh of paint on a wall.*)

13.

(*1989. as MAEVE speaks, MAY and COLIN get dressed.*)

MAEVE DIXON: see now i don't believe in all that nonsense. when it's your time, it's your time. and i'll tell you what, this earthquake, it was nothing compared to the other one. 1906. i remember it, sure i do. i remember the fire more. that came after. i was six years old. my mother died in that fire. may fitzgerald, that was her name. she was a dancing girl. my father, was a gravedigger by trade. don't know how they met. my mother passed before i could ask and my father, well you wouldn't ask my father that sort of thing.

(*MAY and COLIN fade away.*)

MAEVE DIXON: i'm the oldest of six, and the only girl. i was born in 1900. i'm 89. i don't feel 89. inside, i feel about 22, 22, and sassy. i worked all my life, is why. i was a bookkeeper at perfection curtain cleaners, 14th and mission, owned by a jewish family, the kleins. before that i was a seamstress at levi strauss, and before that i was at new method laundry. trucks'd come with linens from the hotels downtown, sheets so many sheets. hard work, hot all the time and your hands'd get red and chapped from the bleach, and your feet'd ache from standing, your back, too. i made sixty-five cents an hour and that was pretty good back then. had enough for this and that, movies at the el capitan, dancing, i used to love to go out dancing. the avalon at sutter and van ness, walahans on market. i danced to benny goodman at the world's fair on treasure island. o could i dance. still can. i'll dance with you now, girl, boy, i don't care, it's all the same to me. no, i don't mean it that way. goodness no, no no. hm. that was a good time. the girls i worked with, there was hazel, hazel schumer. she got married, married a butcher, big fat man. all the other girls, i don't know. the only one i keep up with is irene. she still lives here in the mission with her brother, rinaldo. she doted on that boy, i'm telling you, o and he was a devil, spoiled like nobody's business. he turned out alright in the end. he owns a shop on valencia, selling antiques and memorabilia. takes care of her now. irene, she's not doing so good. she gets confused. she looks at me sometimes like she's looking for clues to a puzzle, like i could say the right word and everything, everything would snap into place and be right again. sometimes irene, she says the strangest things.

(*IRENE D'AMATO slowly becomes visible. young like she was back in 1928.*)

MAEVE DIXON: last time i went to visit, she said she'd just seen flora o'shea, this girl we used to know, lived in the neighborhood, been dead for years, killed when she was just sixteen. never found out who did it, never found out why. we get old, and flora stays just the way she was, young so young. we were that young once. and i'm thinking this to myself and irene, she says, wait, maeve, look. look. can't you see her? it's flora. she's been with me my whole life long. like a word on the tip of my tongue, like a secret thing i can almost hear, a whispered thing, a magic spell. i can almost hear it if i listen hard enough.

(*an echo of TRICIA's song. FLORA appears.*)

IRENE: what if the dead could talk, maeve? what if they could? what would they tell us? what would they say?

(*FLORA and* IRENE *are two women staring across a field of time, a field of space. the song gets stuck in an endless groove. a phrase repeats. a cosmic loop. it grows in volume and distorts, explodes.* FLORA *fills with light, as if the blood in her veins was light, as if her skin was see-through. the light gets so bright, it spills beyond the edges of her body and swallows up everything in its wake. then darkness. in the darkness, we hear the sound of a room full of people. the noise of musicians tuning their instruments. the screeching feedback of a microphone. light on* JAVI NUÑEZ, *master of ceremonies. he wears a tuxedo. he holds a brass trophy. he speaks into the microphone.*)

JAVI NUÑEZ: luhluhluhluh-ladies and jehjehjehgent-gentlemen, puhpuhplease guhguhguhgive a wuhwuhwuhwuhwuhwuh-wuhwarm, warm, hand of applause, they duhduhduhdeserve it, ladies and gentlemen—my puhpuhpuhpuhpleasure to introduce to you now, the muhmuhmuhmambo champions for 1957: cuhcuhcuhcouple number 14, hernan sandoval and gloria kantor.

(*applause. the band starts up. mambo music.* JAVI NUÑEZ *walks backward into the void, receding from view. spotlight on* HERNAN SANDOVAL *and* GLORIA KANTOR. *they wear tags with the #14.*)

14.

(*a dance hall in the mission. 1957.* HERNAN *and* GLORIA *mambo in an orb of light. they mambo like pros. a parentheses of bliss and synchronized movement. the mambo music ends. radio static. frank sinatra. janis joplin. santana. bits and pieces of music from the last thirty years slip by. track #10 on the retsin cd "sweet luck of amaryllis" begins. enter* MILDRED NUÑEZ. *she's wearing a coat. she has a shopping bag. she's on her way to somewhere else. she watches* HERNAN *and* GLORIA, *a flicker of recognition. and then she keeps going. enter* TOBIN SCHUMER, *a punk kid from kenosha, wisconsin. he has a mohawk. he wears an old leather jacket and ripped up, dirty jeans. his face and hands are bruised. it's 1989 and he's faraway from home.* GLORIA *and* HERNAN *come to a stop. they look at each other, studying each other's faces, touching each other's faces so they won't forget, and then they slowly, reluctantly exit.* TOBIN *watches them go. he's alone. the music continues. he feels his way through the abandoned space, the residue of people from long ago still clinging to the walls and floorboards. the flicker of ancient light fixtures, frayed wires in the wall. enter* JERRUSHA FITZGERALD *unseen. he approaches* TOBIN, *and gently rifles through his pockets, pulling at the seams, a ghostly pickpocket looking for his stolen gold. he extracts some papers, a torn piece of paper with phone numbers, a folded up flyer for a band, a condom, some gum, a key chain. a wad of crumpled bills. he counts them.)*

JERRUSHA:
    one. two. three. four. five ones.
    a five. that makes ten.
    eleven. twelve.
    thirteen. fourteen.
    fifteen.

(TOBIN *turns around, but* JERRUSHA FITZGERALD *is invisible to him.* JERRUSHA *walks past him into the night. the dance hall has transformed into a graveyard.)*

15.

(*light on* COLIN DIXON. *he's digging a grave.* TOBIN *watches him. the sound of the shovel sinking into dirt.* MILDRED NUÑEZ *unpacks her shopping bag. cakes and sugar skulls. she sets them on a gravestone and exits, as* JAVI NUÑEZ *slowly emerges into view.)*

COLIN DIXON: mildred nuñez. pretty thing, ain't she. works in the old folks home where the old mission dolores used to be. my wife may used to live there. well, she wasn't my wife no more by then. and she wasn't may neither. she was going by some other name, calling herself mary something. sparkle, sparkle, sparks. mary sparks, that was it. she had this whole story about being some mormon, being the oldest living mormon. mormon, christ. off her nut she was, but i knew it was her. could see it in her eyes. used to tell our kids she died in a fire, but that wasn't true. she just ran away is all, ran away and had herself a life, a whole other life. marry a dancing girl, you're gonna get dancing feet, dance their way straight out your front door.

(*JAVI NUÑEZ is devouring the cakes and sweets left for him. powdered sugar on his fingers, crumbs falling down his chin.*)

COLIN DIXON: see there, that's mildred's father over there. hahahavi nuhnuhnuhnez. huhuhhow ya duhduhduing, hahahavi? poor fuckin yorick. yeah that'd be you, ya dead fuck. eat up, ya sorry fuck. ah i shouldn't make light of the dead. poor sap. back to heaven, back to hell. go. git.

(*JAVI exits.*)

TOBIN SCHUMER: if he died, that would mean, i mean that would mean he's dead.
COLIN DIXON: i see you're a quick thinker. what's your name, quick thinker?
TOBIN SCHUMER: tobin.
COLIN DIXON: tobin. the hell kinda name is that? tobin what?
TOBIN SCHUMER: schumer.
COLIN DIXON: schumer huh. there's a schumer over there. i buried him a while back. big fat man. duggans had the casket custom made. had to have a special crane lower him into the ground. you could be kin. distant kin, by the looks of it. your hair just stay up like that or what?

TOBIN SCHUMER: i gotta spray it. then i use a little gel and baby powder, makes this kind of paste.

COLIN DIXON: that's very interesting. i myself, i opted for a more timeless style. styles come and go, see, mine remains eternal.

(COLIN *takes out a mango from his pocket, and a knife. he begins slicing the fruit.*)

COLIN DIXON: mango? you like mango? food of the gods, i'm telling you. (*offering* TOBIN *a piece of mango.*) here ya go.

TOBIN SCHUMER: no. thanks.

COLIN DIXON: what are you? some kinda fussy eater?

TOBIN SCHUMER: i'm not hungry.

COLIN DIXON: suit yourself. (*COLIN eats.*) mmmm. sweet. ripe. you don't know what you're missing.

TOBIN SCHUMER: who's it for?

COLIN DIXON: hell if i know. i just dig the holes. could be worse, i suppose. find things sometimes. found this. pried it loose from the fingers of its previous owner. once i found a beautiful mother-of-pearl box, inlaid wood, beautiful. buried treasure i'm thinkin to myself. colin, i'm thinkin to myself, colin my boy, you got it made. you'll never lift a shovel again, easy street. opened it up and you know what i found? a human heart. swear to god. a mummified human heart. looked like a large turnip, but it was some poor fuck's heart. does that scare you?

TOBIN SCHUMER: no.

COLIN DIXON: somebody slicing you open, cracking open your rib cage and ripping out your fuckin still-beating heart, sticking it in a fuckin box, that don't scare you.

TOBIN SCHUMER: no.

COLIN DIXON: you're quakin in your boots, ya lyin fuck. course i'd be scared, too, if i were you, scrawny as you are. put you in a ring with a bag of bones, my money'd be on the bag of bones. look at you, like a bird you are, a fuckin egret, a gentle breeze'd knock you over. you call those arms, look at those skinny, bird arms. how much do you weigh, birdboy?

TOBIN SCHUMER: enough to knock you upside the head, old man.
COLIN DIXON: ah that's good. very good. very good. i underesti-
mate you, birdboy. you got moxie. i like that. you ain't from
around here, are ya. i can tell by your shoes. you got farmboy
shoes. looks like you've been walking all over the city in those
farmboy shoes.
TOBIN SCHUMER: i was looking for my friend.
COLIN DIXON: girlfriend?
TOBIN SCHUMER: no, she wasn't, it wasn't like that. we were gonna
meet up at this old church. this old burned out church.
COLIN DIXON: 15th and dolores. yeah i know it.

(*a blur of flesh and hair. the image gradually comes into focus. it's
the face of a young girl seen close up. her eyelids are shut tight and
flickering. she's dreaming. as COLIN DIXON talks, an echo of
FRANK WILDER surfaces. something in his stance, in how he
moves. it's a ripple on the surface.*)

COLIN DIXON: frank used to live there, up in the belfry, him and
the pigeons. frank wilder. don't even know if that was his real
name. what's real, what's not, what's somewhere in between,
who can say. crazy bastard, frank was. mean, too. claims he
killed a chinaman way back when. claims he killed two girls,
stabbed them, kept stabbing them, over and over again. some
girl from the neighborhood, and some girl who ran away.

(*the sleeping girl opens her eyes. the image of the girl fills the
whole space. her face is the universe. her eyes are huge. they blink.
they blink. TRICIA emerges from out of the girl's retina, out of the
dark, black pupil of her eye.*)

COLIN DIXON: i am the darkness. i am the darkness that makes the
daylight sweet. i am the silence underneath. i am the silence
that makes the song a precious thing, more precious than anyone knows. the way he said it, might've been a hundred years
ago. might've been just yesterday. no way to know for sure. you
know frank wilder? o you'd remember him if you met him. he's

missing an eye, see. lost it in a fight with some punk kid. lucky shot. struck a nerve. he's got a glass eye now. pops it out at night, fits inside the socket smooth against the bone. you might not know it to look at him. you'd have to look long and hard, and then, even then you wouldn't know for sure, what he sees, if he sees anything at all.

(*TRICIA's voice like an echo grazing your skin.*)

TRICIA: remember.
COLIN DIXON: she never showed, your friend, did she?
TOBIN SCHUMER: no she, no, she didn't.
COLIN DIXON: it happens—
TRICIA: remember—
COLIN DIXON: all kinds of things, anything can happen. hazards of the road. travel together part of the way. part of the way you travel alone.

(*COLIN slowly begins to fade away. the sound of a train, a low rumble that gets louder as it goes. TRICIA comes closer. TOBIN and TRICIA in the middle of the night. a memory.*)

TOBIN: tricia?
TRICIA: see it?
TOBIN: tricia?
TRICIA: see, see the light. it's coming.
TOBIN: we were on the side of the tracks waiting to hop the train. milwaukee west to st. paul, then straight shot west cross the dakotas, idaho, all the way to tacoma, hitch south to san francisco, all we wanted was to get to san francisco. night. the moon half full. heard it before i saw it, a mile away now, less, i could see the light getting closer and closer, i could feel the ground trembling, shaking, closer and closer till it was all of a sudden bearing down, bearing down on us, fuel and sparks and the smell of metal, ten tons of steel rumbling past, so loud, so loud it hurt.
TRICIA: now. tobin, now.

TOBIN: i can't.

TRICIA: come on.

TOBIN: i can't. i can't. i'm scared.

TRICIA: all you have to do is follow me, run, just keep running, and when i say, lift yourself up and hold on, hold on tight, climb the ladder, pull yourself over, and you're there, you're safe. it's okay, it's alright. listen, you hear that. i can hear you breathing. i can hear your heart beating. don't be scared. up there, you'll see, you're moving so fast now, faster than a rocket, faster than anything, past the edge of town, past the stockyards and the water tower, past the cornfields and the billboard signs, all the places you remember, all the people you've ever known, asleep in their rooms, your mom and your dad and your brothers and your sisters, everybody you used to know, the first girl you kissed, remember, the taste of her lips, grape soda and peppermint, remember, and her eyes, remember, how she looked at you, everything in her eyes, till all that's left is the sound of the train and the sky, there is so much so much sky.

(*the sound of the train becomes so loud. a blur of metal speeding through the night.* TOBIN *is fading away.* TRICIA *is by herself. the train transforms into a river. rushing metal turns into rushing water.* TRICIA *steps into the current. and is gone.*)

16.

(*the retirement home where the old mission dolores used to be.* MARY HOLLAND SPARKS *as she was at the beginning. she and* DETECTIVE VICTOR OLVIDADO *are in the middle of a conversation.*)

MARY HOLLAND SPARKS: sixteen sweet sixteen. sixteen years old. same age i was when i got married to my first husband. my first husband was a gravedigger and crazy. he was, he was crazy. (*pause.*) why do you think they ran away?

VICTOR OLVIDADO: i don't know.

MARY HOLLAND SPARKS: lots of reasons, lots of reasons why. what happened to the boy?

VICTOR OLVIDADO: he went back, he went back home.

MARY HOLLAND SPARKS: strange. traveling all those miles trying to get away, ending up back where you started.

VICTOR OLVIDADO: mrs. sparks—

MARY HOLLAND SPARKS: no. please. call me mary. or may, you could call me may. may fitzgerald.

VICTOR OLVIDADO: is that your real name?

MARY HOLLAND SPARKS: each one's as real as the next. depends on which reality we're talking about. (*pause.*) they never found who did it, did they.

VICTOR OLVIDADO: no.

MARY HOLLAND SPARKS: and that troubles you. after all these years, troubles you still. you take it to heart.

VICTOR OLVIDADO: i would like to know. i would like to be able to put it to rest. i would like to do that.

MARY HOLLAND SPARKS: i knew a little boy once, beautiful little boy. he knew shakespeare by heart. he'd stand right there, recite shakespeare for me. all those mighty words in such a tiny soul. i'd close my eyes and listen, listen to the words. malcolm xavier keene. he must be all grown up by now. (*pause.*) stabbed she was, i read about that, stabbed in that old church, and i think about that, i see it, i see it, can't get it out of my mind, close my eyes and i can see it, i can still see it. patricia.

VICTOR OLVIDADO: people called her tricia. tricia sullivan.

MARY HOLLAND SPARKS:
tricia. tricia. flora. may.
mary. may. flora. tricia.
flora. tricia. mary. may.
and i was here. and i was here. remember me.

VICTOR OLVIDADO: mrs. sparks—one of your nurses, miss nuñez, you told her you saw something, maybe you know something.

(*MILDRED appears.*)

MARY HOLLAND SPARKS: mildred? i tell mildred all kinds of things. told her i was a hundred and sixty-seven years old, told her i was the oldest living mormon, that i sailed to san francisco on a schooner. i tell her all kinds of things.

VICTOR OLVIDADO: do you tell her the truth?

(*MARY HOLLAND SPARKS smiles. a smile like a hand opening up with a shiny pebble inside.*)

MARY HOLLAND SPARKS: i like you, detective. you like to solve things. i can tell. except see now, some things they don't get solved. not the way you think. (*pause.*) tell me, you know mildred. you know her from before.

(*TOMAS appears. an echo of* MILDRED *and* TOMAS *when they were young.*)

VICTOR OLVIDADO: she, she used to go out with my uncle, my uncle tomas.

MARY HOLLAND SPARKS: it didn't last.

VICTOR OLVIDADO: it was a long time ago. they were just kids.

MARY HOLLAND SPARKS: young love.

VICTOR OLVIDADO: it was before my time.

MARY HOLLAND SPARKS: i like stories. i bet you do, too, your line of work. i like to know about people, strangers. pass a person in the street and i think: what've you seen, who were your kinfolk, your first love, the thing you fear, what was that thing, that thing that marked you, carved its name in the inside of your heart. (*pause.*) whatever happened to your uncle?

VICTOR OLVIDADO: he's had a difficult life.

MARY HOLLAND SPARKS: bad luck.

VICTOR OLVIDADO: bad choices.

(*TOMAS exits.*)

MARY HOLLAND SPARKS: now that's something, see, a young man'd say. come talk to me about choices in thirty, forty years, talk to me about choices. some folks have rotten luck. some folks are born under a lucky star. luck. fate. chance.

(*VICTOR OLVIDADO begins to recede from view. MILDRED exits. as she does, TRICIA SULLIVAN enters. the two women pass each other. a flicker of recognition.*)

MARY HOLLAND SPARKS: that she and he crossed paths that day, what do you call that other than fate.

(*enter COLIN DIXON. he crosses slowly to the grave.*)

MARY HOLLAND SPARKS: hadn't seen him in so long, thought he'd moved on, passed away, and then i see him through my window, see him walking towards that girl, and i knew, i knew it was him. like an angel of death. i knew in an instant, i knew. cut her up like he almost did me. like he did that girl a lifetime ago, another girl, like the one i used to be. crazy, he was crazy.

(*COLIN DIXON picks up his shovel, and exits into the night. TRICIA SULLIVAN remains.*)

MARY HOLLAND SPARKS: luck. fate. chance. wait. wait. seventeen reasons. you know that sign? course you do, you grew up around here. i always liked that sign. i liked the mystery. i liked to wonder. that's where i saw him, this chinaman i used to know, right by the old seventeen reasons sign.

(*IGNATIUS LIU appears.*)

MARY HOLLAND SPARKS: told me my fortune once, stopped in the middle, something spooked him and he just took off. imagine running into him after all these years. chinaman, i said, tell me my fortune, i've been waiting a lifetime to hear my damn fortune, tell it to me now. you know what he said to me? death, he said. i saw death. death by knives, death by fire, death by the hand of a crazy man. is that all, i said to him. hell, that ain't nothing. let death come, let him knock on my door. we'll dance the dance, we'll do the do. i cheated him once, i'll cheat him again. i'll run away. there's a thousand ways this story could end, it don't have to end in a grave, it don't have to end like that. i know crazy and i know scared, and it don't have to end like that. it can end a thousand other ways. it can end with the chinaman. he can be the last thing you see. he finds you in the dark, he finds you and he takes your hand, and then the two of you, you start to rise up, lighter than air, higher and higher, you can't believe it, you want to laugh it feels so strange, it feels like nothing else you know, and your mind, your mind is racing, all the things, so many things, but you've already gone so far, you're floating away faster and faster. i watch until i can't see anymore. i watch until there ain't nothing left but the memory, like a song you used to know.

(*TRICIA SULLIVAN extends her hand, an echo of MAY FITZGERALD when she asked her to have her fortune told. IGNATIUS LIU takes her hand, and they disappear into eternity.*)

17.

(*the "17 reasons" sign appears, ghostly scaffolding. beyond the sign, night sky. the SUNSET SCAVENGER appears as he did at the beginning of the play. he gently places his hand on the video image of the seventeen reasons why sign. flash. it disappears.*)

END OF PLAY

Cowbird

By Julie Marie Myatt

Are You My Mother? by P. D. Eastman, copyright © 1960 by P. D. Eastman. Copyright renewed 1988 by Mary L. Eastman. Used by permission of Random House Children's Books, a division of Random House, Inc. Please note that permission to reproduce two lines from *Are You My Mother?* in *Cowbird* does not imply permission to recite the book in the performance of the play. No portions of this book may be read from or enacted in either amateur or professional performances of this play without formal permission from Random House, Inc., and the payment of a royalty.

No performance or reading of this work *Cowbird* in any medium may be given without express permission of the author. Inquiries regarding performance rights, publication, or duplication of any kind should be addressed to: Julie Marie Myatt, 2448 28th Street, Santa Monica, CA 90405.

⇒ BIOGRAPHY ⇐

Julie Marie Myatt's *Cowbird* premiered in February 2002, at Eye of the Storm Theatre in Minneapolis, Minnesota, and was directed by Casey Stangl. Myatt has had other plays produced in New York, Los Angeles, Minneapolis, and Actors Theatre of Louisville. Her ten-minute play *Lift and Bang* is published in *30 Ten-Minute Plays by 2 Actors from Actors Theatre of Louisville* by Smith & Kraus, and *What He Sent* is published in *The Best American Short Plays, 2000-2001* by Applause Books. She received a Walt Disney Studios Screenwriting Fellowship in 1992-93, a Jerome Fellowship at the Playwrights' Center in 1999-2000, and a McKnight Advancement Grant for 2001-2002. Myatt's other plays include *August Is a Thin Girl, The Pink Factor, The Sex Habits of American Women, Alice in the Badlands,* and *49 Steps to the Sun.*

⇒ PRODUCTION HISTORY ⇐

Cowbird by Julie Marie Myatt
Produced by Eye of the Storm
February 14-March 17, 2002
Directed by Casey Stangl

Cast

LORNA . . . . Sally Wingert
MICHAEL . . . . Casey Greig
CELIA . . . . Briana Kennedy-Coker
BEN . . . . Eric Sumangil
BURT . . . . Terry Bellamy
MAGGIE . . . . Claudia Wilkens

Designers & Technical Staff

Dramaturg . . . . Kristina Halvorson
Production Stage Manager . . . . Margaret Schneiders
Set Designer . . . . Nayna Ramey
Lighting Designer . . . . Jared Grohs
Sound Designer . . . . C. Andrew Mayer
Costume Designer . . . . Sarah Wilcox
Props Designer . . . . Robert-Bruce Brake

Eye of the Storm Theatre

Eye of the Storm Theatre (EOTS) discovers passionate new voices and produces new plays that speak to audiences demanding theatre of vision, clarity, exhilaration, and risk. EOTS presents new plays by today's finest playwrights, with a dual focus of producing world premieres and bringing to the Twin Cities "hot" new plays on the national scene.

Founded in 1991, Eye of the Storm Theatre is "a vital, critically important theatre for the Twin Cities," according to Cynthia Gehrig of the Jerome Foundation. EOTS combines a reputation for quality with a keen eye for discovering exciting new voices. Despite our modest budget, we consistently gain access to award-winning new plays on the national scene that provide audiences with thought-provoking entertainment. Our production of Edward Albee's *The Play About the Baby* was the third production in the nation of this provocative play. Plays such as *The Beauty Queen of Leenane, How I Learned to Drive*, and *Quills* have explored family dysfunction, incest, and censorship. The success of these productions shows EOTS' ability to obtain early production rights to plays in demand around the country, and be the first to provide these exciting entertainments to Twin Cities audiences.

EOTS' commissioning program is a crucial element of the company's vitality. The world premieres developed by EOTS have achieved national recognition: *The Big Slam* has been produced at fifteen theatres across the country, including the prestigious Woolly Mammoth Theatre in Washington, D.C., and A Contemporary Theatre in Seattle; *Hate Mail* was produced at New York's Primary Stages, optioned by Fox Theatricals for a national tour, and has had twelve productions; *Heckler* has been produced in Los Angeles and Philadelphia; last season's *Cowbird* was in the Lincoln Center Director's Festival in New York last summer; this season's *Fair Game* already has a major production scheduled at Philadelphia's City Theatre in 2003.

In 1999 EOTS expanded its commissioning program with Seed the Storm, a festival of new works. Four writers are commissioned to create the "seed" of a new play that may grow into a future EOTS production. Following the festival EOTS chooses one or two seeds to develop into full-length works. Seed the Storm increases the number of writers and projects in development and greater diversity—in gender, age, ethnicity, geographic base, and artistic style—among the artists with whom we collaborate. Seed the Storm deepens our involvement with our audience by including them in our development process.

—Casey Stangl
Artistic Director
Eye of the Storm Theatre
2003

➤ SETTING AND CHARACTERS ⭅

Characters*

LORNA COTES . . . . 45 years old
BERT . . . . late 40s, big man
MICHAEL . . . . 25 years old
MAGGIE . . . . late 60s
BEN . . . . 23 years old, thin
CELIA . . . . 19 years old

*Play is intended to be cast multiculturally/multiracially, representing the many cultures/races of North America.

Setting

Santa Monica, California
July 1999

Cowbird *Molothrus*

"Abundant, increasing in West; often in mixed flocks with black-birds. Once known as 'buffalo bird,' now attends livestock, inhabits fields, farmlands. Deposits eggs in other species' nests; host bird raises cowbird chicks, often at the expense of own young."

—All the Birds of North America

— ACT I —

Scene 1

(*A dark, tacky bar. Night. The sounds of people laughing and talking. A young* MAN *sits at the bar;* MICHAEL; *handsome, but weary and worn for being only twenty-five years old.*

MICHAEL *lights a cigarette.*)

CUSTOMERS: (*Off.*) Hey LORNA!

(*Lights up on* LORNA COTES. *She's mid-forties, well-dressed, attractive. She struts in waving to her friends.*)

CUSTOMER: (*Off.*) Where've you been, girl!
WOMAN: (*Off.*) Where'd you go for so long?
MAN: (*Off.*) Who'd you meet?
WOMAN: (*Off.*) What'd you buy?
　　What'd you bring me?
　　Were you alone?
MAN: (*Off.*) Who was he?
LORNA: You know I never kiss and tell . . . Who wants to buy me a drink? All these questions are making me thirsty. You folks make talking to my mother seem like decent conversation. (*A drink sits in front of her.*) Now there's a welcome wagon. (*She drinks it down. Moans with pleasure. Holds up the empty glass.*) Who's next? Huh? Did you really miss me? (*She sees another drink on the bar.*) Now we're talking. (*LORNA taps* MICHAEL's *drink in thanks, and takes a sip.*) To you, handsome. (*MICHAEL smiles quickly, and shyly averts his eyes back to his beer.*) What's your name, kid?
MICHAEL: Uh . . . Michael.

— 375 —

LORNA: You look like an uh Michael.

MICHAEL: I do—

(*A huge man pushes between* LORNA *and* MICHAEL. BERT. *He picks* LORNA *up off her bar stool.*)

BERT: There she is!

LORNA: I thought you were still on the road.

BERT: No, that was you! Feels like you've been eating well out there, huh?

LORNA: I may have splurged. Once. Occasionally.

BERT: You look great.

(*He admires her figure and tries to kiss her cheek.*

LORNA *coyly avoids him.*)

LORNA: Not tonight, darling.

BERT: Why not?

LORNA: Busy.

BERT: With who?

LORNA: Since when do I have to explain my time to people? Jesus. I would have got married for that.

BERT: Since you started filling out that dress. Wow. It's enough to make me—

LORNA: Sorry. No.

BERT: Guess what I bought while you were gone?

LORNA: A new car.

BERT: How'd you know?

LORNA: You buy one every time I leave.

BERT: I get lonesome.

LORNA: What is it?

BERT: Chrysler.

LORNA: Ooo. Convertible?

BERT: Nice night.

LORNA: Convertible?

BERT: Maybe.

LORNA: Bert . . .

(*BERT slowly exits, waving the keys, keeping his eyes on LORNA.*

LORNA returns to her cocktail. Feels MICHAEL staring at her.)

LORNA: So uh Michael . . . you in college?
MICHAEL: Me?
LORNA: You said your name's Michael, isn't it?
MICHAEL: Yes.
LORNA: You in school?
MICHAEL: Why?
LORNA: Why not. Seems like a good idea.
MICHAEL: Why?
LORNA: People are impressed by it. All that learning. Mind expansion.
MICHAEL: I finished.
LORNA: Well. Doesn't that just cock your pistol.
MICHAEL: I graduated. A couple of years—
LORNA: So . . . what are you doing with yourself now?
MICHAEL: I'm just—
LORNA: Besides sitting around here . . . killing innocent young ladies like myself with your wild good looks.
MICHAEL: Nothing.
LORNA: Oh. Interesting. Now that takes a lot of time, doesn't it?
MICHAEL: What?
LORNA: Doing nothing.
MICHAEL: What do you do with yourself?
LORNA: Plenty.
MICHAEL: Like what?
LORNA: I'm not drunk enough. (*To the bar.*) Anyone got another one for me? Whose party is this anyway? Am I not a sight for sore eyes? Some fellow in Cancun, just the other day, after he stood gazing across the room at me, came up to me and told me that I literally Hurt his eyes. He said that I was so bright, so goddamn luminous that he felt this shooting Pain from his eyes straight down to his heart when he looked my way . . . (*Michael watches as she lights a cigarette.*) So I gave him a pair of sun-

glasses, a visor, and some sunscreen and told him to tell me more. (*She catches his eye. Offers him one.*)
MICHAEL: Thanks.
LORNA: It'll kill you.
MICHAEL: So will boredom.
LORNA: Can't argue there.

(*Another drink for LORNA.*)

LORNA: (*To the customers/bar.*) I can't help it, folks. I love you. (*She kisses the air; to the bar.*) And someday I'll prove it to ya'll. One by one. My bed. My body. No strings attached.

(*MICHAEL watches as she sips her martini. Enjoying every minute.*)

LORNA: (*To the bar.*) OK . . . maybe a Sunday breakfast or two. And some genuine compliments on my fine technique . . . but that's it.

(*LORNA looks around, takes in the room.*

MICHAEL looks around, following her eyes.)

LORNA: Nothing's changed here, I see.
MICHAEL: What?
LORNA: I've been coming here for fifteen years and they've had the same goddamn things on the wall.
MICHAEL: What?
LORNA: Those, those mirror things. Fifteen years of staring at the same faded ostrich asses or whatever the hell those are.
MICHAEL: I think they're vultures.
LORNA: Huh.
MICHAEL: Some call them buzzards.
LORNA: Really?
MICHAEL: Maybe.
LORNA: You a bird specialist?
MICHAEL: No.
LORNA: You won't catch a woman with that bird shit.

MICHAEL: It's just book stuff—I read a lot . . . of books—
LORNA: Good old-fashioned flattery will get you much farther. (*She winks at him, touches his cheek.*) You want to give it a try?
MICHAEL: What?
LORNA: How do I look? (*MICHAEL doesn't know what to say. LORNA laughs.*) I leave you speechless, huh? (*MICHAEL pushes a laugh.*) Well, you wouldn't be the first, sweetheart.

MICHAEL: Uh—

(*LORNA stands.*)

LORNA: A convertible calls. (*She finishes her drink.*) Ahh . . . see . . . that is pleasure. Absolute pleasure. The old Pacific is gonna sing sweet lullabies for me now. Oh yes she will. Wind in my hair. Sea on my skin. "Hello salty girl. I'm back." (*She dabs her lipstick with her napkin.*) See you bird man.

(*She exits.*

MICHAEL watches her go.

MICHAEL slyly picks up LORNA's napkin.)

MICHAEL: Martini please?

(*He presses the lipstick marks left on the napkin against his own lips.*)

Scene 2

(*A loud KNOCKING.*

LORNA's apartment. Morning.

It's one of those Southern California apartment buildings built in the '70s, and the matching furniture hasn't been replaced since.

There's a few fashion magazines around, a couple of dead plants, and a full bar in the built in the corner with bar stools.

A Spanish radio plays in the distance. Birds chirp.

A couple of new nice department store shopping bags are strewn about with boxes of shoes and dresses hanging out.

LORNA enters with a glass of water and a bottle of aspirin.

The knocking continues until LORNA opens the door. Her neighbor MAGGIE stands on the other side of the door with a pile of mail. She's in her late sixties.)

MAGGIE: You're fat.

(LORNA takes the aspirin.)

MAGGIE: Must have been a good trip.
LORNA: Uh huh.
MAGGIE: Ever heard of calling the post office?
LORNA: What time is it?

(MAGGIE enters.)

MAGGIE: You need to water these plants.
LORNA: I thought you were going to do that—
MAGGIE: Running up and down these stairs is no picnic at my age.
LORNA: I'll buy new ones.
MAGGIE: Must be nice. *(MAGGIE wanders over to the bags.)* I don't
    know where you put all this stuff.
LORNA: Thanks for keeping my mail, Maggie.
MAGGIE: Sure.

(LORNA holds out her hands to accept it.

MAGGIE hands over the mail.)

MAGGIE: You have any bread in the house?

LORNA: No.

MAGGIE: Looks like you've been eating something.

LORNA: It's temporary.

MAGGIE: Every time you take a trip, you get fat. Seems like too much trouble to me. I don't like to diet.

LORNA: I know—

MAGGIE: You can learn just as much on TV, you know. You ever watch some of those travel programs? They're pretty interesting. You feel like you're right there.

LORNA: I'd rather be right there.

MAGGIE: Getting fat.

LORNA: Isn't it your lunch time, Maggie?

MAGGIE: I don't know what I'm going to do without bread. My delivery's not till tomorrow.

LORNA: You'll make do.

MAGGIE: They bring my food last now. All my groceries sit wilting in that kid's truck while he smokes cigarettes and shoots the breeze with all the other customers. I've been giving them my business for twenty years.

LORNA: Why don't you go down there and talk to them?

(LORNA *lights a cigarette.*)

MAGGIE: I will.

LORNA: Uh huh.

MAGGIE: I guess I can eat crackers. I've got some saltines in the cabinet from last week. (MAGGIE *looks around the apartment.*) Did you bring me any—

(LORNA *thrust a pack of matches in* MAGGIE*'s hand.*

MAGGIE *reads the matches.*)

MAGGIE: Arizona?

LORNA: Uh huh.

MAGGIE: I thought you went to Mexico.

LORNA: I met a guy from Arizona.

MAGGIE: What was he like?

LORNA: I don't know. Tall. Tan. Rich.

MAGGIE: Does he own this hotel?

LORNA: And seven others.

MAGGIE: Was he anything like that guy from Las Vegas?

LORNA: Who?

MAGGIE: The one that owned all those casinos?

LORNA: No. Arizona was sweeter.

MAGGIE: Really?

LORNA: Much.

MAGGIE: I thought the casino guy sounded nice. He spent a lot on his matches. That's a good sign.

LORNA: I guess.

MAGGIE: Really. Those are still the best I got. Next to the Atlantic City ones you stole in Spain.

LORNA: Right—

MAGGIE: But then I liked that Chicago man you met in London that owned that football team . . . what was his name?

LORNA: Chicago . . .

MAGGIE: You said he was real friendly and sweet, and big. Broad shoulders. Bill somebody.

LORNA: Oh, Chicago. Well—

MAGGIE: Oh Christ. My show's coming on. And I haven't even made my lunch. I guess I'll be eating those damn crackers. Welcome home.

LORNA: Thanks.

MAGGIE: Don't be stomping around up here. Remember. I'm a light sleeper.

(*MAGGIE exits.*

LORNA closes the door and throws the mail on the couch.)

MAGGIE: (*Off.*) A kid came by to see you.

LORNA: What?

MAGGIE: (*Off.*) Some kid.

(*LORNA quickly walks and opens the door.*)

LORNA: Why? (*LORNA shouts up the hall.*) Why?
MAGGIE: *(Off.)* How the hell would I know?
LORNA: What?
MAGGIE: *(Off.)* My show's coming on!

Scene 3

(*The bar.*

LORNA sits with a drink in hand, telling one of her stories.)

LORNA: So I'm running across the ship, in heels, and I look behind
    me, and he's still chasing me, he's still running as fast as he can,
    and I'm running as fast as I can, but I was a high school track
    star you see so I've got the calf muscles to beat him, even in
    three-inch spikes, and he's huffing and puffing over his gold
    chains and Rolex—
BERT: But I thought he was the Captain—
LORNA: He was—
BERT: Why's he wearing gold chains?
LORNA: What?
BERT: That doesn't sound very Captain-like.
LORNA: Why?
BERT: When I was in the Navy, no Captain of any ship I knew would
    be caught dead in gold chains.
LORNA: This is a cruise ship.
BERT: He's still a man of dignity.
LORNA: Not with a fifth of bourbon in his belly.
BERT: Disgraceful.
LORNA: All I could see was this blur of white running behind me
    when I slipped and fell in the pool.
BERT: He shouldn't be Captain.

(*MICHAEL enters.*)

LORNA: I fell in head first and was soaked to the skin when all he did was stand there looking at me.

(*He sees* LORNA *at a table and takes a seat at the bar.*)

MICHAEL: Martini.

LORNA: Didn't even lift a finger to get me out. Luckily, there was a fellow from Texas nearby, and those men love to come to the rescue in such events and he reached down and pulled me out with one big oil-money arm. We spent the rest of the evening drying me off in his cabin.

BERT: You only say these things to make me jealous.

LORNA: You only listen to get jealous. Now, go get me another drink, sweetheart . . . Go.

(*She waves him off to the bar, and sees* MICHAEL.)

LORNA: Michael! Come sit with us. Buy him a drink while you're at it, Bert.

BERT: Why?

LORNA: He's handsome and I want you to. Now go.

BERT: I'm handsome.

LORNA: Of course you are.

BERT: Women tell me that I'm good-looking, Lorna.

LORNA: You are.

(BERT *shuffles off, passing* MICHAEL *on his way to the bar.*)

BERT: She's mine, kid.

MICHAEL: OK.

BERT: I've been waiting five years.

MICHAEL: OK.

BERT: Remember that.

(MICHAEL *sits down at the table.*)

LORNA: "Just do it."

MICHAEL: What?
LORNA: Your shirt.
MICHAEL: Oh, yeah. Nike. My father got it on sale—
LORNA: That's what I always say. Just do it. For Christ's sake.

(*BERT returns to the table, struggling not to spill the two martinis.*)

LORNA: And just drink it. Thanks, Bert.

(*BERT quickly sits as close to LORNA as possible.*)

LORNA: Are you trying to smell me?
BERT: What?
LORNA: You're not trying to smell me again, are you?
BERT: No.
LORNA: Uh huh.
BERT: But you do smell nice. Milky—
LORNA: So, Michael, you live around here?
MICHAEL: No.
LORNA: You on vacation? Come here to explore the wonders of the California coast? Taste the sun? Surf the big ones? I know some guys up in Malibu that can show you—
MICHAEL: No.
LORNA: You just here to drink? (*She taps his glass.*) Well. Then. That'll work. Cheers.
MICHAEL: Oh. Thanks. You're my mother.
LORNA: What?
MICHAEL: You're my mother.
LORNA: Oh . . . you want me to take you home with me?
MICHAEL: No.
LORNA: You want me to tuck you in?
MICHAEL: No—
LORNA: I can tell you a bedtime story.

(*MICHAEL stares.*)

LORNA: Hey . . . hey . . . you ever read that Dr. Seuss book? Where the little tiny bird goes around to all these crazy things—an elephant, a fire hydrant, a bulldozer, an elephant—and he asks every one of them, "Are you my mother?" That's a sweet book.

BERT: I think my nephew has that—

LORNA: It's a great book.

MICHAEL: It is.

LORNA: You should read that, kid.

MICHAEL: I don't need to read it.

LORNA: I didn't say you need to read it, sweetheart, I just said you should. You might enjoy it.

MICHAEL: I know who my mother is.

LORNA: Well, maybe you should be nice and go over there and give her a call. Let her know you're thinking of her. Bert, there's only one olive in here. You know I like two.

MICHAEL: I'm thinking of you . . . at the moment.

LORNA: Might as well be talking to a bulldozer, kid. Bert, get me another olive.

(BERT remains seated as he and the rest of the bar seems to be staring at LORNA.)

LORNA: Hey hey . . . what is this folks, a sideshow? Jesus. Don't you assholes have something else to do than stare at me all night? I mean, I know I am pretty "luminous" . . . some would say "captivating," others have said "irresistible," but please . . . really. Resist me. Go have some fun. Fuck someone at the bar.

BERT: He's your son?

LORNA: Get out of here! And get me a drink while you're at it.

(BERT goes to the bar.

MICHAEL removes a folded piece of paper from his pocket.)

MICHAEL: That's your name, isn't it?

LORNA: I don't have my glasses.

MICHAEL: Lorna Cotes.

LORNA: It's a common name.
MICHAEL: "Born January 5, 1955. Pampa, Texas."
LORNA: It's a large city.
MICHAEL: "Gave birth to a boy on July 8, 1974, in St. Peter's Hospital in Columbus, Ohio."
LORNA: Ohio. Let me think . . . Nope. Never been there.
MICHAEL: "Lorna Cotes' current residence: 1813 Ocean Avenue, Apt. C, Santa Monica, California, 90405."
LORNA: Which one of you turkeys is giving out my address?
MICHAEL: "Birth mother has not responded to search."
LORNA: What search?
MICHAEL: You have a computer?
LORNA: No. I'm more of a people person.

(*LORNA grabs her purse.*)

MICHAEL: You can learn a lot these days.
LORNA: Have you been snooping around my house?
MICHAEL: No.
LORNA: Liar.
MICHAEL: I'm the one with the truth right here—
LORNA: You haven't been coming around my building asking about me?
MICHAEL: No.
LORNA: Then what brings you in here, Columbo?
MICHAEL: I am my mother's son.

(*LORNA gets close to his face. Touches his cheek.*)

LORNA: But not mine. Sweetheart.

(*LORNA laughs and smiles and shakes her head as she exits.*

MICHAEL follows.)

Scene 4

(*A parking lot.*

MICHAEL catches up with LORNA.)

MICHAEL: You know, you're a lot prettier than I thought you'd be.

(*LORNA stops.*)

MICHAEL: I just didn't picture that face ... or the hair. You're much more glamorous really.

(*LORNA laughs. She begins to light a cigarette.*)

LORNA: Look kid, I don't know what you're trying to pull.
MICHAEL: What?
LORNA: This is where I live, where I drink, where I walk, drive, buy my groceries. My place.
MICHAEL: I know that.
LORNA: Then what are you trying to pull?
MICHAEL: Nothing. I just came to meet you.
LORNA: In my bar?
MICHAEL: Beginner's luck.
LORNA: Bullshit.
MICHAEL: It's true.
LORNA: Do I look like a mother?
MICHAEL: I guess not—
LORNA: Hell, we could have even had some fun together. You and me. But this whole mother thing is a real mood spoiler, you know. (*She drops the cigarette and leaves it there.*) And those are my friends in there.
MICHAEL: They're fun people.
LORNA: I think so.
MICHAEL: I didn't mean to—

LORNA: Coming in and announcing to a room full of strangers that I am your mother . . . (*She laughs.*) What makes a kid do something like that?

MICHAEL: Twenty-five years of wondering.

LORNA: Oh really?

MICHAEL: You know how long I've wondered what it would be like to look at your face? To see what color your eyes were? The shape of your mouth?

LORNA: Listen . . . if I were your "real" mother, and I'm not, I would think, and I'm just taking a wild stab at this here, sweetheart, I would think that the whole point of giving you away was that she didn't have to see you again.

MICHAEL: Right.

LORNA: Be reminded.

MICHAEL: Uh huh.

LORNA: You can't just do that to a person.

MICHAEL: Yeah.

LORNA: So, just get yourself back to wherever you came from and sit down with your Mom and tell her you love her. OK?

MICHAEL: What?

LORNA: I'm sure she's a good woman who loves you very much.

MICHAEL: She's dead.

LORNA: What?

MICHAEL: My adoptive mother is dead. She died two years ago.

(*LORNA is silent.*)

MICHAEL: It's true.

(*Silence.*)

MICHAEL: I know. It's pathetic really.

(*LORNA exits.*

MICHAEL watches her go.)

MICHAEL: "How can I move thee? ... Will no entreaties cause thee to turn a favourable eye upon thy creature, who implores thy goodness and compassion ..."

(*MICHAEL stops.*)

MICHAEL: "Believe me, Frankenstein, I was benevolent; my soul glowed with love and humanity; but am I not alone, miserably alone?"

Scene 5

(*LORNA's apartment.*

LORNA paces; anxiously moving about the apartment.

LORNA finally begins to wind down. Lights a cigarette and then pours herself a drink. She takes a seat on the couch.

She finishes the drink. A drop spills on her chest. She wipes the vodka away, feels her full breasts underneath.

She moves her hand down and rubs her belly.)

Scene 6

(*LORNA's apartment.*

MAGGIE enters through the open door.)

MAGGIE: Could you take your shoes off in the house.

(*LORNA enters with a handful of new plants, some mail, and a six-pack of Slim-Fast.*)

MAGGIE: Could you take your shoes off?

LORNA: Why?

MAGGIE: I can't sleep.

LORNA: It's four in the afternoon.

MAGGIE: So?

LORNA: It's still light outside.

MAGGIE: Still.

LORNA: Still what?

MAGGIE: I know you're wearing them.

LORNA: It's my apartment, Maggie. I can wear my own goddamn shoes.

MAGGIE: I don't know why you need to put them on anyway. Any minute there will be some man coming over to take them off for you, won't there?

LORNA: That's my business, Maggie.

MAGGIE: Well, I don't want to listen to it.

LORNA: Then don't.

MAGGIE: A woman your age running around all the time. (*MAGGIE touches the plants.*) These are pretty.

LORNA: Thank you. Now, if you don't mind, I've got bills to pay.

(*LORNA sits down on the couch.*)

MAGGIE: Some people might wonder how you pay those bills.

LORNA: Don't you have a show to watch?

MAGGIE: That's a fancy dress.

LORNA: Yes it is.

MAGGIE: Looks like you paid a good bit for it.

LORNA: I did.

MAGGIE: Must be nice.

(*LORNA begins looking through the mail.*)

LORNA: It is. Now, move along Maggie. I've got business to attend to.

MAGGIE: What kind of business?

LORNA: I don't ask you about your days and you don't ask me about mine. That's the deal. So mosey on down to your piles of clutter and let me attend to mine.

MAGGIE: You could ask me about my life.

LORNA: I could.

MAGGIE: I wouldn't mind.

LORNA: Well, that's interesting, but I won't.

MAGGIE: That kid asked me about my life and I liked it.

(*LORNA keeps looking through the bills.*)

MAGGIE: He was a nervous type, short, but nice.

LORNA: Uh huh.

MAGGIE: He had some questions about you too.

LORNA: Oh did he.

MAGGIE: I didn't have much to tell him of course.

(*Silence.*)

MAGGIE: Told him you've been living here about fifteen years and that you didn't talk to me much.

LORNA: That's right.

MAGGIE: He said he would come back another day.

(*Silence.*)

MAGGIE: I offered him a Pepsi but he said he had to go.

LORNA: Don't you have to go?

MAGGIE: I guess I could. (*MAGGIE doesn't move.*) I keep looking for you on *America's Most Wanted.*

LORNA: Do you?

MAGGIE: I do.

LORNA: Well, I'll let you know if I make it on there. I know you'd hate to miss it. What night's it come on?

MAGGIE: Saturday.

LORNA: I'll keep you informed.

(*MAGGIE heads for the door.*)

MAGGIE: You get a reward for turning people in.
LORNA: You'll be the first to know.
MAGGIE: $50,000.
LORNA: It's yours.

(*MAGGIE exits/closes the door. LORNA puts the mail aside, lights a cigarette and slips off her shoes.*)

Scene 7

(*LORNA's apartment.*

BERT sits across the table watching LORNA *as she sorts through her stack of bills and letters. She tears up the junk mail.*)

LORNA: Don't you have something to do?
BERT: No.
LORNA: You giving up working?
BERT: Uh huh.
LORNA: What? Jesus. Am I growing a chicken out my face? Stop staring at me.
BERT: That kid does kind of look like you.
LORNA: You think everyone looks like me.
BERT: I do not.
LORNA: Every time you see a movie, you tell me so and so looks like me.
BERT: Because they are pretty, not because they are related.
LORNA: Well, if you want to talk genealogy, you'll have to take your ass someplace else. I'm busy.
BERT: It was his mouth or something. His teeth.
LORNA: You're gonna see some teeth on your arm in a minute.
BERT: The way they show when he talks.
LORNA: Hand me my checkbook.
BERT: And his cheeks. You have the same cheeks.

LORNA: I have my cheeks. And you are never going to lay one speck of your cheek next to them again if you don't shut up. Now hand me that goddamn checkbook . . . Bert . . . stop staring at me and hand me that checkbook.

(*BERT hands it over.*)

BERT: His hands look familiar too. Didn't they?

(*LORNA grabs his hand and bangs it on the table.*)

LORNA: He is not my son, Bert. You hear me? So you can either sit there with your trap shut, or you can leave.

(*LORNA lets him go.*)

LORNA: I don't want to listen to you.

(*BERT rubs his hand, as LORNA begins to write a check.*

BERT watches her write, looks around the room, rubs his hand, looks at his hand.)

BERT: I always wanted a son.

(*LORNA points to the door.*)

Scene 8

(*The bar.*

MICHAEL sits at the bar alone with a pitcher of beer.

BERT enters still rubbing the pain out of his hand.)

BERT: A little slow this time of day.

MICHAEL: Yeah.
BERT: No bartender?
MICHAEL: He went to lunch.
BERT: Huh.

(*Silence.*)

BERT: Your father must have been a foreigner.
MICHAEL: What?
BERT: Your father. I don't think he was American.
MICHAEL: Why?
BERT: Lorna doesn't really take to us. She likes things imported.
MICHAEL: I don't know.
BERT: You don't know what.
MICHAEL: Where my father was from.
BERT: Huh.
MICHAEL: Do you?
BERT: What?
MICHAEL: Know anything—
BERT: I barely know where Lorna's from . . . She doesn't like to talk
    much about those things.
MICHAEL: Really.

(*MICHAEL pours him a beer.*)

BERT: Where are you staying?
MICHAEL: In a motel.
BERT: Did you fly out here?
MICHAEL: Drove.
BERT: Where from?
MICHAEL: Pittsburgh.
BERT: Nice town.
MICHAEL: Not really.
BERT: You drive all the way out here just to meet Lorna?
MICHAEL: Uh . . . yes. I guess you could say that.
BERT: That's a long way.
MICHAEL: It is.

BERT: Was it worth it?
MICHAEL: I don't know yet.
BERT: Hell . . . she'll warm up to you.
MICHAEL: You think so.
BERT: If she's your mother.
MICHAEL: She is.
BERT: She's bound to love you.
MICHAEL: I'm not looking for her love.
BERT: Of course you are.
MICHAEL: I'm not.
BERT: What do you want?
MICHAEL: Do I have to want something?
BERT: You drove across the country.
MICHAEL: I'm young. There's a lot to see.
BERT: Huh.

(*MICHAEL nods.*)

BERT: So why you hanging out here?

(*LORNA enters.*)

LORNA: I need a ride to the bank.
BERT: Sit down a minute.
LORNA: I don't drink this time of day.
BERT: Ha. Are you trying to impress your son?
LORNA: No—
BERT: Sit down—
LORNA: He's not my son.

(*MICHAEL fishes through his pockets.*)

MICHAEL: I have baby pictures.
BERT: Do you now? Let's see.
MICHAEL: Some are a little worn.
BERT: Lorna, come look.
LORNA: I'm not interested.

BERT: Everyone likes to look at babies. C'mon.

(*LORNA remains standing by the door.*)

BERT: Will you look at that . . . what a face. What a face.

MICHAEL: Yeah.

BERT: It's perfect.

MICHAEL: I, ah, I did do a few local modeling jobs for baby food.

BERT: No kidding? I'd buy food from your face. I would.

MICHAEL: My parents were stopped on the street. Some guy owned an advertising agency and wanted to use me.

BERT: And look at that one . . . what were you, two or so?

MICHAEL: One and a half.

BERT: Lord.

MICHAEL: My mother made all my clothes.

BERT: That's some outfit.

MICHAEL: It was hell. Look at me.

BERT: I know.

MICHAEL: Might as well be holding a tin cup and dancing to an accordion.

BERT: The hat is a little small.

MICHAEL: I look ridiculous.

LORNA: Bert. Do you mind?

BERT: There's some cute stuff here, Lorna.

LORNA: I'm not interested in cute stuff. I need a ride.

BERT: Oh, look at that . . . is that a hamster you've got there?

MICHAEL: Robert McGee. He eventually ran himself to death on his wheel, but he was sweet. In his way.

BERT: I had a turtle.

MICHAEL: Really?

BERT: Never did come out of its shell.

MICHAEL: They're like that.

BERT: I think my father got it on sale.

LORNA: Bert!

BERT: What?

LORNA: I have got plans.

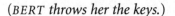

(*BERT throws her the keys.*)

BERT: Go do them.
LORNA: I thought you were taking me to lunch.
BERT: Right. Look at that new bike.
MICHAEL: I won it, actually—
LORNA: Bert?
BERT: Michael, have you eaten?
MICHAEL: Uh. No. Not yet.

Scene 9

(*LORNA's apartment.*

BERT, LORNA, and MICHAEL all look ill.)

BERT: Now that was something.
LORNA: Ten bucks for a pile of backyard weeds.
MICHAEL: Thanks for lunch. Good organic restaurants are some-
    times hard to—
BERT: Fastest meal I've ever had.
MICHAEL: I guess I was kind of hungry—
BERT: If you two aren't related, then peas don't belong in pods.
    Good Lord. That waiter didn't have time to clear his throat to
    take our order before he was putting down the check.
LORNA: I think there was dirt in my salad.

(*MICHAEL takes in the apartment.*)

MICHAEL: A lot of minerals in dirt. I hear some places in Texas peo-
    ple actually eat the local land—
LORNA: Bathroom's back there.

(*MICHAEL exits.*)

LORNA: He's out of here in five minutes, Bert, or you're never getting near my bed again, much less—

BERT: I like him.

LORNA: Well, good for you. I don't have time for new friends. I've got plenty.

BERT: He's your son.

LORNA: If I've said it once, I've said it fifteen fucking too many times, that kid is not my son.

(*A KNOCK at the door.*)

LORNA: I'd think I'd know if I had been anyone's mother. Don't you?

(*Another KNOCK.*

LORNA *opens the door. BEN, 23, stands on the other side.*)

BEN: Lorna Cotes?

LORNA: I'm not buying.

(*LORNA tries to close the door.*)

BEN: I think you're my mother.

LORNA: Sorry?

BEN: My mother.

(*MICHAEL enters from the bathroom.*

BEN *sneaks through the door.*)

BEN: You're Lorna Cotes?

LORNA: Maybe.

BEN: Well . . . I was born June 20, 1976, in Louisville, Kentucky? I was adopted by Dr. Benjamin and Margaret Goldberg?

LORNA: And?

BEN: Six pounds six ounces?

LORNA: Is that supposed to mean something to me?

BEN: Well, you're my mother.

LORNA: I'm not.

BEN: I think you are.

LORNA: You're mistaken.

BEN: No . . . no I'm not . . . I got it all right here . . . (*BEN stares at her.*) Don't you remember?

LORNA: No.

BEN: Twelve hours of labor?

LORNA: And?

(*BEN pulls up his shirt.*)

BEN: I have a birthmark on my stomach?

LORNA: Please. (*She pulls down his shirt.*) I don't want to see your skin.

BEN: My head was covered in hair?

(*LORNA walks away from him. BEN follows.*)

BEN: My eyes were closed shut.

(*LORNA won't look at him.*)

BEN: My father must have been Asian or—

LORNA: I don't care. I'm not a DNA specialist.

BEN: I didn't think you were, ma'am.

LORNA: So why don't you take your hair and spotted stomach and this boy over here. (*She grabs BEN and pulls MICHAEL to the door.*) And get out of my house. I'm not interested in your birthmarks or your story.

MICHAEL: Do you have records with you?

BEN: Uh huh.

MICHAEL: Let me see them.

(*BEN hands the papers over to MICHAEL. LORNA tries to rip them from his hands but MICHAEL holds on.*)

LORNA: This is not a fucking orphanage—
BERT: They know that—
LORNA: Obviously they don't, Bert, because I am being invaded here. You see that?! I'm not interested in any Oliver fucking Twist breathing down my neck! So take your papers and dates and ounces and pounds and your goddamn desperate eyes out of here—
MICHAEL: It's her alright. I've got the same—

(*MICHAEL pulls the paper from his back pocket.*)

LORNA: This is my house!

(*LORNA pushes them out the door. Slams and locks it behind them.*)

BERT: Lorna.

(*BERT stands staring.*)

LORNA: Don't look at me like that.

(*LORNA grabs the bottle of booze.*)

Scene 10

(*The hall.*)

BEN: No father.

(*MICHAEL and BEN stand comparing papers.*)

MICHAEL: Same here. Nothing.
BEN: Did you ask her?
MICHAEL: I don't know if she knows.
BEN: Really?

MICHAEL: Does that surprise you?
BEN: Well, she slept with the guy. They had sex.

(*MICHAEL laughs.*)

BEN: What?
MICHAEL: I'm guessing she's slept with many.
BEN: Why? What's she like?
MICHAEL: Well . . . the best that I can tell, she's pretty friendly. Likes
    to drink. Kind of funny. Unless you tell her she's your mother.
BEN: Huh.
MICHAEL: Things kind of went downhill from there.

(*Silence.*)

BEN: My mom gave me the plane ticket out here.
MICHAEL: Really?
BEN: For my birthday.
MICHAEL: Nice.
BEN: Yeah, but I've been out here for a month and this is the first
    chance I've had to meet her.

(*MICHAEL nods.*)

BEN: Half my summer is almost gone.
MICHAEL: I guess so.

(*Silence.*)

BEN: My mom's afraid I'll never come back.
MICHAEL: No worry of that, huh?

(*MICHAEL and BEN stand staring at each other.*

MICHAEL lights a cigarette. Offers one to BEN.)

BEN: No, thanks.

(*MICHAEL puts the cigarettes away.*

BEN checks his watch. Silence.)

BEN: Do, do you have a birthmark?
MICHAEL: No.
BEN: I didn't think so.

(*They stare at each other.*)

MICHAEL: Are you afraid of heights?
BEN: No—
MICHAEL: Well, I'm not afraid of all heights. Just the really tall ones.
BEN: I hate eggs.

(*Silence.*)

MICHAEL: I like them.
BEN: Bacon?
MICHAEL: With the eggs.
BEN: Do you wear glasses?
MICHAEL: No. Do you?
BEN: Contacts.
MICHAEL: I'm an insomniac.
BEN: Really?
MICHAEL: Yeah.
BEN: That's too bad. I used to wet the bed.
MICHAEL: Really?
BEN: Not—not anymore.
MICHAEL: You like your parents?
BEN: What?
MICHAEL: Your parents. Are they nice?
BEN: Oh. Yeah. Sure. They're great.
MICHAEL: Yeah?
BEN: I love them.
MICHAEL: That's good.
BEN: You?

MICHAEL: You want a beer?

BEN: No.

MICHAEL: Do you drink?

BEN: Not, not often. Never really—

MICHAEL: Do you want to?

BEN: I don't think so.

MICHAEL: Well. Hell. What's a brother for?

Scene 11

(*LORNA's apartment.*

BERT now sits at the table, but still looks away from LORNA.

LORNA sits on the couch with a bottle of vodka.)

LORNA: Whining at me and sniffing around like two fucking lost puppies.

BERT: They seem like good—

LORNA: I'm not talking to you.

BERT: Fine.

LORNA: I lead a quiet life, don't I? I mean, I don't go around looking for trouble or talking about myself or bragging about things, do?

BERT: Well, yes, sometimes—

LORNA: Shut up.

BERT: Occasionally.

LORNA: Since when can boys show up and grab on to your fucking dress hem and scratch into your eyes with their voices and tell you You are their mother? Since when can they do that? Just walk in like some kind of mailman and announce that they are delivering themselves to you, like it or not, and you've got no say in the matter?

BERT: Are they your kids?

LORNA: What's it matter?

BERT: It matters to them, Lorna—

LORNA: Why are you still here?

BERT: I thought you might want some company—

LORNA: What's it matter what I want? Huh? Seems it doesn't matter, does it? It's all about them. What they need. I am not responsible for them. I am not.

BERT: Why'd you have them?

LORNA: That's none of your business.

BERT: You had them, gave them away—

LORNA: To good families! To good families. To lonely fucking couples! People foaming at the mouth for babies! Those kids are lucky! And they come back here looking me in the eye like I did something wrong!

BERT: That's not what they're doing—

LORNA: They want to know Why . . . they want me to sit them down on my knee and rub their foreheads and tell them I did what was best for all of us and then they want me to touch their cheeks and tell them I love them and that never a day has gone by that I haven't thought of them . . . and then they want me to take them into my arms and cry and tell them how much I've missed them and how sorry I am, they want me to smooth down their hair, tell them what fine men they've become . . . but I won't do it! I won't.

BERT: Then don't.

LORNA: I won't. That's not what I'm here for. No sir. That's not my part. I gave birth for Christ's sake—I may have given birth to those kids but that's it. They are lucky! Don't they see that! One day in a doctor's office and they could have been air. Scraped clean. Could have been tossed into a bucket of red blood clots. The end. They could have been nothings. But no. No. That's not what happened. Sacrifices were made. A body was stretched and pulled out of shape just to house them. Screams of pain were shouted through clinched, gnashed teeth just to bring them forth. But they are here, aren't they? They are here. Because of me.

BERT: You are responsi—

LORNA: You don't bother the stork once it's done. No sir. You don't come asking for more. You don't come till up the cabbage patch. They already got all they are getting from me. That's it. Breath of life is all you get from me, kids.

BERT: Fine.

LORNA: I'm not talking to you.

Scene 12

(*The beach.*

MICHAEL and BEN sit with beers in hand. MICHAEL's shirt is off. He's got scars on his chest.)

MICHAEL: Look at that . . . that bird only has one foot.

BEN: I wonder what happened to the other one.

MICHAEL: I don't know.

BEN: Maybe it was born that way. I think that happens sometimes.

MICHAEL: He doesn't seem to mind, does he.

BEN: No.

MICHAEL: A little one-legged Casanova. Horny bastard. He probably told her he was Jonathan Livingston.

BEN: Who's that?

MICHAEL: A famous seagull.

BEN: No . . .

MICHAEL: He's got his own book.

BEN: Really?

MICHAEL: He's a spiritual bird.

BEN: Huh.

MICHAEL: What about you?

BEN: What?

MICHAEL: Your parents raise you religious or anything?

BEN: We're Jewish.

MICHAEL: You like it?

BEN: I guess so.

MICHAEL: You guess so.

BEN: I don't know anything else.

MICHAEL: You like wearing that, that, that yarmulke?

BEN: You get used to it.

MICHAEL: I hear it's a good religion. If you're into that.

BEN: What?

MICHAEL: That.

BEN: You're not?

MICHAEL: No . . . It's like trying to catch a fucking fly in a box. You have to believe that if you caught it and it's in there . . . you just have to believe it's in there.

BEN: Why?

MICHAEL: Because if you don't believe it's in there . . . and you try and open the box to make sure, maybe it'll fly out. Gone. You gotta believe it's in there or you may lose it, right?

BEN: I don't know—

MICHAEL: No. Might as well leave the fly alone. And the box.

BEN: Your parents aren't religious.

MICHAEL: The closest my father ever got is when he said, Goddamn it! as his hand went across my face.

BEN: Huh.

MICHAEL: He wanted a quieter son.

BEN: And your Mom?

MICHAEL: She wanted a quieter life.

BEN: And you?

MICHAEL: What?

BEN: What do you want?

MICHAEL: We don't look like brothers, do we.

BEN: No. I guess not.

MICHAEL: Let me see your hands.

(*They hold out their hands beside each other.*)

MICHAEL: Let me see your feet.

(*They both unfold their legs and put their feet side by side.*)

BEN: I wonder who we look like.

Scene 13

(*LORNA's apartment.*

LORNA's asleep on the couch. BERT is gone.)

MAGGIE: *(Off.)* Lorna? Hey, Lorna? (Maggie bangs on the door.) Lorna! Open up!

(*LORNA finally comes to. Stumbles to the door.*)

LORNA: What?
MAGGIE: *(Off.)* Open up!

(*LORNA opens the door. MAGGIE stands holding the arm of CELIA, 19, who's trying to wrestle her way out of MAGGIE's grip. She wears an old backpack and looks as if she's been on the road for too many of those 19 years.*)

MAGGIE: She says she's yours.
CELIA: I didn't say anything.
MAGGIE: You did too. You said your mother lived in the building.
CELIA: How do you know it's her?
MAGGIE: Look at you.
CELIA: So?
MAGGIE: Look at her.

(*CELIA looks LORNA over. LORNA is disheveled.*)

CELIA: I look like that?
MAGGIE: There's certainly something familiar there.
CELIA: I think I'm much prettier.
MAGGIE: You do, do you? (*MAGGIE compares the two.*) Well, yes, well, maybe you're right.

(*LORNA closes the door.*)

LORNA: No one looks like familiar here!

(*LORNA listens, panicked by the door.*

She waits, then opens the door.

CELIA stands on the other side.

LORNA doesn't close the door. Remains staring.)

CELIA: Take a picture. It lasts longer.
MAGGIE: Oh my.
LORNA: Take a hike Maggie.

(*LORNA moves away from the door, CELIA walks inside.*

CELIA looks the apartment over as LORNA looks her over.

CELIA sets down her backpack.)

LORNA: You're not staying here—
CELIA: I didn't say I was.
LORNA: Keep it on.

(*CELIA puts it on her back.*)

CELIA: Bitch.
LORNA: What?
CELIA: Nothing.

(*LORNA tries to clean herself up. Adjust her hair. Her dress.*)

LORNA: What do you want?

(*CELIA sees her heels by the couch.*)

CELIA: Nice. (*She slips off her clogs and puts them on.*) Same size. How do I look?

LORNA: Take them off.

CELIA: Why?

LORNA: Your feet are dirty.

(*CELIA slips them off.*)

CELIA: Well then. Can I use your shower?

LORNA: No.

CELIA: I could use a shower.

LORNA: You're not staying here.

CELIA: Did I say I was?

(*CELIA picks up objects around the room.*)

LORNA: Look—

CELIA: Celia.

LORNA: Celia—

CELIA: Do you like it?

LORNA: What?

CELIA: My name?

LORNA: I don't know—

CELIA: They said they told you what it would be.

LORNA: Who?

CELIA: My parents. When they gave you the check, they said they told you my name.

LORNA: I don't remember.

CELIA: Celia E. Brown. The "E" doesn't stand for anything. Did they tell you that?

LORNA: I don't know—

CELIA: My parents just liked the letter. Do you like it?

LORNA: What?

CELIA: "E"?

(*LORNA stares at her.*)

CELIA: I tell people it was taken from the eye doctor's chart. So I
could always be seen.

(*LORNA looks away.*)

CELIA: Mother.
LORNA: Don't call me that.
CELIA: What?
LORNA: Don't call me that.
CELIA: But—
LORNA: Please.
CELIA: It's true. I'm here. Look at me.
LORNA: I know.
CELIA: Look at me—
LORNA: I know. Isn't that enough?

(*CELIA sets down her backpack and sits beside LORNA on the
couch.*)

LORNA: What do you want?
CELIA: I want you to look at me.
LORNA: Why?
CELIA: Please.
LORNA: Why?
CELIA: I need you to tell me things.
LORNA: I see you.
CELIA: Look at me.
LORNA: I said, I see you!
CELIA: Do you?
LORNA: Yes.
CELIA: Do you?
LORNA: Leave me alone. I lead a quiet life—

(*CELIA presents her body to LORNA.*)

CELIA: Do you see my, my fingers?
LORNA: I don't bother people—

CELIA: Look at them. They were tiny when you saw them last time, weren't they? Grabbing things? They're big now. Strong. They're the same fingers. Grabbing—

LORNA: I mind my own business—

CELIA: See my hair. It comes from you. Tangled. My lips. Hungry and cold. My eyes.

(*LORNA keeps her eyes covered.*)

CELIA: Scared and vacant. My lashes. They grew from you. Dark. Long. Flirtatious—

LORNA: Please—

CELIA: My belly.

LORNA: No—

CELIA: My feet. Look at them.

LORNA: No.

CELIA: See my feet. They want to run like yours.

LORNA: I don't care.

CELIA: They want to run away all the time.

LORNA: Please—

CELIA: Tell me why they want to run.

LORNA: Don't do this.

CELIA: Tell me why.

LORNA: Please leave—

CELIA: Tell me why they ache at night. Your blood pumping through them—

LORNA: No.

CELIA: Mother—

LORNA: Please, girl. Stop.

CELIA: Tell me why they look like yours.

LORNA: I'm not going to tell you I'm sorry—

CELIA: Tell me why they look like yours and it doesn't matter.

LORNA: I'm not going to apologize.

CELIA: Tell me why my feet cry at night when they are alone. Why they sleep with others they don't even know.

LORNA: I'm not going to lie.

CELIA: Tell me why I am your daughter and I don't even know you.

LORNA: I won't make excuses.
CELIA: Tell me why I am your daughter and you don't love me.
LORNA: I don't know who you are.
CELIA: Tell me why I want to rip your heart out and throw it away.

(*LORNA finally looks at her.*)

LORNA: I am not sorry.
CELIA: Tell me why I want to crawl back inside you.
LORNA: I did nothing wrong.
CELIA: Tell me how you sold me.
LORNA: I had to live.

End of Act I

— ACT II —

Scene 14

(*The street.*

MICHAEL and BEN stumble drunk arm-in-arm across the stage.)

MICHAEL: That's right.

BEN: How many times?

MICHAEL: Oh, that's not important.

BEN: Did they try and find you?

MICHAEL: Oh, no, I always went home. Eventually.

BEN: Why?

MICHAEL: I don't like the cold much.

BEN: No.

MICHAEL: Or hunger.

BEN: No.

MICHAEL: A bed is nice too.

BEN: I would never run away.

MICHAEL: You would if there was a fist coming at you.

BEN: Maybe.

MICHAEL: Let me tell you something, Benjamin, from one brother to another—You ever read *Frankenstein*?

BEN: No.

MICHAEL: If there's one thing I know about, it's people. I've got eyes like a hawk for watching people, and I think that if anyone were to come ten feet within your soft soul with an object meant to harm your, you—how tall are you?

BEN: Why?

MICHAEL: Don't worry. Look at me. You can always be a late bloomer—

(*BEN lets go of MICHAEL.*)

BEN: Maybe, maybe my dad was short.
MICHAEL: He could be a dynamo.
BEN: Sure.
MICHAEL: If Lorna wanted him, hell. Right?
BEN: I'll ask her.
MICHAEL: You do that.
BEN: What are you going to ask her?
MICHAEL: Oh, well, you know. The usual.
BEN: Usual what?
MICHAEL: Usual son to mother questions concerning birth control and did she ever consider using it.
BEN: Oh.
MICHAEL: You think that's too much?
BEN: No. But, what do you think she's going to tell you?
MICHAEL: Some romance story.
BEN: Then why ask her?
MICHAEL: I'm a hopeless romantic.
BEN: Hey. Me too.

Scene 15

(*LORNA's apartment.*

LORNA enters from the bedroom and finds CELIA sleeps curled up on the couch.

LORNA approaches her. She touches a piece of CELIA's hair. Smells it.

She grabs a blanket and begins to put it on CELIA, but in doing so, hesitates. She throws the blanket on a chair.

She lights a cigarette. Grabs her keys, and exits.

CELIA wakes.)

Scene 16

(The hall. A line of doors. A baby cries offstage.

LORNA rushes forward and falls into a drunk MICHAEL and BEN.

There's little space to pass.)

LORNA: Where are you going?
BEN: Home—
MICHAEL: Where are you going?
LORNA: You get him drunk too?
MICHAEL: You going to ground us?
LORNA: Let me through.
MICHAEL: Please ground us. Make us stay home.
LORNA: Let me through.
MICHAEL: Let Dr. Frankenstein through!
BEN: I think I'm going to be sick.
MICHAEL: "Oh! My creator, make me feel happy; let me feel gratitude towards you for one benefit! Let me see that I excite the sympathy of some existing thing; do not deny me my request! . . ."
MAGGIE: *(Off.)* What's that noise?
BEN: I feel sick.
MAGGIE: *(Off.)* Lorna?
BEN: I mean it—
LORNA: Not here—
MICHAEL: That's my boy.
BEN: Oh God—

(BEN starts to heave.)

MAGGIE: *(Off.)* Who's out there? I can call the cops, you know?
LORNA: Mother fucker.

(LORNA grabs BEN's arm and unlocks her apartment door.)

Scene 17

(*The sound of* BEN *vomiting offstage.*

LORNA's *apartment.*

MICHAEL *stands trying to light a cigarette.*

LORNA *enters pulling* CELIA *out of her bedroom.*)

CELIA: I wasn't going to steal anything.
LORNA: Keep your hands off my stuff.
CELIA: I was just looking at it. (CELIA *sees* MICHAEL *before* MICHAEL *focuses on her.*) There's no crime against looking.
LORNA: Depends what you're looking for.
CELIA: You're a little young for her, aren't you?
MICHAEL: You jealous?
CELIA: Not yet.
MICHAEL: Don't worry then, Sunshine.
LORNA: None of this sunshine talk in here, kids. I'm not running a day-care center. Get moving.
MICHAEL: What's your rush?
LORNA: I'm not here for your entertainment.
MICHAEL: You see me clapping?
LORNA: I don't know how you got my name and address, but I want it back. You hear? You're not taking any of it with you.
CELIA: I was just looking.
LORNA: A woman's got a right to her privacy.
MICHAEL: A kid has a right to meet his mother.
CELIA: His mother?
MICHAEL: Yeah.
CELIA: You're his mother?
LORNA: It's yet to be confirmed.

(BEN *enters from the bathroom wiping his mouth and pale.*)

BEN: Can, can I lay down?

LORNA: Jesus! Does this place look like a shoe?

MICHAEL: If the old woman has some kids—

LORNA: I am not old.

CELIA: He's yours too?

LORNA: So he says.

CELIA: Damn.

LORNA: So you all say.

CELIA: I have proof—

(*LORNA pours herself a drink.*)

LORNA: Listen, you three, I didn't ask for you here, did I? Did I? Did I send out invitations? Did I send out notices to come spend your goddamn summer vacation scratching around my door, looking for love?

MICHAEL: I am not looking for love—

CELIA: That's not why—

LORNA: Bullshit. That's what you all want.

CELIA: How much did you sell them for?

MICHAEL: What?

CELIA: She got $20,000 for me.

MICHAEL: No shit?

CELIA: Under the table.

MICHAEL: See, now that's interesting to me because all these years I just assumed I was left at the wrong doorstep.

CELIA: I'm sure she got some money for you.

LORNA: You're not sure of anything.

(*CELIA holds up a contract.*)

CELIA: I am sure that I am standing in my mother's apartment. I am sure that my mother sold me for $20,000 on August 9, 1979. I am sure that my father is unknown. I am sure that you were told my name before I was removed from the delivery room and placed in my parents' arms. I am sure that no contact was made with me after that day. I am sure no cards or presents were ever sent for my birthday. Or Christmas or any other holiday for that matter. And, I am sure that my child will never see a two-page bill of sale—

LORNA: That is not what that—

CELIA: An *agreement* never to come claim her, with my name and signature and price on her head.

LORNA: Don't be so sure until you've been there.

CELIA: I am there.

(*LORNA is silent.*)

MICHAEL: A price. Now that's an interesting subject. How much did you get for me?

LORNA: I would like you all to leave now.

MICHAEL: See, that never even occurred to me, Mom, because I just assumed I was some orphan my parents took pity on in a sea of tiny beds, and they thought they could do with me what they will. A shitty home is better than none . . . but now, see . . . now it makes sense that really they didn't get what they paid for, and I know how they hate that, and that must have been terribly disappointing. Not to mention, a bad investment.

LORNA: It wasn't that simple.

MICHAEL: Oh, but I think it was, Mom.

LORNA: Don't call me that.

MICHAEL: But Ma, the thing I want to know is . . . what I want to know is what gave you the right to bring a new child into the world, with his bloody skin and bare butt in the air and his eyes closed shut and his mouth still wailing to heaven as they cut the cord—who gave you the right to bring him forth and then decide he'd be better off in the arms of strangers?

LORNA: I gave me the right.

MICHAEL: I see. And is that a halo I see around your hair or just a bad case of bed-head?

LORNA: You're here, aren't you?

MICHAEL: Yes. This is true. I am here. But your head, this room, my head and the four of us combined, are not big enough to hold all the horrors and loneliness I endured with those strangers and if you for one moment think you are some angel of mercy,

I think you better have yourself another drink because I am here to tell you, you are WRONG.

LORNA: They wanted a baby.

MICHAEL: You think every couple that can't have a baby together deserves one?

CELIA: If they have the money?

MICHAEL: Right. Yes. If they have the money?

LORNA: I think they should have the chance to have one, yes. I gave them that.

BEN: I like my parents—

MICHAEL: You are not God—

LORNA: No, but I gave them something beautiful—

MICHAEL: You sold some babies because you could, but you have no right to claim that what you did was always in the best interest of the child. No. No right. I am here to tell you that you were WRONG.

LORNA: How could I know that?

MICHAEL: You couldn't. I guess you couldn't. But the least you could do is take some responsibil—

LORNA: What do you want me to do? Hug you?

(*MICHAEL bats the drink out of her hands.*)

MICHAEL: Look me in the eye! That's what I want you to do! Look me in the fucking eye!

(*LORNA looks at him.*)

MICHAEL: "How dare you sport thus with life!"

LORNA: What?

MICHAEL: I am your son! You made me!

LORNA: You want me to kiss you?

MICHAEL: I want more!

LORNA: More what?

MICHAEL: I want to be happy.

LORNA: Me too.

MICHAEL: Why did you have me?

(*Silence.*)

MICHAEL: For profit?

(*Silence.*)

LORNA: Go figure it out. (*LORNA opens the door.*) Go out there and figure it out. Make yourselves proud. All of you. Go walk the earth. Jump the moon. Crawl into someone's arms. But not mine.

CELIA: Are there more?

LORNA: Why? You want to call them up? Bring them over? Peck me to death?

BEN: We wouldn't do that.

CELIA: Are there more?

LORNA: What's it matter?

MICHAEL: See again, what interests me about you, Madre, is that you still seem to lack certain obvious emotions or regard or Responsibility concerning your children—

LORNA: Listen—

MICHAEL: We continue to ask you questions about you, your past, our lineage, and you still seem unaware that it is of great importance to us.

LORNA: And you seem to lack the obvious awareness that I don't care. No matter how many *Frankenstein* quotes you throw at me. You are not a monster.

MICHAEL: How do you know?

(*LORNA notices something wet on her shirt. Across her chest.*)

LORNA: It's not in your blood.

MICHAEL: I'm not so sure . . . But, still, you didn't see how I was raised, now did you?

(*LORNA hides the spot with her arm.*)

CELIA: How many others are there, Lorna?

LORNA: You found me. You can find them.

BEN: I just want to find my father.

LORNA: If you do, tell him I said hi.

BEN: OK—

MICHAEL: There's not one single thing, not one bit of yourself you'd like to impart upon us, your dear children? Your own flesh and blood? From your very own womb?

(*LORNA thinks.*)

LORNA: Maybe one thing.

(*All three stand looking at her. Waiting.*)

LORNA: I don't love you. (*LORNA holds the door.*) I never did.

(*Slowly they file out.*

LORNA closes the door behind them and checks her shirt. It's wet through.

Milk has started to pour from her breasts.)

LORNA: No . . . Oh no you don't.

MAGGIE: (*Off.*) What's all the commotion down here?

LORNA: No. I won't have it.

(*LORNA takes off her shirt. Her bra is soaked with milk.*)

MAGGIE: (*Off.*) Hey Lorna? What's going on in there?

LORNA: Nothing!

(*LORNA covers herself. She's panicked.*)

MAGGIE: (*Off.*) Who were all those kids? Your kids?

LORNA: I don't have time for you, Maggie.

(*LORNA puts the blanket up to her chest.*

LORNA picks up the phone.)

LORNA: Bert . . . come get me . . . I'm just asking you to . . . because
    I need you to come get me . . . I am being invaded again . . .
MAGGIE: *(Off.)* Lorna!
LORNA: *(In phone.)* I'm being swarmed, Bert.

Scene 18

(*The beach.*

MICHAEL, CELIA sit staring at the water.)

MICHAEL: Guess there won't be cake.
CELIA: Or balloons.
MICHAEL: Who's the father?
CELIA: Of?
MICHAEL: The one in your belly.
CELIA: Oh. Would you know him?
MICHAEL: Lucky guy.
CELIA: Thanks.
MICHAEL: Too bad incest is so unpopular.
CELIA: Right.
MICHAEL: I could have made a move on you.
CELIA: I wouldn't have stopped you.
MICHAEL: See?
CELIA: We've got trouble in our genes.
MICHAEL: Lust in our loins.
CELIA: Hunger in our hearts.
MICHAEL: Adultery in our underpants.
CELIA: Sorry.
MICHAEL: I'm a crappy boyfriend anyway.
CELIA: I'm unfaithful.
MICHAEL: I cry.

CELIA: I'm jealous.
MICHAEL: I don't mix well at parties.
CELIA: I make scenes.
MICHAEL: I drink too much.
CELIA: I'm pregnant.
MICHAEL: I'm moody.
CELIA: It could have been wonderful.
MICHAEL: Paradise.

(*BEN enters with a stack of papers.*)

BEN: I want to go home.
MICHAEL: Why?
BEN: Look at this.
MICHAEL: How many?
BEN: Twelve.
CELIA: No.

(*CELIA grabs the papers.*)

BEN: I've never felt so lonely in all my life.
MICHAEL: You're young. Have faith.
BEN: I feel miserable.
MICHAEL: They'll be plenty more of that.
BEN: I want my mother.

(*MICHAEL looks over CELIA's shoulder. They read the paper together.*)

CELIA: "Michael, July 8, 1974, Columbus, Ohio"
MICHAEL: "Ben, June 20, 1976, Louisville, Kentucky"
BEN: "Celia, August 9, 1979, Bedford, New Hampshire"
MICHAEL, CELIA: "Alice, December 4, 1982, Norfolk, Virginia"

(*BEN joins in.*)

MICHAEL, CELIA, BEN: "Kate, December 15, 1984, Virginia Beach, Virginia" . . .

Scene 19

(*LORNA's apartment.*)

LORNA: And then there was Kate and she wasn't born right and they put her away . . . she wasn't what any of us expected so we just had to put her away. So I, well I . . .

MICHAEL, CELIA, BEN: *(Off.)* "Emma, May 3, 1987, Raleigh, North Carolina"

LORNA: But Emma. She was fine. I just was so happy she was fine.

MICHAEL, CELIA, BEN: *(Off.)* "Pete, April 7, 1989, Atlanta, Georgia"

LORNA: I got a lot of money for Pete.

BERT: Why?

LORNA: They really wanted a boy.

MICHAEL, CELIA, BEN: *(Off.)* "Paul, September 23, 1991, Phoenix, Arizona"

LORNA: Paul didn't cry for hours. They almost wanted their money back. But then he wailed. I could hear him across the hall and them trying to quiet him.

MICHAEL, CELIA, BEN: *(Off.)* "Star, October 12, 1993, Santa Fe, New Mexico"

LORNA: They wanted to call her Star and I couldn't say anything. She looked nothing like a Star . . . she was more plain. Grounded. More of a Sam really . . .

MICHAEL, CELIA, BEN: *(Off.)* "Bette, October 11, 1995, Flagstaff, Arizona"

LORNA: Her parents were older and they had a friend named Bette and they thought she looked just like her. Her hands were tight fists I remember. A boxer. She punched the air.

MICHAEL, CELIA, BEN: *(Off.)* "Jack, February 7, 1997, Eugene, Oregon"

LORNA: It was a difficult birth. I was in labor for thirty hours. It had always been so easy, and then when Jack finally came, I fell asleep before I got to see him . . . and . . .

LORNA, MICHAEL, CELIA, BEN: "Lily, July 1, 1999, Portland, Oregon"

LORNA: Her skin was like a hazelnut. She was very quiet. Sweet. Round. Smiling. (*She passes a glance to BERT.*) I like the name Lily. It was my mother's name. (*LORNA touches her breasts and they are still soaked through with milk.*) I didn't mean to hurt them, Bert.

BERT: I know.

LORNA: A woman has to live. People want babies.

BERT: Yeah.

LORNA: Some people will do whatever they have to to get them. Really.

BERT: Sure.

LORNA: I can have them. It's easy for me.

BERT: Sure.

LORNA: It's not so easy for everyone.

BERT: I know.

LORNA: A woman's got to live. Support herself. I don't have other skills.

BERT: Well—

LORNA: I didn't go to college. I didn't even finish high school. I could pick cotton. That's it.

BERT: Huh.

LORNA: Shit. This is what I could do and they're here.

(*BERT is silent.*)

LORNA: Right?

BERT: Right.

LORNA: Answer me.

BERT: I did.

LORNA: What difference does it make how they got here? . . . Bert?

BERT: What?

LORNA: What difference does it make?

BERT: What's your mother's name again?

LORNA: Lily.

BERT: Are you sure?

LORNA: Of course I'm sure.

BERT: Positive?

LORNA: Yes!

BERT: Why are you getting angry with me?

LORNA: I think I know my own mother's name.

BERT: You do?

LORNA: Yes!

BERT: Sure now?

LORNA: Yes!

BERT: What difference does it make?

LORNA: Fuck you.

BERT: She's just some lady—

LORNA: I went to visit Kate—I, I visit her when I can. I send her clothes and the doctors told me it wasn't something I did wrong. They promised me. I made sure of that—

BERT: Some woman—

LORNA: Michael's parents made it easy. They looked so, so . . . Norman Rockwell; scrubbed and white-fenced and she was mild and matronly and he grinned and sold insurance and they had already bought the station wagon outside—

BERT: She was just your mother—

LORNA: And then, then eventually, the more I had, and the more exotic I made the kids, the more glamorous that baby looked in wealthy arms, and the more money they'd pay just to have it for themselves . . . and the people found me . . . begging for babies . . . the couples just found me and would pay anything for a newborn. Anything—

BERT: Lily, you said her name was?

LORNA: Desperate for a newborn of their very own.

BERT: She wasn't important to you—

LORNA: Those kids have a mother.

BERT: They have two.

LORNA: I'm not the one that needs them!

BERT: What do you need?

LORNA: To enjoy my life.

BERT: That's it?

LORNA: My life. That's not much to ask.

BERT: They're not trying to take it away from you.

LORNA: Yes they are. They are. They want pieces of it. They want reasons and stories and names and pictures and faces and skin colors and eye colors and freckles and birthmarks and memories and explanations I didn't save for them. I didn't even keep them for myself. That's not what I do. I don't hold on to things like that, I just run through them. I like it that way. I like the way I do things and the money all those couples gave me let me do it. It's not that complicated. They wanted something they couldn't make themselves, and I gave it to them. Like, like a shoe smith. I gave them the right fit . . . but now all these goddamn shoes are walking back here asking me what type of leather I used and why didn't I wear them myself and which goddamn cow forked over the skin. I want my privacy back. I want my body back. They look at it and they steal something from me and then something starts to hurt. I feel this pull in my stomach and my tits, look at my tits . . . but my mind . . . my mind feels the same way I did when I turned over in that delivery room with every one of them . . . it feels fifteen miles down the road with a cigarette in my hand and two year's rent in my pocket and they aren't getting near it. They can take my tits with them, suck away . . . I won't be using them . . . but they are not getting the goods, you see . . . they're not getting the girl with it . . . this is what keeps Lorna Cotes alive and free and they aren't getting it.

BERT: Fine.

LORNA: I didn't mean to hurt them.

BERT: I know.

LORNA: I didn't.

BERT: I heard you.

LORNA: Take me to the hospital, Bert.

BERT: Why?

LORNA: Something's ripping me apart.

Scene 20

(The street. A motel sign flashes in the background.

MICHAEL, CELIA, *and* BEN *stand with suitcases and backpacks beside them.)*

MICHAEL: We could start a band instead.
BEN: Or a basketball team.
CELIA: Our own cult.
MICHAEL: A traveling circus . . . trapeze artists . . . The Lost Lorna Twelve.
BEN: I hate traveling.
CELIA: Clowns scare me.
BEN: I'm allergic to peanuts.
MICHAEL: I'm . . . well. Heights are not my . . .

(BEN checks his watch.)

BEN: I told my parents I'd be home on the next plane.
MICHAEL: Don't be a stranger.
BEN: I won't.
CELIA: Call us when you get home.
BEN: I will.
MICHAEL: And don't forget to brush your teeth and say your prayers.
BEN: I won't.

(BEN picks up his suitcase. It's heavy in his arms.)

MICHAEL: Hey, you know what I think?
BEN: What?
MICHAEL: I think your dad must be someone huge.
BEN: You think?
MICHAEL: Oh yeah. I think he's probably a king somewhere or something.
BEN: No . . .

CELIA: I think Michael's right. I see royalty in you.

BEN: You do?

MICHAEL: Something we don't have.

BEN: Really?

CELIA: We're, we're just common chicken stock.

MICHAEL: Run of the mill.

BEN: What is it?

CELIA: Is it his hair, Michael?

MICHAEL: Well, that's certainly nice, but I think it's more than that.

CELIA: Right . . . right . . . something in his face?

MICHAEL: It's certainly a noble face, great nose—

CELIA: Oh yes. And eyes.

MICHAEL: Strong.

CELIA: Definitely.

(*BEN touches his nose.*)

MICHAEL: But you know, I think it's in his shoulders. His shoulders have a stance all their own.

(*BEN takes a look at himself.*)

CELIA: They are going places.

MICHAEL: Indeed. They are. I think your father must be a great man, Benjamin. You are the product of some excellent genes.

CELIA: Grade A.

MICHAEL: It's written all over you.

BEN: Really?

CELIA: In gold.

MICHAEL: It surrounds you.

BEN: Wow. You know what's funny?

MICHAEL: What?

BEN: My parents are always telling me to stand up straight. Keep my head up. Always.

MICHAEL: Are they?

BEN: "Such a great mind and big heart is wasted on a guy who can't hold it up high."

MICHAEL: They sound like smart people.
BEN: I thought they were just nagging me.
CELIA: They're lucky to have you.
MICHAEL: Don't let them forget it.

(*They stand in silence.*)

MICHAEL: Take care of yourself. Keeps your nose clean.
BEN: You too.
MICHAEL: Are you trying to tell me what to do, little brother?
BEN: No.
MICHAEL: I don't want to have to kick your ass.

(*BEN turns to CELIA.*)

BEN: Good, good luck with your baby.
CELIA: Thanks.
BEN: He's the lucky kid.
CELIA: You think so, huh?
BEN: He's got one, two . . . five uncles. Six aunts.
CELIA: Right.

(*BEN picks up his suitcase.*)

BEN: I'm going to tell my mom about you guys. She won't believe it.
MICHAEL: You don't have to tell her about the drunk part.
BEN: Are you kidding?

(*BEN smiles as he walks offstage.*

MICHAEL reaches and pulls CELIA to him and kisses her.)

MICHAEL: The forbidden fruit is always sweeter. Isn't it.
CELIA: Where'd you learn to kiss?
MICHAEL: What do you mean?
CELIA: You nearly took my teeth out.
MICHAEL: I did not.

CELIA: You did. You can't get a girl like that.
MICHAEL: I've gotten lots of girls like that.
CELIA: Uh huh.
MICHAEL: They throw themselves at me—

(*CELIA grabs him and kisses him. He doesn't want to let go.*)

CELIA: Now that is a kiss.
MICHAEL: Uh huh.
CELIA: Remember it.
MICHAEL: I'll try.
CELIA: And don't waste it on just anybody.
MICHAEL: Huh?
CELIA: They'll think you're easy.
MICHAEL: Uh huh.
CELIA: Believe me.
MICHAEL: Sure.
CELIA: Michael?
MICHAEL: Yeah?
CELIA: Do me a favor?
MICHAEL: What?

(*He moves in to kiss her again.*)

CELIA: Tell me it's all going to work out.
MICHAEL: What?
CELIA: Just tell me I can be a good mother.
MICHAEL: You can.
CELIA: How do you know?
MICHAEL: Well . . . you like babies, right?
CELIA: Yes.
MICHAEL: See. There's a start.
CELIA: I guess. Fuck. (*CELIA begins to cry.*) Fuck.
MICHAEL: C'mon, Celia.
CELIA: I'm gonna fuck up.
MICHAEL: No. You won't.
CELIA: I will. I fuck things up. All the time.

MICHAEL: You won't this.

(*Silence.*)

MICHAEL: Hold out your arms.
CELIA: What?
MICHAEL: Hold out your arms.

(*CELIA holds out her arms.*)

MICHAEL: Nice, long arms. Wow. Strong?

(*CELIA makes a muscle.*)

MICHAEL: Yes. Very strong. Good. Now do this. (*MICHAEL makes a cradle with his arms. CELIA copies him.*) OK. Now sway your arms back and forth. (*CELIA sways her arms, as if a baby is inside.*) Uh huh. Great. Now whisper in your baby's ear. Softly. "I love you."

CELIA: "I love you."
MICHAEL: Softer than that.
CELIA: "I love you."
MICHAEL: "I always will."
CELIA: "I always will."
MICHAEL: "You're the most perfect child there is."
CELIA: "You're the most perfect child there is."
MICHAEL: "I'll never leave you."
CELIA: "I'll never leave you."
MICHAEL: "I'll never hurt you."
CELIA: "I'll never hurt you."
MICHAEL: "I'm your mother."
CELIA: "I'm your mother."
MICHAEL: "Aren't we lucky?"
CELIA: "Aren't we lucky?"
MICHAEL: "You're home."
CELIA: "You're always home."

Scene 21

(*Hospital room.*

LORNA lays in bed sleeping. BERT sits in a chair beside her.

MAGGIE enters with a rather wilted flowering plant.)

MAGGIE: Since when did cabs start costing twenty bucks just to go one way?

BERT: Hey Maggie.

MAGGIE: One way!

BERT: Thanks for coming.

MAGGIE: Well, pretty much spent a month's worth of groceries just getting over here but I didn't want her to think I don't care about her or something. (*She sets the plant down. It loses a few leaves.*) Four dollars they wanted for this thing. How's she doing?

BERT: Alright. She's coming in and out of sleep—

MAGGIE: They take everything out?

BERT: No.

MAGGIE: Well, it would be easier if you ask me. Might as well just rip it all out and forget about it.

BERT: Maybe—

MAGGIE: She's no spring chicken and she sure as hell doesn't have any plans for a family, no, I know she's not that type, so why not just take it all out.

BERT: She might feel empty.

MAGGIE: Pssh. No. I had a complete hysterectomy twenty years ago and I felt fine. But of course, we didn't have much of a choice then.

(*BERT is silent.*)

MAGGIE: She'll be alright. She's a tough old bird. Nice hospital. Wonder how much a night they want for this room.

LORNA: (*Sleepy.*) None of your business.

MAGGIE: Well, there she is.

LORNA: Hi Maggie.

MAGGIE: How're you feeling?

LORNA: I'd love a drink.

MAGGIE: You know it cost me twenty bucks for the ride down here?

LORNA: Really?

MAGGIE: It's ridiculous. You'd think I could ride in a limo or something with those prices.

LORNA: Thanks for coming.

MAGGIE: Oh, well, you know. You look good.

LORNA: Thanks.

MAGGIE: And you'll heal real fast.

(*LORNA nods.*)

MAGGIE: It's sure quiet at home now without you.

(*MICHAEL enters carrying a single flower.*)

MAGGIE: And no kids running around the halls.

LORNA: Uh huh.

MAGGIE: I'm still watching for you on TV.

LORNA: Thanks. Hey Bert, you want to give Maggie a ride home.

BERT: Oh. Yeah.

LORNA: I'd appreciate it.

BERT: Sure.

MAGGIE: I just got here.

LORNA: I don't want you to miss your shows.

MAGGIE: Oh, that's alright—

LORNA: Is it Saturday night?

MAGGIE: I guess I should get back. I really don't like the smell of this
place anyway. Smells like some disease is gonna sneak in and
grab me while I'm here.

LORNA: Uh huh.

MAGGIE: Makes me feel old.

LORNA: I know.

MAGGIE: Well then. (*MAGGIE touches LORNA's hand and then awk-*

wardly kisses LORNA's forehead.) You feel better now.

LORNA: Thanks.

MAGGIE: I'll water your plants.

(*LORNA nods as they exit.*

MICHAEL moves closer.

She sneaks a cigarette from under her pillow and lights it.

She takes a deep drag.)

MICHAEL: That'll kill you.

(*LORNA keeps smoking.*)

LORNA: So will a lot of things.

MICHAEL: I guess so.

LORNA: But hell . . . what do I know, I've got enough drugs in me to fly a horse. (*Silence. LORNA puts out the cigarette. Getting sleepy again.*) A present, huh?

MICHAEL: I heard you were here.

LORNA: Nice.

(*MICHAEL tries to hand her the flower as LORNA is falling asleep. He begins to set in on her chest—*)

LORNA: You're no monster, Michael.

(*LORNA grabs his hand instead.*

LORNA falls asleep.

MICHAEL remains holding her hand.

He studies her hand in his.)

MICHAEL: "A mother bird sat on her egg . . ."

(*He brings her hand to his cheek.*

He recites the book Are You My Mother? *by P. D. Eastman, word for word, by heart.*

He tells LORNA *the story in her sleep.*

As he finishes the last line, " . . . And you are my mother," *he lays his head on her lap.*

She opens her eyes.

She is awake.

BLACK OUT.)

End of Play